Welfare in Ireland

Welfare in Ireland

Actors, Resources, and Strategies

Michel Peillon

Westport, Connecticut
London

Library of Congress Cataloging-in-Publication Data

Peillon, Michel.
    Welfare in Ireland : actors, resources, and strategies / Michel Peillon.
      p. cm.
    Includes bibliographical references and index.
    ISBN 0–275–97288–7 (alk. paper)
    1. Public welfare—Ireland. 2. Ireland—Social policy. I. Title.
  HV250.3.P45   2001
  361.9415—dc21   2001016358

British Library Cataloguing in Publication Data is available.

Library of Congress Catalog Card Number: 2001016358
ISBN: 0–275–97288–7

First published in 2001

Praeger Publishers, 88 Post Road West, Westport, CT 06881
An imprint of Greenwood Publishing Group, Inc.
www.praeger.com

Printed in the United States of America

The paper used in this book complies with the
Permanent Paper Standard issued by the National
Information Standards Organization (Z39.48–1984).

10 9 8 7 6 5 4 3 2 1

Copyright Acknowledgments

The author and publisher gratefully acknowledge permission for use of the following material:

Chapter 5, "Other Forces in the Field," is based on M. Peillon's "Bourdieu's Field and the Sociology of Welfare," *Journal of Social Policy* 27(2): 213–229 (revised). Reprinted by permission of Cambridge University Press.

An extract from M. Peillon's "Welfare and State Centralisation," *West European Politics* 16(2): 105–121. Copyright © 1993. Reprinted by permission of Frank Cass.

Excerpts reprinted by permission of Sage Publications Ltd from M. Peillon, "A Qualitative Comparative Analysis of Welfare Legitimacy," *Journal of European Social Policy* 6(3): 175–190. Copyright © 1996 Sage Ltd.

Extracts from M. Peillon's "Support for Welfare in Ireland: Legitimacy and Interest," *Administration* 43(3): 3–20. Copyright © 1995. Reprinted by permission of the Institute of Public Administration, Ireland.

Contents

List of Tables

Acknowledgments

I would like to express my appreciation for the help that I received while working on this book. Margaret Burns, administrator of the Council for Social Welfare, spared neither time nor effort to guide me through the present-day social teaching of the Catholic Church. Paula Carey, research officer at the Irish Congress of Trade Unions (ICTU), facilitated my consulting the full range of ICTU annual reports. Dr. Tom Inglis read Chapter 4 of the book and offered most cogent and useful comments. Whatever clarity the text may possess is largely due to the uncompromising editing of Denise Peillon.

Welfare in Ireland

Introduction

A sociological approach is defined by the questions that it asks about its subject matter. But sociological questions have rarely been asked about the Irish welfare state. Welfare studies often rely on concepts, frameworks, and methods that have been developed by sociologists but do not answer sociological questions. Yet, contemporary social theory is addressing this theme of welfare institutions and practices. They are now recognized as significant elements of the contemporary world, participating in the dynamic of modernity. This book puts forward a sociological analysis of welfare institutions and practices in Ireland.

The welfare system, meaning the set of existing social policy programs, cannot be understood in its own terms as a separate domain of activity. It must be placed in its wider social context. But the necessity of grasping the processes that fashion this sphere of activity from outside does not lessen the need for comprehending its internal dynamic. The emphasis on its insertion within the social structure should not lead to a neglect of its specific logic. The concept of welfare field, loosely derived from Bourdieu's work, has been chosen to perform this double task: inserting welfare institutions within Irish society and accounting for their internal logic. The way that the concept of field has been elaborated by Bourdieu brings right to the fore this dual aspect of insertion and specificity. It focuses on the main forces that shape welfare institutions, the strategies that they adopt, and the goals that they pursue. Formulated in its simplest way, for Bourdieu a field refers to a particular domain of activity in which a struggle takes place. The issue at the core of the struggle relates, within each field, to the generation and distribution of a type of resource, either material or cultural, which Bourdieu calls capital. The activity of those who operate in the field is determined by their position in the structure of domination according to which the field is organized. The strength of such a model of analysis is gauged by its capacity to deal in a unified way with a range of questions that are usually analyzed separately and treated as discrete issues.

This book also focuses on some of the comparative issues with which the welfare studies literature has been concerned. It embarks on a comparative analysis on the basis of the investigation of the Irish case. A single case can be significant in two different ways. It may provide an exemplary illustration of a general idea or type of explanation, or else, it does not fit in any particular framework and stands as a counterexample. The significance of the Irish welfare system does not rest on the fact that it offers an exemplar of an established analysis or theory. For a time, the issue of welfare development dominated comparative welfare studies. The factors influencing welfare effort, and the mechanisms involved, the major forces at work have all been delved into. The analysis of the Irish case throws some light on questions that have been raised in this context. The Irish welfare effort has followed a strange trajectory. Once a welfare laggard, Ireland quickly caught up with more economically developed European countries; but when economic prosperity came to Ireland in the second half of the 1990s, Ireland found itself once more a welfare laggard, this time in the midst of plenty. For this reason, no conventional explanation of welfare development easily applies to Ireland. The growth of Irish welfare has certainly not followed the path that one would expect on the basis of economic or industrial development. In a similar way, Ireland does not confirm the "social democratic" account of welfare development, in that the latter is not accounted for by the strength of the labor movement. As we see later, Ireland does not fully support the view that the state plays a prominent and autonomous role in the development of welfare.

The significance of the Irish welfare system, as a case in comparative studies, rests mainly in its counterpoint value. The issue of welfare effort, which monopolized attention for a long time, has more recently been replaced by an interest in the qualitative differences that exist between welfare systems. The question has become: What kind of welfare system is it? Ireland is not easily placed in the established classifications of welfare systems that have been put forward. The attempt to categorize Ireland as a semiperipheral country does not appear convincing either, as its welfare system has moved close to that of the core countries. But Ireland proves useful as a case study of the welfare mix: of the way the state, market mechanisms, voluntary organizations, and the informal sector are combined. Ireland displays interesting features in this regard. Central powers and voluntary organizations are associated in Ireland in quite a unique fashion. The Irish social security system is one of the most centralized in Europe, along with a loose welfare mix in the provision of many social services: the state pays the costs of such services but enjoys very little control over the way that services are delivered. This occurs, for instance, in relation to education and health.

The unusual features of the Irish welfare system enhance its significance in another way. For instance, Ireland provides a good opportunity to study in detail the role of the Catholic factor in welfare development, the way that the Catholic Church has shaped welfare institutions. Ireland has also been engaged in a policy of what may be called "welfare corporatism," in which the level of social benefits is negotiated as part of a national deal involving wage increases and taxation. This phenomenon can be fruitfully investigated in the Irish context. Either as an exception to a general pattern or else as exhibiting quite distinctive features, Ireland has much to contribute to a comparative understanding of welfare. It may be used to enrich, complement, qualify, modify, or even challenge some of the results of comparative welfare studies.

As its third goal, this book aims at giving, in an informative and accessible manner, an overview of welfare in Ireland. It is sketching a broad picture, painted with bold strokes. Such an exercise is not without dangers. It does not offer a meticulous representation of welfare activity but an angle, an interpretation that is theoretically conditioned. Its intellectual pertinence comes inevitably with a price.

The first chapter sets the base from which the analysis proceeds; it provides a general picture of the Irish welfare system and selects a range of features that mark it in a significant way. Being in possession of this descriptive account, the reader is presented with the intellectual tools utilized in the analysis. Chapter 2 gives a summary of the work of Pierre Bourdieu and explains how this framework is used for the study of the welfare field in Ireland. It points to the major actors operating in the field, the resources that they mobilize and the strategies that these collective forces follow in order to maximize the resources that they seek to generate in the field. It is contended that this framework offers an efficient tool to analyze the Irish welfare system.

Part 1 focuses on the collective actors in the welfare field. Chapter 3 investigates the logic of state intervention, as it endeavors to generate the symbolic capital of legitimacy that it needs to secure its position in society. This capital of support materializes only to the extent that the state delivers welfare benefits acceptable to other forces in the field. It pays for this legitimacy in hard currency, which is extracted from society and comes itself with a legitimacy cost. Possibly more than in other countries, the state in Ireland is concerned with optimizing the rate at which material capital is converted into symbolic capital.

Chapter 4 examines the position of the Catholic Church in the Irish welfare system. The church has traditionally occupied a central position in the provision of social services but a marginal position in the provision of social security. It acts in the welfare field on the basis of a double capital of power (in the form of control over a range of institutions) and legitimacy. It requires from its participation in the welfare field both material capital from the state and continuous control over welfare institutions. However, the position of the Catholic Church in the welfare field has been eroded, and it now aims at generating a symbolic capital that bolsters its position in Irish society.

Chapter 5 considers the strategy and goals of collective actors that have played a less central role in the Irish welfare field, but by no means an insignificant one. The trade union movement strives to improve welfare benefits and services for its members, but also for those who have become welfare-dependent and socially marginalized. Employers, as significant contributors to the Social Insurance Fund, promote their own policy of containing social expenditure. The feminist movement has, to a large extent, shaped some of the services directed at women. A kind of parallel welfare system has actually emerged to cater to their specific social needs. These collective actors exchange their support to state policy for improvements in welfare benefits; they are concerned, in a straightforward way, with converting their political support into material capital.

Part 1 of the book identifies the main players in the Irish welfare field and their practices. The dynamic that is induced by these practices and strategies is considered in Part 2. Chapter 6 assesses the relative weight of the various collective forces that have contributed to welfare development in Ireland. To do so, it focuses on significant advances or landmarks in the Irish welfare system and pinpoints in each case the configuration of relevant factors. In fact, different configurations of forces seem to operate in various social policy contexts and programs.

Chapter 7 examines the welfare mix in Ireland and points to the existence of several such mixes. The historical compromise between church and state is now breaking down, and the Catholic Church is engaged in a delicate shift in its participation in the welfare field. Welfare corporatism has emerged as a very significant feature in which the state and the social partners agree on a package of economic and social policy measures. Finally, the state is revising its links with numerous voluntary associations in the sector of personal services and promoting a more formal and contractual relationship. But in all these welfare mixes, the state remains the central player, and, through them, it seeks to generate symbolic capital.

Chapter 8 discusses the nature of the Irish welfare system, mainly in the light of Esping-Andersen's classification of welfare regimes. This type of analysis is useful as a way of understanding the place of welfare in society, but less so for grasping the internal dynamic of the welfare system. For instance, the issue of commodification points to a link with the economy; the configurations of welfare mixes emphasize its connection with the political system; the redistributive impact of social programs is linked with the socioeconomic structure. The analysis of these features allows us to place the welfare system in its context, that is, to outline its mode of articulation to other domains of Irish society. This issue is further investigated in Chapter 9, in relation to the impact of Ireland's peripheral character. How has this peripherality influenced the development of welfare in the Irish context? This peripheral location has determined the way that welfare is positioned in society.

In the Conclusion, the main results of the analysis are recapitulated, with a particular focus on assessing the framework utilized in this study. It emphasizes what the concept of the welfare field allows us to say about welfare in Ireland. It is implicitly claimed that this study provides a unified overview of welfare in Ireland, something that has been strikingly missing; that it identifies the factors that shape welfare and reconstructs the logic of action of the major players; and that it accounts for the main features of welfare in Ireland. Readers will have to trust their own judgment in deciding if these claims have been upheld.

1

Welfare in Ireland:
Features and Trends

The idea of a welfare system assumes a level of unity that is not necessarily warranted. The degree of coherence, that is, the extent to which social policy programs are animated by a clear principle that unifies them, varies considerably from country to country. Some welfare systems appear very systematic, and others far less so. Furthermore, social policy programs within the same country do not necessarily follow a similar path of development. This does not mean that one should not investigate the possible trends that social policy programs undergo in a particular country or even the transformations of welfare systems in general. It merely implies that we should proceed with caution.

This chapter presents an analysis of the structure and dynamic of the welfare system in Ireland. It is organized around five main themes. The patterns of development are investigated in order to work out to what extent and in which form the Irish welfare system has grown. Do we observe a centralizing trend in the provision of social benefits? Has the Irish welfare system passed from an emphasis on assistance for those in need toward the implementation of the insurance principle? Or is it introducing universal benefits? Have social policy programs become more generous? We may add a further question that has emerged in the recent past and which concerns the trend toward the individualization of social benefits: Is Ireland also moving in this direction? These issues and themes form the focus of this chapter. It endeavors to produce a clear picture of the structure and trajectory of social policy programs in Ireland. We are not yet concerned with accounting for such features and trends. We simply set up the scene, and subsequent chapters develop the analysis further.

PATTERNS OF DEVELOPMENT

The Irish welfare system has been growing for most of the last fifty years. But this development did not occur without fluctuations and reversals. Different indicators have been used to measure what is sometimes referred to as welfare effort. Although not without its problems, welfare development is conventionally indicated by the percentage of national wealth spent on social policy programs. It represents at least a measure of commitment to welfare. Table 1.1 presents the figures for social expenditure in general and also for the main social programs in terms of the Gross Domestic Product (GDP).

Table 1.1
Social Expenditure as Percentage of GDP

	Social Expenditure	Income Maintenance	Education	Health	Housing
1950	14.7	4.8	2.9	2.8	4.2
1955	15.5	5.8	2.9	3.3	3.6
1960	14.0	5.7	3.2	2.9	2.1
1965/66	15.80	5.87	4.04	3.15	2.74
1970/71	19.10	7.31	5.03	4.38	2.38
1975	27.50	10.72	6.12	6.53	4.13
1980	29.78	10.99	6.54	8.61	3.64
1985	29.69	13.57	6.12	7.02	2.98
1990	23.90	11.40	5.27	5.91	1.32
1995	22.92	10.45	5.00	6.03	1.44

Sources: 1950 to 1960: Maguire 1987, table 3: page 464; 1965 to 1995: *National Income and Expenditure* various years.

This table reveals several phases in the development of the Irish welfare system. It started from a low basis, with only 14 percent of the GDP dedicated to the public provision of social benefits and services in 1950. One observes a slow, but regular, growth from then on across the range of social policy programs (although housing does not follow any trend and appears quite erratic). Welfare grew significantly in the 1970s for all social policy programs. It peaked in the early 1980s, and the trend turned downward during the 1990s.

The Irish welfare system experienced its most dramatic development in the 1970s and acquired its most crucial features during this period. The old health service, based on dispensaries, was replaced by free access to general practitioners for low-income categories, and, soon after, free hospital services were granted to all. During the 1970s, too, education was transformed by free secondary schooling and the introduction of community schools, not to mention the expansion of the third-level sector. Finally, during that time social security was extended to all employees. These constitute landmarks in the history of social policy. But economic growth was faltering in the aftermath of the oil crisis of 1973, and these new services and benefits were, to a large extent, paid for with borrowed money. This could not be sustained for long.

The development of welfare in Ireland, chiefly in the 1970s, may have given the impression that Ireland was catching up with its European partners and that its welfare effort went beyond what would be expected on the basis of its economic development, as measured by its level of industrialization or its per capita income. Several commentators have stressed this point: "The Republic's social services are highly developed in relation to income per head and degree of industrialization" (Coughlan 1984: 38). Reference is routinely made to the fact that Ireland has a welfare state that is on a par with countries that possess a far higher national income (Breen et al. 1990: 99). The evidence suggests that, although a lot poorer than its European partners, Ireland produced a welfare system that was only slightly less developed than those of its partners in Europe. In 1975, for instance, Ireland lagged behind most European countries, but not that far behind. More significantly, its welfare system had outgrown that of other peripheral European countries, such as Finland, Greece, Portugal, and Spain. But its welfare effort peaked in the mid 1980s, then declined and more or less stabilized. Ireland now finds itself among the European laggards; countries that, like Finland and Spain, were once peripheral have clearly moved ahead. This trend is explained not so much by a decline of welfare benefits but by Ireland's exceptional economic growth during the 1990s. Ireland is not using this newly created wealth to maintain its welfare effort. Having reached a level of economic development that comes closer to the European average, Ireland is not keeping up its welfare effort. Table 1.2 gives a general indication of the comparative evolution of welfare effort in Europe.

Table 1.2
Social Protection Expenditure as Percentage of GDP

	1975	1980	1985	1990	1994
Belgium	24.2	28.1	29.0	26.7	27.0
Denmark	6.1	28.7	27.8	29.7	33.7
Finland	29.8	18.6	24.6	25.6	34.8
Germany	—	28.5	28.1	26.9	30.7
Greece	25.8	—	—	20.5	16.0
France	22.9	25.9	28.8	27.8	30.5
Ireland	19.7	21.0	24.0	20.3	21.1
Italy	22.6	22.8	22.5	24.0	25.3
Luxembourg	22.4	26.0	25.4	25.9	24.9
Netherlands	28.1	29.9	31.1	32.2	32.3
Norway	18.5	20.3	—	29.0	28.2
Portugal	11.0	10.1	16.1	17.0	19.5
Spain	11.7	16.1	18.0	20.7	23.6
Sweden	26.2	32.0	33.3	35.8	—
United Kingdom	19.4	21.4	24.5	23.0	28.1

Source: *Eurostat*, various years.

The growth of the welfare system in Ireland can also be measured by the widening of its coverage. Most people, although by no means all, are nowadays insured against a range of contingencies. The extension of social coverage has followed a general pattern:

Initially, coverage was limited to workers in particularly strategic industries or in peculiarly dangerous occupations. Mining, for example, was often one of the first industries to be covered. Legislation was subsequently extended to cover all industrial workers, thence to rural/ agricultural workers and so to dependants and survivors of insured workers. In the later stages, coverage was extended to the self-employed and thence characteristically to the generality of the population (or at least to all those recognized as citizens) without further discriminating criteria. (Pierson 1991: 115)

A similar extension is observed in Ireland.

The coverage of Irish social policy programs has spread out considerably over time, but only slowly. Originally, the Irish welfare system catered exclusively to the poor: it offered relief to those who were in dire need. Only in 1952 did a compulsory social security scheme insure manual workers and low-paid employees against disability and unemployment. This was followed in 1974 by the removal of the income ceiling for the participation of employees in social security schemes. At the same time, flat contributions and benefits were replaced by pay-related ones. This meant that the bulk of full-time employees were now included in a unified social security program. Some large social categories still remained outside the net: mainly self-employed and part-time workers.

The process of extending coverage for social policy programs proceeded further with the significant inclusion of the self-employed in 1988 and of part-time workers in 1991 into the social insurance network. It must be recognized, however, that the extension of social insurance to the self-employed was effectuated in a roundabout way. The conditions of their contributions and their entitlements differ from those of employees. On the basis of a reduced contribution, they became entitled to a limited range of benefits, primarily old age and widows' pensions. This introduced major differences in the modalities of participation in the national social insurance scheme and defeated the coherence and unity of "social solidarity." More essentially, some categories of people are not yet included in this framework of social insurance: "However, significant numbers of workers remain excluded from cover: in particular 20,000 low-paid self-employed, over 30,000 'scheme' workers, at least 18,000 assisting spouses and relatives, and about 12,000 employees earning below the earning threshold—which make a total of 80,000 atypical workers (seven per cent of all those at work) excluded from social insurance" (Cousins 1995: 55). One should add all those who, like housewives, do not participate in a direct way in the labor market and who, for this reason, do not contribute to social insurance and have no entitlements other than through their husbands.

The extension of social security coverage is clearly recorded in Table 1.3, which traces the increase in the number of insured people. It displays the impact of the measures taken in 1973 and 1988 on the number of people insured. In 1973, the income ceiling for social insurance was removed, and all employees, manual and non-manual, in the public and private sectors contributed to the social insurance fund. The impact of this measure is indicated by the substantial increase in the numbers insured between 1970 and 1975. In 1988, self-employed people were brought into the social insurance net, and this is reflected in another dramatic increase in coverage between 1990 and 1995.

Table 1.3
Coverage of Social Policy Programs

	Insured Numbers
1955	726,000
1960	710,000
1965	744,000
1970	796,000
1975	969,000
1980	1,034,000
1985	1,333,300
1990	1,436,427
1995/96	1,858,492

Note: The figures must be interpreted with caution, as the same individual can be registered several times as insured. For this reason, they do not allow computing a rate of social insurance coverage.

Sources: *Report of Department of Social Welfare* and *Statistical Information on Social Welfare Services*, various years.

Table 1.4
Recipients of Social Welfare Payments by Social Policy Programs (1995)

Total Old Age	252.947
Total Widows, Widowers, and One-parent Families	176,017
Child-related Payments	4,976
Illness, Disability, Caring	137,155
Unemployment	283,939
Miscellaneous	17,298

Source: *Statistical Information on Social Welfare Services*, various years.

Table 1.4 shows that two social policy programs dominate in terms of the number of recipients. Old age pensions and unemployment transfers account for over 60 percent of the coverage, followed quite far behind by widows' pensions and one-parent family, as well as illness and disability recipients. This does not include social services, such as education or health, which further extends welfare coverage.

"Over the twentieth century, as we have seen, the Irish social welfare system has expanded to such an extent that there can be very few members of the population who are not affected by it at some stage in their lives, whether through payment of contributions or receipts of benefits" (Cousins 1995: 151). Some commentators have relied on this significant extension of welfare coverage to argue that the Irish welfare system is moving toward the universalist model and that it provides social benefits on the basis of rights: "The progressive enhancement of social rights is a basic trend running through the changes that Ireland has experienced since 1960" (O'Connell and Rottman 1992: 205). They point to the fact that all citizens have come to enjoy virtually equal entitlements to a comprehensive range of social services and benefits. The expression used, "virtually equal entitlements," should be seen as a euphemism. The authors define the notion of social citizenship in terms of rights that proceed from membership of the national community: "Social citizenship refers to the bundle of social rights—to welfare, equality and security—to which citizens are entitled, unconditionally, by virtue of their membership of the national community" (O'Connell and Rottman 1992: 205). But the access of most Irish people to social benefits and services is not unconditional and certainly does not derive from Irish citizenship (or even from residence on Irish territory). In the past, access to social benefits hinged on the assessment of needs. A determined shift toward social insurance has meant that most social benefits are now received on the basis of social contributions. In fact, the Irish welfare system contains very few universal benefits, that is, benefits enjoyed as of right. A children allowance has been given, at an early stage, for each child, independently of income or contribution to a social security fund. Primary and secondary education could also be presented as a universal social benefit, in that education is offered free of charge to all children. This universality was established from an early stage for primary schooling. It was introduced in 1967 for secondary schooling. In 1997, the fee for third-level institutions was also removed, although one would hardly call universal a benefit that depends on academic selection. Overall, the range of benefits enjoyed on the basis of right, either because of citizenship or because of residence in Ireland, remains quite small; they do not amount to a movement toward universalism. Some social services are organized on a universal basis, but social security as a whole stays outside the ambit of universal access.

"Over the past three decades social citizenship rights have steadily expanded. In our view, this expansion of social rights constitutes a fundamental dynamic shaping contemporary Irish society, but neither the trend nor its significance has been sufficiently recognised" (O'Connell and Rottman 1992: 205). This statement about the existence of a dynamic of social right expansion overstates the case. The idea that welfare entitlements in Ireland are increasingly based on rights mixes two very different arguments. The first argument concerns the steady extension of welfare coverage to a point where most of the population, but by no means all, is covered by social security programs. However, this takes place not through the granting of automatic entitlements for all but mainly through social insurance schemes that require regular contributions. These insurance schemes are complemented by social assistance programs that rely on means tests and represent, in a sense, the opposite of universal benefits based on rights. This outlines the second argument, which relates to the mode of access to social benefits and services. The concept of social right does not apply to the coverage of social policy programs but the basis on which one enjoys social benefits. Most social benefits are not organized on such a principle. By and large, the Irish welfare system originated as a social assistance system; the policy of shifting the Irish welfare system onto an insurance basis has only partially succeeded. The universalist orientation has always remained marginal within the Irish welfare state. At best, one can say that the Irish welfare system has retained a mix of assistance, insurance, and universal access to social benefits.

PERSISTENT DUALISM

One is often told that welfare in Ireland has been progressively developing into a full-fledged insurance system. The inclusion of the population into the framework of social insurance would sever the link between welfare and poverty; a widening social insurance net marginalizes social assistance. The Commission on Social Welfare (1986) explicitly called for an extension of compulsory social insurance to cover practically the whole population.

Social assistance involves the provision of social benefits and services to those who are considered to be in need. Means tests determine the entitlement of applicants to a range of social benefits. Social insurance, on the contrary, implies that people pay a percentage of their income to a social security fund; their contribution entitles them to draw benefits in case of sickness, unemployment, or old age. Such benefits depend on an adequate level of contributions. The distinction between assistance and insurance remains very clear, but in practice one easily passes from one to the other. For instance, employees contribute to a social insurance fund that protects them if they become unemployed. But the coverage against unemployment does not last very long, and after some months these unemployed people lose their social insurance entitlements. Their subsequent eligibility for unemployment assistance is not granted automatically, and their access to social benefits becomes means-tested.

A first indication of the trend in terms of the balance between social assistance and social insurance is given by the number of welfare recipients under each heading (Table 1.5). One notes a dramatic shift toward social insurance between 1946 and 1966. A peak was reached in 1980, with 60 percent of welfare recipients covered by social insurance schemes. But the trend reversed after that, and the relative weight of social insurance significantly weakened in the 1990s.

Table 1.5
Recipients of Social Insurance and Social Assistance Payments

| | Insurance | | | Assistance |
	Number	%	Numbers	%
1947	56,926	19.3	237,748	80.7
1966	170,090	50.0	170,090	50.0
1971	211,273	52.6	190,415	47.4
1976	292,876	57.8	213,619	42.2
1980	330,000	60.0	220,000	40.0
1985	398,632	55.0	325,530	45.0
1990	382,843	52.2	350.454	47.8
1995	405,727	48.3	466,605	51.7
1997	422,435	48.5	447,917	51.4

Sources: Commission on Social Welfare 1986; *Statistical Information on Social Welfare Services*, various years.

A similar pattern is observed in relation to the relative proportion of expenditure channeled towards social insurance and social assistance (Table 1.6). Once more, social insurance expenditure increased significantly up to the early 1980s and then dwindled during the 1990s. In 1995, social insurance expenditure for old age and widows' pensions accounted for close to two-thirds of total expenditure for insurance welfare. On the other hand, more than three-quarters of welfare expenditure for unemployment fell into the social assistance category. The Irish welfare system has not moved from a residual model of social policy to a social insurance model; it has not produced a straightforward transfer from assistance to insurance.

Table 1.6
Social Expenditure by Social Assistance and Social Insurance Programs

| | Social Insurance | Social Assistance |
	%	%
1945	22	55
1955	28	46
1965	46	28
1975	51	32
1980	56	32
1985	53	36
1990	47	41
1993	44	45

Source: Cousins 1995: table 1, 29.

The proportion of social expenditure dedicated to social assistance was reduced mainly because of the introduction of a children's allowance. Social insurance started only in the late 1950s, peaked around 1980, and declined in relative terms after that. In that sense, any attempt to present the transformation of the Irish welfare system in terms of a transition from an assistance-based system to an insurance-based system does not correspond to the reality of the situation, unless one chooses to interpret the sharp decline of social insurance expenditure (which in 1993 was as low as 45 percent) as a short-term aberration, explained by the difficult circumstances in which Ireland found itself at that stage. This reversal is conventionally explained by the sharp increase in the numbers of recipients of means-tested unemployment assistance, itself related to the growth of long-term unemployment. Even a glance at Tables 1.7 and 1.8 reveals that unemployment was mainly responsible for the reversal of this trend. The figure for unemployment assistance increased dramatically in the early 1990s, to stabilize and decrease afterward. But no social program has registered a determined shift toward social insurance.

Table 1.7
Insurance and Assistance in Old Age Pensions

	Social Insurance		Social Assistance	
	Numbers	%	Numbers	%
1980	97,382	42.8	130,077	57.1
1985	108,892	46.3	126,058	53.6
1990	122,945	50.9	120,632	49.0
1995	134,940	53.3	118,007	46.6
1997	141,815	55.7	112,482	44.2

Source: Statistical Information on Social Welfare Services, various years.

Table 1.8
Insurance and Assistance in Unemployment Transfers

	Social Insurance		Social Assistance		Smallholders
	Numbers	%	Numbers	%	Numbers
1980	47,264	42.6	43,203	38.9	20,342
1985	88,211	39.4	118,498	53.0	16,510
1990	58,644	27.6	140,318	62.1	13,020
1995	61,122	22.8	196,792	73.4	9,997
1997	60,867	25.6	167,892	70.8	8,309

Source: Statistical Information on Social Welfare Services, various years.

The growth of social insurance represents the outcome of a deliberate policy. The first social insurance scheme was launched in 1911 by the British government. It replaced the Workmen's Compensation Act of 1897 and the Old Age Pension Act of 1908. It set up compulsory insurance against unemployment and sickness for manual workers and low-paid, nonmanual workers. The majority of benefits under the National Insurance Act 1911 applied to Ireland, but medical benefits were exempted. The Catholic Church and sections of the Irish medical profession opposed the introduction of such a program. The insurance principle clashed with some material, political, and ideological interests at the time.

Additional insurance was provided in 1935 with the widows' and orphans' pensions and, in 1942, with the wet-time insurance for the building trade. But the significant step in the development of social insurance occurred with the introduction of the contributory old age pension. The Social Welfare (Insurance) Bill of 1950, enacted in 1952, created a common fund for unemployment, sickness, widows' and orphans' pensions. In 1960, a contributory old age pension scheme was introduced for employees below an earning ceiling. The range of social insurance payments and benefits was further extended to cover a retirement pension payable at age sixty-five (1970), an invalidity pension for persons with a long-term capacity (1970), a death grant (1970), and a deserted wife's benefit (1973). In 1973, the insurance principle was reinforced in two ways. First, pay-related supplementary payments linked earnings, contributions, and benefits. Furthermore, all employees were now included in the social insurance net. Only in 1978 was pay-related social insurance (PRSI) fully established. However, it did not last long; the pay-related schemes were reduced all through the 1980s and eventually abolished in 1994. Another significant expansion of social insurance took place in the late 1980s and early 1990s. Social security insurance was first widened to encompass self-employed (1988) and then part-time workers (1991), who had till then remained outside the social security net.

The extension of social insurance was never such that social assistance disappeared as a significant feature. We have already seen that the first social insurance program was curtailed when applied in Ireland because of the opposition of some powerful groups in Irish society. Medical benefits were excluded in the 1911 insurance program and primary health care never developed afterward as an insurance-based scheme. Economic circumstances in Ireland in the 1980s greatly increased the reliance on assistance payments. Several means-tested schemes were initiated in this period: a preretirement allowance, a lone parent's allowance (1990), and a carer's allowance. It appears difficult, then, to interpret the transformation of the Irish welfare system as a staightforward replacement of social assistance by social insurance. Instead, one observes a dual welfare system, with a changing balance between assistance and insurance programs. The emphasis on means-tested benefits has not been removed or even marginalized. Both types of programs still form the main elements of the welfare system in Ireland.

THE CENTRAL POSITION OF THE STATE

Social expenditure is financed on a tripartite basis. But this not does not mean that the respective contributions of the three main partners, the state, employers, and employees, are pitched at the same level. Social expenditure relies, to a large extent, on public finance. Table 1.9 gives the breakdown of the source of financing for social expenditure from the 1950s. At that time, the state paid close to three-quarters of all social expenditure, but it has slowly declined since. The contribution of employers to the financing of social welfare benefits has remained more or less at the same level, while the contribution of employees has increased with the introduction of social insurance, stabilizing at a rather low level.

Table 1.9
The Financing of Social Expenditure, in Percentage

	State	Employers	Employees	Other
1950	70.1	22.3	6.2	1.7
1955	71.3	21.5	5.4	2.0
1960	72.8	21.2	5.0	1.0
1965	67.7	23.5	7.9	1.1
1970/71	63.7	18.9	16.5	1.2
1975	57.8	25.9	15.4	0.6
1980	63.2	24.5	11.16	0.9
1985	64.5	22.2	12.43	0.8
1990	59.0	24.2	15.5	1.0
1995	62.8	22.2	14.4	0.8

Sources: 1950 to 1965: Maguire 1987: 467; 1970/71 to 1995: *National Income and Expenditure*, various years.

The pattern has not dramatically changed over this long period, despite the fact that the social insurance element of the welfare system has been considerably expanded. However, the financing of social insurance has itself radically altered over the last half century. The most dramatic change has been the increasing participation of employers, who paid one-third of social security in the 1950s and now contribute close to two-thirds. The contribution of employees has stood at roughly a similar level, close to one-quarter. The state has considerably reduced its own payment, which reached a low 6 percent in 1990. The self-employed are now participating in the social security scheme. The relative weight of the contributions of the various categories is given in Table 1.10. The state is significantly decreasing its involvement in the financing of social insurance, but only marginally its contribution to social expenditure. The failure to shift the welfare system from assistance to insurance accounts for that. The state takes full financial responsibility for all social assistance programs in Ireland, as well as paying most of the cost of social services (education, health, and personal social services). Its financial stake in welfare remains high for this very reason, despite its withdrawing from social insurance contribution as such. But the line that separates state contributions and other contributions is not that clear. Most employees treat social insurance contributions as another form of public taxation.

Table 1.10
The Financing of the Social Insurance Fund, in Percentage

	Self-employed	Employers	Employees	State
1950	33.8	27.7	30.8	—
1955	33.3	30.9	29.8	—
1960	30.3	26.2	38.5	—
1965	30.0	28.1	39.5	—
1970	35.5	29.8	32.6	—
1975	48.1	28.7	22.3	—
1980	54.5	21.5	23.7	—
1990	63.8	26.2	5.9	3.7
1995	61.0	23.4	11.1	4.5

Sources: 1950 to 1980: Maguire 1987: 467; 1990 - 1995: *Statistical Information on Social Welfare Services*.

Most social welfare schemes are run by the Department of Social Welfare. The history of income maintenance schemes could be interpreted as one in which the responsibility for a range of programs has been progressively taken over by central authorities. In the 1908 act, the administration of the pension schemes was handed over to local pension committees. In 1911, "approved" societies were trusted with the task of administering the National Insurance Act. These voluntary societies were amalgamated in the National Health Insurance Society in 1933. At that time, too, the obligation of providing relief for the unemployed passed from local authorities to the National Exchequer. Nevertheless, the relief of the poor by local authorities was consolidated in 1939. Local authorities have progressively been divested of their welfare function, particularly of social assistance. In 1986, the responsibility for funding the supplementary welfare allowance scheme was entirely reallocated to central government, and local authority funding was abolished. This represented the final stage in a long process of transferring responsibility for such funding from local authorities (as under the 1838 Poor Law) to central government.

The picture appears quite different in relation to social services, such as education and health. The state had to come to terms with the Catholic Church, which claimed control over such areas of activity. This resulted in a historical compromise in which the various churches were allowed to set up and run schools and hospitals as they saw fit, albeit within a framework established by public authorities. Nonetheless, the latter financed such services to a large extent. This compromise is being dismantled for a range of reasons that are analyzed at a later stage. But the position of the state remains pivotal. Local authorities have seen their involvement drastically reduced in the provision of educational and health services, although some regional agencies have been established in which local councils are represented. Seamus Ó Cinneide (1993: 100) dryly notes that the "invocation of subsidiarity" has never stopped the state from being highly centralized. If at times "etatism" has been seriously challenged in relation to social services, the Catholic Church or other forces in Irish society have never shown too much concern with its growth in income maintenance. One may venture that the control of the state over social security matters was not challenged because nobody was in a position to organize its financing.

TOWARD MORE GENEROUS WELFARE BENEFITS?

The Commission on Social Welfare, which carried out a systematic review of the welfare system in Ireland, gave as one its main recommendations the increase in the rates of social welfare benefits. Its recommendation was justified mainly in terms of alleviation of poverty, particularly high in Ireland compared to most other European countries. This underlines, at least implicitly, the lack of generosity that is associated with welfare payments. Rates of welfare benefits are determined through a clash between two main requirements: the need to set these at a level that removes welfare recipients from poverty and the need to provide an incentive to seek work. These two principles form the main parameters within which welfare levels are decided and around which a conflict of interest crystallizes. The commission also recommended that social benefits, which are insurance-based, be fixed at a level about 10 percent higher than social assistance payments.

The trend in the level of benefits is not easily measured, as numerous income maintenance schemes rely on their own criteria and set different levels of payment. However, an analysis of unemployment benefits or old age pensions indicates the trend. In the 1970s, old age pensioners formed a high proportion of those living in poverty; those who depended on old age pensions obtained a level of income that did not sustain an adequate standard of living. Nearly a third of households headed by an elderly person had an income below half the average income in 1973, and 44 percent failed to reach the 60 percent line of national income. In 1987, only 8 percent of such households did not enjoy an income above half this average (Callan, Nolan, and Whelan 1994: 66, 67). The authors of this study concluded that the increased value of old age pensions has constituted a major factor in this transformation. Old age pensions rose in value by 107 percent in real terms between 1973 and 1987, when average industrial earnings increased by only 88 percent. Furthermore, more people nowadays are benefiting from noncontributory pensions, which are slightly more generous. For all these reasons, welfare payments have effectively reduced poverty among the elderly. This conclusion does not apply to unemployment benefits. Households with an unemployed head are most exposed to the risk of falling into poverty: 58 percent of such households receive an income below half the average industrial income.

The welfare system is meant, at the very least, to ensure a minimum standard of living. But this does not stop welfare recipients from experiencing poverty. Those most at risk are, in descending order, recipients of unemployment assistance or supplementary welfare allowance; unemployment or disability benefit; noncontributory and old age pensions, and those with a widows' or old age contributory pensions (Callan, Nolan, Whelan 1994: 71–72). Despite the high proportion of resources being devoted to this task, the Irish welfare system does not effectively move welfare recipients out of poverty. This is explained by the magnitude of the task that it is asked to perform.

The preceding comments and analyses relate to 1987. But the situation has since changed, mainly in terms of the relative level of welfare benefits. For instance, short-term unemployment benefit was valued 12 percent higher than the rate for long-term unemployment assistance in 1987. This has been reversed, with long-term unemployment assistance now higher than unemployment benefits. Furthermore, pay-related benefits have been phased out. Nevertheless, the increases in social welfare payments have remained in line with, or slightly above, inflation, but below average earnings. From 1990, welfare payments have outdistanced the consumer price index, but they have not fared that well in relation to average industrial earnings. These comments apply with greater force to long-term payments. For instance, the rates of payment for long-term unemployed have increased significantly faster than the consumer price index but slower than average industrial earnings (Department of Social Welfare, various years).

Welfare payments have increased in real terms from the 1980s on. Most commentators make statements to this effect. But this could still mean that such payments do not protect from the risk of poverty, which is conventionally defined as a percentage of average income. To put this issue in a comparative context, it has been contended that "[o]n a comparative basis....Irish social welfare rates are generally more generous relative to average earnings or income than those in the UK, but if anything below the average for EU [European Union] countries as a whole" (Kennedy 1997: 136).

INDIVIDUALIZATION

While the solidarity of preindustrial society was founded on ascribed status, industrial solidarity demands a more direct sense of community membership. Historically, this sense of membership has relied on the granting of citizenship. Citizenship means that all members of the group enjoy a range of rights and are protected by a common law. Citizenship must be seen as a statement of equality, at least within the boundaries of the group. This analysis was put forward by T.H. Marshall (1950), who stressed that full membership in a modern society involves the enjoyment of three types of right. Civil rights uphold individual freedom (freedom of speech, thought, and faith; right to own property; right to justice) and equality in front of the law. Political rights relate to political enfranchisement and guarantee the freedom of participation in the political process: a right to vote, join political organizations, and seek political office. Finally, membership in the modern community is also associated with the enjoyment of social rights, through which a meaningful participation in collective life is made possible. These rights include economic security, access to education, entitlement to work, and enjoyment of health services. Civil rights were the first to be granted, but not without a great deal of difficulty. Political rights, initially confined to the aristocracy, were progressively broadened: first to the middle classes, then to the working classes and finally to women. Similarly, social welfare was at first restricted to the needy (or even destitute); it was later extended to the working class, and eventually to the whole population. Social services do not simply sustain citizenship; the granting of social rights would provide the last element in the elaboration of the modern community.

Citizenship implies a mode of participation in the public domain that remains independent from ascriptive links (family, ethnic group, religious beliefs, etc.). Through the enjoyment of a range of rights, social, economic, and cultural differences are, in a sense, negated or, rather, transcended. In that sense, citizenship upholds universal values, but a universalism that does not erase social and cultural differences. It acts, instead, as a framework that endorses such differences and allows them to coexist harmoniously.

Historically, most welfare systems have been constructed on the basis of a gender bias and were designed to sustain the family unit. This ideology of "familism" upholds the view that the responsibility of looking after the material needs of wife and children rests on the husband, while women assume responsibility for caring within the family. This has also been referred to as the "male breadwinner model." In such a perspective, welfare claims are made for the family as a whole. Social policy programs aim at maintaining the male breadwinner family unit; they intervene when support is required in order to compensate for its temporary or permanent collapse. In such an ideology of familism, welfare expenditure is meant to assist the "caring mother" and her children. Support is granted either on the basis of the husband's participation in the labor force or else, if the husband does not or cannot fulfill his function, to alleviate acute need and destitution. In both cases, the married woman enjoys no independent right to welfare benefits. Her claim depends on the rights of the husband, which have to be established by his insurance contributions or else on a plea of poverty, but not as of right. In that sense, such women do not enjoy social rights as citizens.

Such a male breadwinner model has been central in shaping the Irish welfare system. The Irish Constitution of 1936 placed a great deal of emphasis on the protection of the family. Article 41 (1) stated: "In particular the State recognises that by her life within the home, the woman gives to the State a support without which the common good cannot be achieved." Article 41 (2) continues: "The State shall, therefore, endeavour to ensure that mothers shall not be obliged by economic necessity to engage in labour to the neglect of their duties in the home" (Conroy Jackson 1993: 75). This provided the ideological and legal underpinning for organizing the welfare system on the basis of such a view of the family: one in which the husband/father works outside the home, while the wife/mother takes care of the family. She depends on her husband to ensure her own economic well-being and that of her children. The fundamental inequality of men and women in relation to social benefits derives from this basic premise of the welfare state in Ireland.

Social policy benefits are tailored to ensure minimal living conditions for the family unit and to protect the family in case of serious difficulty experienced by the breadwinner: unemployment, disease, death, and so on. Married women staying at home—and they are close to half a million—have access to social benefits, such as pensions, not in their own right but only as wives and mothers. As dependents of their husbands, they are not entitled to any protection other than what they derive from their legal relationship to an insured husband. The 1975 Social Welfare Act and the Social Welfare (Consolidation) Act of 1981 defined wives as dependent if they were simply living with their husbands. The methods for payment of welfare benefits confirmed women's subordinate status within the home. Up till 1985, the father, rather than the mother, received allowances and benefits for dependent children.

By and large, married women at home continue to have access to social benefits either because their husbands are protected by social insurance schemes or else through social assistance schemes. But social assistance distributes benefits on the basis of a notional familial income, which varies according to the number of adults and children in the family. Little individualization of social benefits has occurred in this context. The full individualization of housewives would require a universalist welfare regime. But universally based social benefits remain quite rare in the Irish context: only children's allowance, primary and secondary education, and hospitalization belong to this category. At the same time, one can imagine an individualized assistance scheme, in which benefits are granted on an individual basis, for all who satisfy the required conditions but independently of familial status. In such circumstances, the individualization of assistance would not overcome the marginalization of welfare recipients.

In 1991, according to the Census of Population, women formed roughly 45 percent of the workforce, and married women, 15 percent. Of the total population of 700,844 (excluding widows), 30 percent (215,612, to give the exact figure) of married women participated in the workforce. Married women in the labor force, who numbered close to a quarter of a million in 1991, are entitled to social security benefits in their own right and on the same terms as those applied to married men and single women. But the removal of unequal access to social benefits does not mean equalization in practice. Social insurance schemes often lead to married women's not receiving the same level of benefits. This derives from the conditions of participation of women in the labor force. The reliance on part-time work and the interruptions of employment for familial reasons translate into lower social benefits for women. In Ireland, as in most countries relying on social insurance, women do not fare equally in relation to social welfare, even if they enjoy similar formal entitlements.

A range of "women's benefits" has been introduced since the late 1960s and early 1970s, directed at deserted wives, prisoners' wives, and unmarried mothers. They were all social assistance payments, with the exception of the deserted wife's benefit, which was automatically granted. In 1973, a social welfare allowance was started for unmarried mothers. It constituted, for all practical purposes, an allowance for housework and child care, and this was paid for sixteen years. But claimants could not register for unemployment or take up employment. For that reason, they did not accumulate a contribution record for social security benefits. They were also prohibited from cohabitating with a male partner, contributing further to their isolation as a special category of social welfare recipients. In 1990, a new social security measure for lone parents streamlined six different social welfare schemes; it initiated a single, unified, lone-parent social welfare allowance, available to women and men in the categories covered.

It would seem that such women are now treated as individuals, not on the basis of any dependence. However, it has been argued that such an individualization is very limited or even deceptive. All such women are not perceived as autonomous individuals but as passive victims of misfortune (McDevitt 1987). These social welfare schemes cater specifically to widows, deserted wives, unmarried mothers, prisoners' wives, and elderly spinsters, but not for men in comparable situations. These schemes are still based on a perception of a woman as dependent, as a person who, deprived of the support of a man, needs state support. Far from enhancing autonomy, such schemes implement Article 41 of the Constitution and encourage single parents to stay at home and out of the labor market (Conroy Jackson 1993). They replace dependence on a husband by dependence on the state. In a similar way, it has been noted that Ireland stands alone in providing a special welfare scheme for deserted wives and in considering marital breakdown as a risk that has to be covered by the social security system (Callender 1988: 3).

Such women are entitled to social benefits more or less as a right, in the sense that they obtain it without means testing, but not on the basis of citizenship. "Women formerly entitled only to Home Assistance were eligible for payments in their own right but ultimately on the basis of their family status (as wives, mothers, daughters) rather than on their citizenship" (Yeates 1997: 157). This means that individualization in such a case does not produce full gender differentiation, for it is justified in terms of a family model that is still inspired by the breadwinner model. Once more, full differentiation would probably require a universalist type of welfare system.

Ann Coakley contends that the Directive on Sex Equality from the European Community opened up the prospect of gender equality based on social insurance and even citizen gender equality. But she points out that the aim of "individualising married women in social welfare resulted in many contradictions, when it was imposed on a familist model that assumed women's dependency within marriage" (Coakley 1997: 181). Individualization refers to the process by which welfare entitlements are determined on the basis of individual status, rather than a familial one. The granting of personal rights to each spouse individually promotes greater equality in relation to social benefits. But the implementation of the principle of gender equality in welfare created its own problems. The Irish government took more than fifteen years to implement this EU directive, as granting equal welfare benefits to married women required fundamental changes in the very structure of social welfare. In any case, this equalization was directed only at those women who participate to the labor force. Marital status remains crucial for all assistance-based schemes, and it is mainly under such schemes that married women staying at home relate to welfare services. Nevertheless, the 1986 reforms started a process of individualization of welfare entitlement.

A great deal of pressure was exercised, originating from the EU but also from feminist and poverty groups, to replace the current male breadwinner model with an individualized model of social welfare entitlements. The introduction of more individualized entitlements for women has proceeded only slowly and has created its own problems, but the trend is in this direction. Individualization would not in this case necessarily indicate an empowerment of women but, on the contrary, manifest the still-potent ideology of familism and seal their dependence on a patriarchal state.

CONCLUSION

This chapter has outlined the main features of the Irish welfare system and has traced the path of its development. It is also meant to form the basis for at least an implicit comparative analysis, in which Ireland is assessed in the context of the welfare experience of European countries. Welfare in Ireland has been looked at under five main headings, and each one is supposed to stress a significant aspect of the Irish welfare state. Such an outline does not claim to be complete, and other significant features are considered in the course of the analysis. It simply provides a starting point.

Ireland comes across as a reluctant welfare state. A late starter by European standards, it quickly made up some ground and, despite its relative economic underdevelopment, appeared to lift itself to a level close to that of other, richer European countries. But this welfare effort dwindled in the 1980s in the face of serious economic difficulties. The welfare drive did not resume with the relative prosperity of the 1990s, as the new wealth was not channeled into an additional welfare effort.

The Irish welfare system is characterized by a deep dualism between assistance and insurance. Although the Irish state committed itself to move away from social assistance and create a social security program based on social insurance, this has not really happened. A more universalist orientation, in which social benefits are enjoyed as of right, has never been considered a serious option.

The state remains absolutely central in the running or administration of social policy programs. Although the welfare mix has varied over time and according to programs, the central state occupies a crucial place. It has, from the start, administered the social security scheme. The declining presence of the church has meant that the traditional welfare mix in education and health is changing, and the state is acquiring greater weight. The latter is also negotiating a new deal with voluntary organizations providing personal social services. It seeks to establish a more contractual relationship with them in which the quality of their services would be closely scrutinized. The state is also engaged in a partnership approach at the national level in which economic and social goals are balanced against each other.

Social benefits in Ireland are to a large extent based on social assistance, but they do not appear ungenerous. This is particularly true in relation to public old age pensions, which have lifted most senior citizens in Ireland above poverty. However, this relative generosity has not succeeded in overcoming the widespread poverty that exists in Ireland.

Finally, a transformation is taking place in the philosophy that underlies the Irish welfare system. Family-oriented and meant to uphold the viability of the family unit, the welfare state in Ireland is slowly and reluctantly moving toward a more individualized allocation of social benefits, with less and less reference to the conventional family unit. This transformation has been triggered by external forces, mainly by the pressure to end gender discrimination in relation to welfare, a demand that has been articulated by the feminist movement, adopted by the European Commission, and, in a sense, imposed on Ireland.

This chapter started with a general statement about the way that the welfare system of advanced societies is developing. Welfare development took place in Ireland quite smoothly at first but then in an erratic manner and with more lows than highs in the recent past. But growth has occurred, with wider coverage of many schemes and more generous social benefits. However, social assistance has shown great resilience and has not been replaced by social insurance. Furthermore, the introduction of pay-related schemes has been rather short-lived. The Irish welfare system has displayed no great inclination to adopt universal social benefits, with possibly the exception of a limited assertion of individual rights as the basis for access to welfare benefits.

A broad outline of social welfare in Ireland has been sketched. It does not claim to offer a comprehensive overview, and its features have been emphasized quite selectively. This descriptive account sets the scene for a deeper analysis.

2

Bourdieu and the Welfare Field

Pierre Bourdieu has elaborated an ambitious theoretical framework in which the concept of field occupies a central place. A field refers to a sphere of activity that possesses distinctive characteristics. This represents, in a sense, the main claim of his approach: each area of social activity displays its own features and proceeds according to its own dynamic; it cannot be assimilated with another type of activity. A social field, according to Bourdieu, constitutes an objective structure, that is, a configuration of social positions within which individual agents are distributed. This structure is always defined as a structure of domination in which some agents are located in dominant positions. A dominant or dominated position is determined by the amount of capital controlled by respective participants. Bourdieu uses this concept of capital in a loose way, for it does not necessarily correspond to material wealth. He makes a fundamental distinction between material and cultural capital, but he also added other types of capital as his analysis developed. A particular emphasis is placed, as we will see, on what he labeled symbolic capital. The structure of the field is decided not only by the amount of capital enjoyed by the relevant social agents, but also by the composition of capital. Bourdieu has put forward a typology of social classes according to the amount and composition (material/cultural) of capital.

The field is analyzed by Bourdieu as a structure of domination in which social forces are engaged in a struggle. The very presence of such a struggle implies that something is at stake in this social arena and that participants are struggling over some significant issue. The struggle in a particular field revolves mainly around the control over a particular type of capital. Bourdieu asserts that those in dominant positions in the field are interested in the reproduction of the existing structure; other agents strive to secure a different distribution of the relevant capital.

A high price is required for entering a field. Participants possess a stake in the field and they control sufficient capital to operate as an effective social force. The activity of these agents in the field reflects rather directly the position that they occupy in it. They adopt strategies that endeavor to maximize their gains, and these gains relate to the control and enjoyment of the capital that is at stake in the field. But these agents do not only follow strategies; their practices mirror the schemes of perception and behavior that have been acquired through socialization and experience. The habitus corresponds to a set of assimilated dispositions and orientations; it provides a quasi-automatic sense of the state of play in the field.

This idea of social field as put forward by Bourdieu has been presented as a conceptual way of acknowledging the specificity of different social situations. Each field possesses its own logic. However, the concept of field is not meant to offer disconnected analyses of various aspects of social life. Although differentiated and specific, a field should not be seen as autonomous. It is connected with other fields and belongs to a hierarchy of fields. The analysis of each particular field cannot be effectuated in isolation from the broader context. Fields are fenced; strategies and practices, beyond this boundary, cease to be determined by the struggles that take place in this arena. But the capital generated in a particular field becomes a crucial resource in another, possibly higher field. The analysis of a field is ultimately conducted in terms of its contribution to the structure of society in general.

It may be useful at this stage to illustrate these rather general considerations about the concept of field with some examples drawn from the work of Bourdieu himself. He has shown, for instance, a sustained interest in the topic of art. The art field includes different groups, each endowed with various amounts of economic, cultural, and symbolic capital. These agents are mainly concerned with ascertaining what can legitimately be viewed as artistic activity and establishing a hierarchy of artistic production. The art field would lose its autonomy without a belief in the value of artistic production, as clearly distinct from its economic value. The ability of artists to define artistic value appears central to the struggles in the field, in which artists, clients, critics, gallery owners, and so on participate. The symbolic capital associated with artistic production is generated by deciding what is valued as art and, consequently, the relative value of various types of artistic production. Both represent central issues in this field of forces and struggles.

Some cultural practices are considered superior, and others inferior. This is best illustrated by Bourdieu's study of art museum attendance. Visiting an art museum or attending a theater or an opera performance marks out the "cultured class." This type of cultural practice is defined as superior, even by those who do not engage in it. Bourdieu would contend that there is nothing superior about such cultural practices. The very manner of visiting art museums is also subjected to the distinction between high and low culture. The immediate appreciation of "great art" is contrasted with the use within the museum of devices and pointers to help those who do not have the easy relationship to art enjoyed by the initiated. The dominant class views as culturally superior that which constitutes its own cultural practice. The grid of perception through which a work of art makes sense and is appreciated is learned mainly in the family setting. But art appreciation is presented instead as an innate gift; the superiority of a cultural practice appears in this way natural, "in the nature of things."

Bourdieu is guided by the idea that the tastes, habits, and lifestyles of social groups partake of strategies in a competitive social struggle. An aura of superiority is assigned to some lifestyles; a cultured taste is set against a mass taste, and the amount of cultural capital that one acquires depends on engaging in cultural practices that participate in the cultured taste. This is what Bourdieu calls "distinction." The marking of difference is organized around the contrast between distinguished and popular tastes. When members of the popular class visit museums, they prefer exhibitions of decorative art, furnishing, historical clothing, and so on. They relate to aspects of artwork that have to do with its concrete features, with how much work is involved in it. In a similar way, they use photography as a record of family life and differ in that from the middle class. These cultural tastes generally correspond to levels of schooling and are associated with class.

Bourdieu has extended his interest to the field of literature. The literary field is analyzed as a structure of domination, that is, as an arena in which some people occupy a dominant position and others, a dominated one. This is manifested in the hierarchy of types of literary creation, according to how worthy they are. Various agents are involved in the field: authors, of course, but also editors, readers, critics, and so on. These agents adopt a range of practices that, to a great extent, sustain the existing structure of the field and reflect tastes and standards that social agents have internalized. The definition of this specialized symbolic capital and the autonomy of the literary field itself, that is, the capacity to define literary value within this field, represent the stakes in the literary field.

Bourdieu also referred to a field of sport, in which the stake becomes the definition of legitimate sport practice and the legitimate use of the body. This invokes a range of dichotomies implicated in determining the symbolic value of different kinds of sportive activity: amateur versus professional sport; the practice of sport versus the spectacle of sport; popular versus elite sport, and so on. The struggle over the hierarchization of ways of practicing sport relates once more to the fundamental issue of social distinction, through which, according to Bourdieu, the culture of the dominant groups becomes the dominant culture and reinforces their position in the structure of society.

Bourdieu also mentioned the fields of philosophy, of religion, economy, science and politics. But he is particularly known for his work on education. The educational field is concerned in a direct way with the production of cultural capital, mainly in the form of credentials. It contributes to the reproduction of society, of the way that capital is distributed. More precisely, education ensures the legitimation of the existing structure of domination. This is achieved when those who acquire the cultural capital appear to merit it simply because they are the most talented. The distribution of cultural capital, once legitimated, is transformed into symbolic capital. Those who do well at school are presented as inherently gifted. Success at school accrues not to those who have already assimilated the right cultural dispositions but to those who are "gifted." Such an "ideology of the gift" hides the fact that schools strengthen social privileges. Cultural struggle revolves around the legitimation of the social order and, as such, of the dominant position of some groups over others. Privileged groups strive to justify their privileges by cultivating a sense of "innate" superiority, of the superior values and standards that they embody. Schools are viewed as a crucial channel through which the culture of the dominant class assumes the status of the dominant culture. For Bourdieu, schooling confers an official seal on those who are already endowed with this dominant culture because of their background. Those children are, of course, rewarded at school and increase further their cultural capital through education. Those who are, from the start, far removed from the school culture because they have no affinity with it acquire little of the cultural capital that is granted by the school.

Bourdieu has never shown any great interest in welfare studies, but his general approach can be used to develop a sociological analysis of welfare. His frame of analysis is best treated in this context as an instrument that allows us to think about the way that welfare operates. The statement that welfare represents a field of activity implies that it is best analyzed in its own terms, as a specific domain of activity. This provides a useful starting point.

WELFARE AS FIELD

The welfare state is sometimes defined, in a very literal way, in terms of the relationship between administrative agencies and clients (Offe 1984). The state is always involved in one way or the other in the provision of social benefits and services, but the degree of this involvement fluctuates greatly. The welfare system engages not only the state but also market mechanisms and many agencies within the civil society: it forms a mix. Welfare systems differ not only according to how "developed" they are but according to the way that their diverse elements are connected. Consequently, the welfare state does not entirely hinge on the relation between state administration and clients. Although a crucial agent, state administration does not monopolize the provision of social services. Once this point is accepted, the welfare field must be seen as extending beyond the bureaucratic field, with which it nonetheless overlaps.

Only those who can mobilize the relevant resources are able to take part in the struggles around which a field is organized. These resources are conceptualized by Bourdieu as capital, which is, of course, unequally distributed. The position of an agent in the field is characterized by the volume and the type of capital to which it has access. Bourdieu considers four types of capital:

- economic capital, which corresponds to material wealth;
- cultural capital, which covers educational credentials and cultural goods;
- social capital, which refers to the mobilization of people through connections, social networks, and group membership;
- and, finally, symbolic capital which is the form taken by all types of capital when their possession is perceived as legitimate.

Although all these types of capital form resources in all fields, their hierarchy varies from one field to another. The accumulation of one particular kind of capital represents for Bourdieu the stake of the struggles in one particular field.

The whole conceptual apparatus elaborated by Bourdieu turns around considerations of power. Fields are presented as structures of domination, within which diverse forces operate and struggle. Capital is power, or, rather, it is a resource that yields power. Symbolic capital itself comes very close to the notion of legitimacy. But this omnipresence of power in Bourdieu's work has its drawbacks, for it appears in very different shapes and forms and, although used extensively, is not deeply probed into. This occurs mainly because power is presented as a generalized resource.

Two fields are more explicitly linked with power. The basic structure and hierarchy of all other fields derive from the overarching field of power. Bourdieu sees this central structure of domination in terms of the opposition between those rich in cultural capital but poor in economic capital and those rich in economic capital but poor in cultural capital.

[T]he field of power is the space of relations of force between agents or between institutions having in common the possession of the capital necessary to occupy the dominant positions in different fields (notably economic or cultural). It is the site of struggles between holders of different powers (or kinds of capital) which, like the symbolic struggles between artists and the "bourgeois" in the nineteenth century, have at stake the transformation or conservation of the relative value of different kinds of capital, which itself determines, at any moment, the forces liable to be engaged in these struggles. (Bourdieu 1996: 215)

Bourdieu also includes in his analysis a political field, which is organized around access to a capital that is specifically political. This field is, at times, presented as a market where diverse political products are on offer: "the political field is the site where political products, issues, programmes, analyses, commentaries, concepts, events, are generated in the competition between the agents who are engaged in it, and between which ordinary citizens, now reduced to the status of 'consumers,' must choose" (Bourdieu in Accardo and Corcuff 1986: 123; my translation). But the political struggle for the monopoly of symbolic violence, for the right to formulate the law, also takes place within the political field. It concerns the appropriation of the political capital "which allows those who possess it a form of private appropriation of public goods and services (residences, cars, hospitals, schools, etc.)" (Bourdieu 1994: 33; my translation).

The introduction of this political capital brings us closer to the welfare field, whose dynamic would not make sense if we did not add political capital to the list of relevant resources considered by Bourdieu. The control over the delivery of a particular social program constitutes both a resource within this welfare field and a major stake within it. Political capital also involves a capacity to speak authoritatively for a large category of people who, furthermore, can be mobilized collectively for exercising pressure. This political resource is used, for instance, to influence the level of welfare benefits.

But another "power resource" matters in the welfare field: the capacity of agents in the field to accede to individuals in order to mold their behavior. This capacity is required by a range of social policy programs. It represents a special form of power and needs to be added to the resources that form both a resource and a stake in the welfare field. This form of power capital belongs to another intellectual tradition, associated with the work of Michel Foucault, but it can be conceptualized in terms of Bourdieu's framework. In the past, people such as doctors and priests possessed the cultural and symbolic capital that enabled them to patronize those with whom they dealt and command access to their privacy. This relationship was elaborated on the basis of a habitus organized around trust and deference. Nowadays this power of access to individuals is more likely to take place within a bureaucratic field and it mobilizes the "state capital," which, as we will see, constitutes a concentration of diverse types of capital.

WHAT IS AT STAKE IN THE WELFARE FIELD?

The structure of a field corresponds to the distribution of capital whose possession enhances the chances of appropriating the capital that forms the stake in the field. Bourdieu's work on education and on the cultural field in general clearly points to the accumulation of symbolic capital as the central stake. He further equates symbolic capital with legitimacy: when the possession of any kind of capital is justified not only in the eyes of those who benefit most from its distribution but also in the eyes of those who are most deprived of it.

The idea that the welfare state produces legitimacy and mass loyalty has been central to the analysis of the emergence and development of the welfare state. One may turn to Habermas (1987) in order to clarify this view. He puts forward a fairly conventional analysis of the welfare state and analyzes it in terms of the pacification of class relations. The latter occurs through mechanisms of compensation. Employees are pacified, as private consumers, by material rewards; voters are pacified, as clients of welfare agencies, through social benefits. Habermas underlines here the trade-off on which rests the welfare state: social rewards are exchanged for compliance with the economic and political requirements of the system. Habermas gives us an important insight into what is at stake in the welfare state. For him, the welfare state represents an institution through which legitimacy is exchanged for monetary rewards. He is talking about the conversion of one kind of resource into another type.

The theme of conversion occupies a central position in Bourdieu's framework. He has pointed out the changing value of the diverse elements of cultural capital, such as diplomas. For him, the relative value of a particular type of capital represents a stake in the struggle: social agents with a specific type of capital must ensure the recognition of its value. They use the capital that they possess in order to maximize the capital that counts in a particular field. The stake concerns the rate of exchange of one type of capital into another. Bourdieu explicitly develops this theme of convertibility in the context of his analysis of the field of power: "[T]he field of power determines the relative value of different kinds of capital (for instance, the 'rate of exchange' between cultural and economic capital)" (Bourdieu 1994: 56; my translation).

This theme of convertibility is quite frequently referred to but never systematically elaborated. Bourdieu has acknowledged the difficulty of formulating precise statements in this respect. He wrote: "For instance, I constantly raise the problem of conversion of one kind of capital into another, in terms that do not completely satisfy even me....What are the laws governing that conversion? What defines the exchange rate at which one kind of capital is converted into another?" (Bourdieu 1993: 33–34). The quest for such general laws is bound to remain elusive. The main parameters for the conversion of types of capital are set in the field of power. But the concrete modalities of this conversion and the exact rates at which they are effectuated depend on the particular fields in which they occur. "That is, at the very least, the extent and ease of convertibility must be quite different in different contexts" (Calhoun 1993: 68). Calhoun is referring here to the historical variability of this conversion. But the citation also suggests that capital conversions are more crucial in some fields than in others. It is here postulated that the conversion of forms of capital appears particularly central to the welfare field. This occurs mainly because the state, which occupies a central place in the welfare field, possesses what Bourdieu calls a meta-capital. "The concentration of different kinds of capital....leads to the production of a specific type of capital, a state capital, which enables the State to exercise its power over the various fields and over the different kinds of capital, more particularly over the rates of exchange (and, consequently, over the relations of force between those who possess them)" (Bourdieu 1994: 109; my translation). For this reason, all major kinds of capital are involved in the welfare field, and their conversion forms the core of agents' strategies.

The rate of conversion between economic and symbolic capital represents the main stake for the state in the welfare field. It has to ensure the highest level of legitimacy for its social expenditure. But diverse agents in the field operate with different types of capital: doctors, teachers, social workers, sometimes priests, those at the receiving end of welfare benefits. They also aim at converting the resources that they possess into the kinds of capital that they seek to accumulate. The stakes in the welfare field are multiple. Instead of considering that agents in the field mobilize their resources to accumulate the capital that forms the stake of the struggle in the welfare field, it seems preferable to envisage a situation in which various types of capital are converted into each other, simultaneously.

AGENTS AND HABITUS

Agents are able to act in the field only because they possess the necessary resources to produce effects within it. They hold a position in the structure of the field as determined by the type and volume of resources that they possess, and this position governs the way that they play within it, but not mechanically or automatically. External conditions shape the activity of agents through a habitus. The latter is sometimes defined as a set of inculcated dispositions; sometimes it is presented as a scheme that provides the categories of perception and evaluation. In any case, the habitus constitutes the principle according to which practices are generated. Through the habitus, agents in the field respond meaningfully to how a situation develops; they improvise a course of action, initiate unexpected moves. They display autonomy and flexibility mainly because they evolve within a world characterized by some looseness. Agents have in this context recourse to strategies as the situation develops, and they steer a course between alternatives. Such strategies do not imply any conscious calculation; rather, they activate dispositions and classifications. Bourdieu has called the habitus "an art of invention" to emphasize that it implies an active and creative relation to the world. It must be pointed out that Bourdieu's framework is sometimes criticized for being deterministic, but this is strongly denied by Bourdieu himself.

In a sense, the habitus represents the point of crystallization of the structure of domination and of the play of power. As the mediating concept between the structure of the field and the practices within it, it translates relations of domination into power, into access to those resources that are at stake in the field. The habitus can be seen as the embodiment of what Bourdieu calls a "cultural arbitrary"; this refers to the classificatory schemes, the mode of interpretation of the social world that the dominant groups uphold and impose. As generative matrix of practices, the habitus already involves the inculcated representations that social agents have of the social world. The practices and strategies generated on the basis of the habitus carry the mark of power in two ways: they manifest the structure of domination that is embodied in the habitus, and they participate in the struggle through which the structure of the field (the distribution of relevant capital) is maintained or transformed.

In the welfare field, the concept of habitus becomes particularly relevant at the point of contact betwen social policy agencies and clients. Welfare agencies and welfare clients belong to a structure of domination, but one that is largely misrecognized. Bourdieu's notion of misrecognition simply indicates, in this context, that the relationship between administrative agencies and welfare recipients, which is organized in terms of control, is misrecognized as caring. Misrecognition is, of course, not accidental: it activates symbolic structures that are incorporated in the habitus and are likely to ensure compliance. But the effectiveness of such a misrecognition should not be exaggerated, for the strategies of control that are used by welfare agencies and to which misrecognition belongs are often met with strategies of resistance. As soon as reference is made to control, mechanisms of resistance to control come into operation. This implies that a system of control is immediately transformed into a site of struggle; such a struggle develops at the interface of the interaction between welfare agencies and welfare recipients.

Strategies of control and resistance should not necessarily be perceived as intentional, for they are enacted through routine practices that are generated by a habitus. Two sets of practices are implicated here: one engendered by the habitus of those who deliver social benefits and services, and the other, by the habitus of those who receive such benefits and have to cope with official agencies. In fact, diverse habitus are probably involved in each category, as both providers and recipients do not form uniform categories. The habitus of either welfare recipients or welfare agents do not simply produce a practice, as if they were mechanically determined by the position in the field. The habitus produces strategies, because it operates in a context of indeterminacy: "The habitus goes hand in glove with vagueness and indeterminacy" (Bourdieu 1990: 77). It produces a "feel for the game": "This 'feel for the game,' as we call it, is what enables an infinite number of 'moves' to be made, adapted to the infinite number of possible situations which no rule, however complex, can foresee" (Bourdieu 1990: 9). This implies choosing the best possible course of action, but not one based on a rational calculation of interest. This "feel for the game" provides an orientation within the context of general dispositions that constitute the habitus. "This word, strategies, evidently has to be stripped of its naively teleological connotations: types of behaviour can be directed towards certain ends without being consciously directed to these ends, or determined by them. The notion of habitus was invented, if I may say so, in order to account for this paradox" (Bourdieu 1990: 9–10).

Within the welfare field, a distinction is drawn between means-tested, contributory, and universal benefits. In the first case, welfare recipients seek access to a range of social benefits and services. They endeavor to obtain the highest possible level of benefits, that is, of economic capital. But as such benefits depend on means tests, they may well respond to the practices of control through strategies of resistance. They also aim at minimizing the stigma that goes with taking up social benefits, to reduce or even eliminate negative symbolic capital. Bourdieu's model of the field applies to this situation. Welfare recipients, although they cannot mobilize resources to act effectively, occupy an objective position in the welfare field. Their position is defined, like anyone else's, by the distribution of the existing capital and also by the access to the capital that such social agents strive to accumulate. However, lack of capital transforms them into objects of welfare. The way that this powerlessness and dependency are experienced may create a habitus, a matrix that routinely generates the practice of welfare clients. This does not mean that welfare recipients necessarily comply with the procedures set up by the relevant agencies. They may turn to a range of strategies in the way that they handle the relevant agencies. The field in which they evolve is still characterized by struggle.

The habitus of welfare recipients is mirrored by that of the officials who deliver such means-tested benefits and services. These officials police access to social benefits, ensuring that only those with a legitimate entitlement receive them. They operate in a field with a political capital, and the exercise of their power immediately produces stigma, negative symbolic capital for their clients. The mechanisms of control and stigmatization become the focus of a resistance that must be overcome or neutralized by the administrative agencies. The position of such administrative agencies in the welfare field leads to the development of an "administrative habitus." This habitus does not correspond to a bureaucratic ethos, which would simply reflect the internal mode of operation of an organization. It is based on the distance that separates, in their objective position, officials and their clients. It is deeply rooted in the structure of the welfare field and cannot be presented as an issue of organizational effectiveness.

The preceding comments do not apply to those benefits that are based on contributions or on social insurance schemes. In such cases, the relationship between administrative agencies and clients conforms to a contract in which rules and regulations are clearly defined. Benefits are calculated on the basis of recorded contributions and leave hardly any room for discretion. One imagines that a rather different habitus emerges in this context for both administrators and clients. The interface of social policy agencies and clients also acquires a very different character with universal social policy programs. The beneficiaries of such services rely on a language of rights, according to which they expect and receive an automatic entitlement to such services. They are mainly interested in the quality of the services to which they are entitled. They are faced by professional providers of services, such as medical doctors or teachers, who enjoy a high level of legitimacy. This does not mean that this situation cannot be conceptualized in terms of control and resistance to control. But this control is more likely to be misrecognized and assumed under the category of care. It activates, in any case, a rather different kind of habitus for both providers and clients.

Far from being uniform, the welfare field is composed of many subfields. One frequently finds, within the same welfare system, some social policy programs that are based on the insurance principle and some that rely on means testing. Each social policy area (of health, education, social security, etc.) not only displays a different structure but activates very different habitus and may involve different stakes, albeit within the context of a similar structure of domination. Even recipients of welfare benefits vary according to their "trajectory," that is, according to the successive positions that they have occupied, according to the changes that they have experienced in the volume and composition of the capital that they possess.

CONCLUSION

Bourdieu conceptualizes most aspects of social life in terms of fields, which constitute sites of struggle over a central stake. The resources used in these struggles and whose appropriation is at stake are defined as types of capital: economic, cultural, social, and symbolic. Each field involves a set of players, of agents who are engaged in practices and strategies on the basis of a habitus. Such an approach can be usefully mobilized to develop a sociological analysis of welfare. The focus is definitely set on the rates at which types of capital are converted in the welfare field. It is argued that such a model satisfies the central requirements of a sociology of welfare, in that it places welfare activities within the wider social context while grasping their internal dynamic. Bourdieu's model does not hold out the only acceptable way of elaborating a general sociology of welfare, but it provides a particularly effective tool to this end.

The model of welfare field derived from Bourdieu's mode of analysis offers a realistic and efficient approach to the elaboration of a sociology of welfare. An appropriate sociological framework demands that welfare institutions and practices are placed in their wider social context and that the internal dynamic of welfare activities is grasped. A perspective that examines the welfare system on its own terms does not meet this requirement. But the social insertion of the welfare system must not lead to a neglect or bypassing of the specific logic at work in the welfare domain. Most perspectives fail to pass this double test. The concept of the welfare field satisfies this double requirement. In a sense, it has been invented for this purpose. The welfare field takes its place within the broad field of social formation, but it also forms a differentiated domain of activity. The differentiation of the welfare field simply means that a specific configuration of agents operates within, and that struggles crystallize around, specific issues and stakes. All these factors set in motion an internal dynamic, a logic of welfare activity. In that sense, the extent of differentiation and autonomy of the welfare field remains an empirical question. The concept of field, as elaborated by Bourdieu, brings this dual aspect of insertion and specificity right to the fore.

A sociology of welfare must also identify the relevant forces that are active within this domain and shape it. Bourdieu's analysis points to the main players in the field and the strategies in which they are engaged. These players include macroagents that clash over the constitution of the field, as well as agents of power and counterpower that manifest themselves at the local level, in the context of the organization and delivery of social benefits.

Part I

Players and Stakes

3

State and Welfare

The welfare system of any particular country can surely not be assimilated to the welfare state, for other social agents participate in a direct way to its shaping and functioning. Reference is conventionally made to the welfare mix, in which the state, commercial organizations, and voluntary associations are all involved in the provision of welfare benefits and services. Yet, the state remains central to the welfare system, and such a comment applies with particular strength to Ireland. The centrality of the Irish state in the welfare field was established in the first chapter. Historically, the state apparatus has been the driving force in setting up the framework for welfare provision. It has, slowly but steadily, expanded the scope of compulsory social insurance and defined the conditions of social assistance. It pays the bulk of the cost of income maintenance and social services. It has retained close control over social security schemes. While not participating in the direct running of many schools and hospitals, it has over the years supervised the delivery of these services.

The state occupies a central position in the welfare field because it brings in the economic resources necessary to sustain a range of social policy programs. This does not mean that the state finances all benefits, as many of them are paid for by the insured. Nevertheless, the state has set up such programs, guarantees them, and underwrites financial shortfalls. It bears the cost of the large noncontributory programs such as unemployment assistance, noncontributory pensions, medical card schemes, public hospitals, and most schools. Some control is exercised over health services and schools, albeit a rather loose one. This seems to point to a distinctive mode of managing social services in Ireland: the state pays most of the costs while delegating responsibility for running them to private associations. To translate this into the conceptual framework that we adopt in chapter 2, the state relies on two main forms of capital to act in the welfare field: economic and power (control) capital.

The state represents a central player in the Irish welfare field. How can we account for its action in this field, and which principles underpin its strategies of welfare development in front of other players? An answer to these questions is attempted in this chapter. It is contended that the state enters the welfare field with a range of resources, which are referred to as capital (mainly economic resources, power and also, to some extent, symbolic capital), and that it endeavors to maximize its legitimacy, that is, to increase its symbolic capital. The determinants of welfare legitimacy are scrutinized in this context. The core of the analysis concerns the conditions that determine the rate at which the state converts its resources into legitimacy, into symbolic capital.

WELFARE AND STATE CENTRALIZATION [1]

It has been widely argued that most social services can be effectively delivered only at the local level. Local authorities assume responsibility for a widening range of social services. Welfare development would then increase the involvement of local authorities in the provision of such welfare benefits, mainly because more and more social services are delivered at this level. However, the adequate provision of such benefits and services remains of great significance for the central state; the way that such benefits are granted and services are performed have consequences for the support enjoyed by the welfare system as a whole and consequently for the state which has become its guarantor. The need for central supervision increases, and local government is brought more and more under the control of the political center. The reliance on local government for the delivery of social services intensifies the interest of the political center in the activities of local government. This interest rests on financial considerations, as the state endeavors to contain or minimize public social expenditure. Furthermore, the central state continues to bear responsibility for social services; inefficient delivery at the local level or uneven quality or levels of benefit produce dissatisfaction directed at the central power itself. The latter acquires, in that sense, a vested interest in ensuring that efficient and standard services are being offered at the local level. In terms of our conceptualization, the state closely monitors the way that its political and economic resources are converted into the symbolic capital of legitimacy. One needs to disentangle all the elements of this argument and test them empirically.

Is It Valid to Assert that the Expansion of the Welfare State Leads to the Direct Involvement of Local Government in the Provision of Social Services?

One accepts without much difficulty that most social services, to reach their clientele in an effective way, are best delivered in the locality. Yet, this does not necessarily mean that local authorities assume responsibility for such services, as diverse institutional devices can be mobilized to ensure such delivery. First, the administrative agencies of central government may decide to set up their own local agencies and operate directly at a local level, under the direct administrative supervision of the central agency or ministry. The responsibility for particular social services is sometimes assigned to agencies created for this particular purpose. These special, separate agencies are given a great deal of autonomy in the way that they function, within the framework prescribed to them. Finally, the delivery of social services may rest on the existing agencies of local government, which have always performed a range of services in the locality. Decentralization does not offer the only possible administrative response to welfare development.

The involvement of local government in the provision of welfare services takes two main forms. Local government agencies assume administrative responsibility for them, or else local authorities contribute to their financing. Some countries rely very heavily on local government for the delivery of welfare benefits, with Denmark leading the field, along with Sweden, Norway, and Switzerland. Other countries largely bypass the agencies of local government; such is the case for the United Kingdom, France, Italy, and very definitely Ireland. In the latter, local authorities bear no responsibility at all for most social security programs. A Social Insurance Fund has been set up to cover mainly old age pensions, widows' pensions, and unemployment. But the fund is administered by the Department of Social Welfare. The same statement can be made for the diverse assistance schemes in which local government has no involvement, either administrative or financial. Local authorities participate in the running of some health services and a minority of schools. They are represented in regional Health Boards and Vocational Education Councils. Although such authorities run the relevant services, they do so under the close supervision of central powers. Furthermore, the financial resources come mainly from central government. County councils bear direct responsibility for the construction and management of social housing, within the financial limits imposed by the central government. Local authorities also decide on the granting of rent allowances.

The comparative study of the link between welfare development and involvement of local government provides some evidence for the existence of such a link: the more developed welfare systems are characterized by the highest level of local government involvement. But this link exists only in the form of a statistical correlation. It does not imply that local government involvement actually increases as the welfare system develops. In any case, Ireland constitutes a definite exception: welfare development has not increased local government involvement in the provision of welfare benefits.

Has an Increased Participation of Local Government in Welfare Produced a Centralization of Power?

Centralization means that power is assigned to central institutions while, in a context of decentralization, noncentral agencies and mainly agencies of local government enjoy a great deal of leeway in their decision making. Local authorities can, in the latter case, operate with great autonomy and choose the way that they fulfill their functions. In that sense, their autonomy is measured by the range of functions entrusted to them. At the same time, centralization and decentralization of power do not constitute absolute facts, and one must envisage degrees of centralization/ decentralization, according to the extent to which the activity of local agencies is supervised or controlled by the central authorities. State centralization may take two forms: an extension of the range of matters that come under the authority of the central agencies of government or else an intensification of the controls that the political center exercises on the local agencies. In both cases, the issue of centralization concerns the nature of the relations established between central government and local government.

B.C. Smith (1985) has identified three dimensions that seem to matter for appraising the extent of centralization/ decentralization. He points to the range of tasks performed by local government; he also mentions the nature of local government revenues; he then turns to the form of central control over local government:

- The first criterion in the measurement of centralization involves the range of responsibilities assigned to local authorities. A possible measure of the functions taken up by local government is provided by the proportion of public servants (or, rather, public sector workers) who are operating at a local level. The proportion of public expenditure that is effectuated at a local level offers another, possibly more accurate way of measuring the range of functions.
- A significant aspect of the relations between central and local authorities concerns the source of revenues for local authorities. It is widely asserted, for instance, that local government depends more and more on financial transfers from central government. Financial reliance on the central state does not necessarily mean loss of autonomy. Grants or subsidies from central government are conventionally divided into specific grants and block grants. The central government subsidizes or even pays entirely for particular social programs, and the money so allocated is spent in the way stipulated by the central powers; in which case, the level of local government autonomy remains very limited. The central state may transfer a certain amount of money, for instance, a proportion of taxes, to the diverse agencies of local government, and the latter decide on how exactly to use this money: this constitutes a block grant.

Ireland must, by all accounts, be considered a highly centralized state. The percentage of public money spent at the local level could be defined, in a comparative context, as middling (around 30 percent). But less than half of the local budget is raised by these authorities, which depend heavily on central grants allocated for specified purposes. Most crucially, the central state exercises very close administrative control over the county councils. It seems that this central control has actually increased over time; the proportion of public expenditure spent by local bodies has steadily declined from the 1950s (Table 3.1).

Table 3.1
Proportion of Public Expenditure by Local Bodies

1955	35.8%
1960	30.7%
1965	29.6%
1970	28.6%
1975	31.4%
1980	29.7%
1985	27.5%
1990	26.9%
1993	26.4%

Sources: Maguire 1987: page 463; *National Income and Expenditure*, various years.

The comparative study of the link between welfare development and state centralization has contradicted the link that was postulated between the expansion of the welfare state and state centralization. It is conventionally argued that the growing direct involvement of local government in the provision of welfare benefits and services (an automatic consequence of welfare development) produces a centralization of power, a need for greater control by the central state. These links were investigated in eight West European countries, and no correlation was observed between the level of welfare provision and the level of state centralization, but it was found that this absence of a link resulted from two strong associations that neutralized each other: one positive between welfare effort and local government involvement and the other negative between the latter and state centralization.

The higher involvement of local government in the delivery of social services is accompanied by a decrease in the level of state centralization. This occurs, in part, because some countries, which turn to local authorities in order to provide welfare benefits, remain very decentralized. More crucially, a central state that exercises a high level of control over local government (a highly centralized state) will often effectively bypass local government to deliver social services. Some, probably most countries with a high level of state centralization do not involve local government in the delivery of social services. Ireland provides a clear illustration of such a situation.

We have already established that Ireland does not typically rely on local agencies for the purpose of delivering welfare benefits. Historically, as the welfare system grew, it did not increase its reliance on local government. Most social services were based on voluntary organizations, mainly religious: this has been eroded but not yet challenged. The central government retained a close control over the various social insurance schemes. The Irish state has always been highly centralized, and this centralization has, if anything, strengthened over time. With its entrenched position, the state opted for a centralized mode of organization of all social policy programs. In a sense, the style of state operation replicated itself in the emerging features of the welfare system. But this did not conform to another style that had characterized the provision of a range of welfare services: a setup in which the state paid for the services but allowed selected private organizations to run such services. The fact that the social security system was shaped in the centralized style (rather than in a mixed style) suggests that administrative style is not merely a matter of choice. It depends on the structure of the field and on the position of the state within it. The presence of the Catholic Church in the provision of social services produces a distinctive context for the conversion of the economic and power capital of the state. The latter practically alone occupies the field of income maintenance. In this field, the weakness of local democracy lowers the legitimacy costs of a centralized provision of welfare benefits. A decentralized provision of such benefits would itself carry high legitimacy costs in a context of weak local democracy. The existence of strong clientelist practices in Irish local government, at the very least, raises the possibility of inequities and biases.

THE LEGITIMACY OF THE WELFARE STATE [2]

The concept of legitimacy is used with considerable looseness. It frequently refers to the capacity of a sociopolitical system to produce and maintain acquiescence from the citizens of the nation-state. It is then equated with support. But, as Weber (1978: 941–948) has emphasized, individuals or groups comply with authority for a whole range of reasons: opportunism, fear, self-interest, apathy, and so on. The concept of legitimacy applies only when consent and acquiescence rest on a belief in the adequacy and fairness of established political institutions. In this sense, legitimacy points toward the beliefs according to which the authority of the central power is justified in the eyes of those who are subjected to it. Some writers demand even more of this concept of legitimacy. They actually refuse to grant any validity to such popular beliefs. The exercise of power can be validated only according to universal values, which have nothing to do with popular feelings. But such a definition of legitimacy remains far too severe and restrictive and would hardly allow for an empirical analysis. It seems preferable to retain the second definition of legitimacy, that of consent based on beliefs and values, as it allows for other sources of support.

People may then support the welfare state on grounds other than norms and beliefs. Support does not require a belief in the appropriateness and fairness of the state's welfare activity. They may even uphold a particular social structure, without having to justify it. They do so, for instance, if they receive from it rewards that they value. One imagines, however, that a process of rationalization takes place and that such individuals or groups soon find good reasons for enjoying their benefits: they end up justifying them. Two general frames of interpretation are then available: either value/belief or self-interest offers a basis for supporting, in a stable manner, an institution such as the welfare state. Other possible sources of support play, at best, a secondary role. If one convincingly shows that self-interest is not implicated in the support for welfare programs, then support depends on beliefs about the rights or wrongs of such programs. In other words, one would be entitled to equate support and legitimacy.

Legitimacy then refers to the principles or values according to which an activity or an institution is successfully justified. Concern about the legitimacy of the welfare state springs from a changing perception of the crisis of capitalism: from conventional economic crisis to a crisis of ideas and beliefs. The welfare state is said to contribute to the reproduction of advanced societies. It pacifies the poor and the unemployed; it neutralizes the possible dissidence of large groups of people; it promotes social integration (Flora and Heidenheimer 1982; O'Connor 1973; Offe 1984). The legitimacy that social welfare generates by performing these functions is assumed to be transferred to the state. In reverse, any weakening of support and legitimacy for the welfare state would significantly add to the difficulties of social reproduction.

P. Rosanvallon (1988) has given several reasons for the alleged crisis of the welfare state, as it is manifested through diminishing support. The most significant difficulty relates to the inherent ineffectiveness of the welfare state. It fails to achieve its two main objectives of protection against risks and income redistribution. In fact, it has been contended that the many promises inherent in the welfare state cannot all be fulfilled, and this intensifies feelings of deprivation (Mayntz 1975). Not only does the welfare system produce its own inequities and disturb accepted income differences and relativities, but the selectivity of welfare programs toward particular groups generates conflicts. The third main difficulty concerns the scarcity of public goods and the unrestricted access of some categories of people to a wide (some would say excessive) range of services. It has to do with the lack of discrimination in distributing benefits. Finally, many people feel that they do not get value for money; the perceived increased cost of services is not matched by improved benefits.

All these factors point to practical difficulties that may well reduce popular support for the welfare state. But they do not indicate a crisis of belief in the rightness of welfare programs and do not, as such, imply a crisis of legitimacy. Other difficulties highlighted about the welfare state come closer to the issue of legitimacy. It is said to erode the motivational patterns of individuals (Habermas 1976). Welfare benefits weaken the perceived relationship between individual performance and well-being. The reliance on welfare damages work incentives and threatens individual freedom. It undermines some of the values that are central to the reproduction of advanced societies. We need to measure the level of support that exists for the welfare state and then ascertain if this support arises on the basis of beliefs and values or on the basis of interests.

In 1990, the International Social Survey Programme conducted a survey of attitudes concerning the role of government for welfare in a range of countries, including Ireland. Some of the questions related to the welfare state or, more precisely, to attitudes on welfare. The questions asked were formulated in the following manner: "On the whole, do you think it should be or should not be the government's responsibility to: -provide health care for the sick; -provide a decent standard of living for the old; -provide a decent standard of living for the unemployed; -give financial help to university students from low-income families; -provide decent housing for those who can't afford it?"

Ireland registered a very high level of support for all welfare institutions (Table 3.2). But the real question concerns the determination of the basis for such a high level of support. This support can be accounted for in terms of two types of interpretation. Support is explained either in terms of values and beliefs that people generally hold about the welfare state or else in terms of what is profitable to them. In other words, support for welfare programs is based on legitimacy or on self-interest. People may support an activity or an institution on the basis of the interest that they have in its existence. The self-interest model assumes that support for welfare programs is determined by the social circumstances of the individual involved. Those in greatest need of such benefits declare themselves more in favor of welfare spending and welfare programs in general. This has been labeled the "need explanation" of attitudes to welfare (Whiteley 1981). Needs are reflected in the interest that people consider that they possess in social welfare. This kind of explanation implies that individuals decide, in a rational way and on the basis of their needs, what their interests are (Taylor-Gooby 1983). In such a perspective, it is assumed that people support an activity or an institution on the basis of the interest that they have in its existence.

Table 3.2
Level of Popular Support for Social Policy Programs

Health Care	99.0%
Old People Pensions	98.1%
Unemployment Benefits	90.6%
Support for Low Income Students	96.1%
Housing	95.7%
Aggregate Index	95.9%

Support for the welfare state on the basis of self-interest has been investigated in several countries. These studies have identified the social circumstances that determine the level of support and guide us in the investigation of Irish welfare support. A study of public support for welfare conducted in Finland has stressed the significance of class position. Manual workers, who generally benefit more from social services, voice more favorable opinions about the welfare state than middle-class respondents (Pöntinen 1988). This finding applies, in fact, to a wide range of countries (Haller, Höllinger and Raubal 1990; Whiteley 1981). For instance, manual workers in England express more support for council housing: the fact that practically only working-class families reside in council houses is not foreign to such an attitude (Taylor-Gooby 1985). In a similar way, low-income categories display more supportive attitudes toward the welfare state than higher-income categories. Coughlin's comparative study reached a similar conclusion about the "lower classes," more supportive of the welfare state than other social classes (Coughlin 1980).

Social circumstances do not only refer to class or income, but also involve demographic characteristics. It has been contended that the gender variable does not influence welfare support to any great extent. Nonetheless, one notes the more positive attitude of women toward the welfare state (Pöntinen 1988). In particular, women endorse more strongly child benefits and single-parent benefits (Taylor-Gooby 1983, 1985). Age also influences welfare interest. One would expect old people to favor state responsibility for pension schemes, although no actual link has been observed there (Pöntinen 1988; Whiteley 1981). On the other hand, younger people, probably with children, are more positively disposed toward family benefits (Pöntinen 1988; Taylor-Gooby 1983). Age would then determine welfare support through the family lifecycle. Those with dependent children indicate more support for child allowances, for expenditure on education, and also for universal health services (Taylor-Gooby 1983, 1985). One imagines in this context that those who are not married or have no children would be less supportive of the welfare state.

One also expects those who, at one stage in their lives, have depended on a particular social service to remain supportive of it. For instance, people who have experienced unemployment tend to favor more generous unemployment benefits (Lewis 1980). Finally, public sector employees display a highly supportive attitude toward the welfare state: indeed, many of them are employed to provide social services such as health and education. To conclude, support for a range of social benefits varies, at least to some extent, according to the relevance of such benefits to respondents, according to the interest that they develop in them (Taylor-Gooby 1983: 176–171).

Beedle and Taylor-Gooby summarized their study of welfare support by emphasizing the homogeneous structure of attitudes to welfare. "The main findings are threefold: first, the most striking impression is of a uniformity in opinions about both the way welfare is financed at present and the way in which it ought to be financed" (Beedle and Taylor-Gooby 1983: 34). Opinions about, or support for, welfare programs do not vary greatly according to social circumstances, but the latter do not entirely lose their relevance: "Secondly, within the overall framework of homogeneous public opinion, a complex inter-weaving of ideas about self-interest, value-judgments about the welfare state, and the social circumstances of respondents is associated with opinions about tax and welfare" (Beedle and Taylor-Gooby 1983: 15). The relevance of needs and interests is partly upheld in the studies referred to previously, but it does not quite match the weight of values and beliefs. Attitudes toward social benefits are "influenced by value judgments to a greater extent than by social circumstances, and the influence appears to be more or less autonomous" (Beedle and Taylor-Gooby 1983: 34). To recapitulate, personal and social circumstances remain secondary in the support for the welfare state. Value judgments exercise an autonomous influence that is far greater than social circumstances. If interest does not play the primary role in shaping the opinions that people form about welfare services, it becomes reasonable to consider that such support is grounded in beliefs and values, that opinions about welfare are organized around basic judgments. Support would then be equated with legitimacy. Does the available information about welfare support in Ireland validate these views?

In the International Social Survey Programme (ISSP) survey mentioned earlier, information is given about the level of support for state responsibility for the following social services: health, old age pensions, unemployment, and housing. All the cross-tabulations reveal a slightly more supportive attitude by women toward welfare programs, when measured in actual figures. However, despite the fairly large sample size (1,005 respondents), the recorded difference never reaches an acceptable level of significance. Gender does not constitute a significant source of variation in the support for the Irish welfare state. It was also anticipated that age would affect, to some extent, support for some social programs. For instance, one would expect greater support from older people for health services and for good pension schemes. In fact, only a very weak relationship is observed in this context. Those over sixty-five display more definite support for public health services and pensions. But the other age categories do not differ much. In any case, the results are not statistically significant. A weak significant association emerges only in relation to support for state responsibility for health care, and it occurs mainly because the over sixty-fives register a more emphatic support than all the other age categories.

It was also considered plausible, on the basis of need and interest, that the marital status (married or living together, as opposed to being single) would make a difference concerning family benefits (which we could not test) and housing. But no significant relationship is recorded. The need explanation also takes into consideration the sector of employment. Not only do consumers of particular social services possess an interest in the welfare state, but so do those who are employed by the state or are in the public sector. One should then observe, on the basis of interest, a higher level of support for welfare state activities among public sector employees. Generally speaking, public sector and private sector employees express a rather similar level of support for the welfare state (with the public sector employees being marginally more supportive). Strangely enough, employees in semistate bodies and the self-employed show a lower commitment. This does not accord with the interest explanation, as it was formulated earlier. The main line of division separates employees (either public or private) from the self-employed. This points to another major difference of interest, between employees and the small property category, as they relate differently to welfare services and benefits. Even then, those employed in the semistate sector disrupt this neat division, as they join the self-employed in their low support.

Class was considered by Pöntenin (1988) to form the most important factor in patterning support for the welfare state. Is such a claim upheld in the Irish context, at least in terms of three main social boundaries: the professional, the other nonmanual, and the manual? The cross-tabulations reveal the existence of a definite class pattern of support for all aspects of welfare services. For instance, the professional category is far less supportive of public health care or of public responsibility for the standard of living of the old. Manual workers particularly favor public support for the unemployed or for social housing. All these differences, statistically significant, broadly confirm Pöntinen's conclusions. But the association remains quite weak.

These results confirm, practically in all respects, Taylor-Gooby's conclusions in his British survey. One finds, first of all, a high homogeneity of opinion. Most people are supportive of the welfare state, and this support varies only slightly according to a small range of factors. The relevance of social programs for categories of people, in terms of need and interest, plays some role in determining the level of support. But such factors must be considered as, at best, secondary (class, income, sector of employment) or even marginal (gender, age, marital status). In that sense, support for the welfare state in Ireland depends more on legitimacy than on self-interest.

THE DETERMINANTS OF WELFARE LEGITIMACY [3]

The relevant literature has clearly identified those social programs that enjoy a high level of support and those that do not. In fact, high support should be seen as the norm, with only a few welfare programs encountering difficulties in mobilizing this. However, this relevant literature loses its clarity with regard to the reasons for various levels of support/ legitimacy. Conventional surveys shed little light on this issue.

In general terms, a distribution of resources can be justified in three ways. People receive what they *need*, what they *deserve* (or merit), or what they are entitled to by *right*. These three principles apply to the distribution of benefits by the welfare state.

- Social services were originally aimed at people who did not obtain sufficient resources on the basis of their efforts. The provision of social housing, unemployment benefits, health protection, and so on is justified by the fact that those people need it.
- The provision of welfare may also be based on merit, if welfare benefits are related to contributions. For instance, a direct relationship is usually established between the number of years that one contributes to a pension fund and the actual level of pension that one receives. The link between costs and rewards is retained, and the principle of distributive justice is upheld. A linkage between benefits and contributions is involved in all forms of insurance schemes in which entitlements depend on contributions.
- As members of the group or citizens of the nation, people are entitled to a range of services and benefits, independently of what they achieve. T.H. Marshall (1950) has recorded the development of rights through which large categories of people are integrated into society. The welfare state is associated with the extension of social rights, which include the right to work, health, education, a minimum level of subsistence, and so on.

The British evidence clearly identifies social programs that enjoy only a relatively low level of popular support (Ringen 1987; Taylor-Gooby 1983, 1985). Unemployment benefits, single-parent benefits, child benefits, and council housing and assistance in general constitute the least favored social services. This lack of popularity is explained, in an ad hoc manner, by several factors. Such programs provide benefits for people many of whom are considered not to need or deserve them. Access to benefits is open to fraud and does not allow for sufficient discrimination (Taylor-Gooby 1985), or the level of benefits is judged to be too high. For one reason or another, these needy social categories are perceived as undeserving (Taylor-Gooby 1988). Low support for social assistance programs has been noted in comparative studies (Coughlin 1980). One expects that benefits that are distributed selectively on the basis of need (with means-tested access) obtain little support. They attract suspicion, because of either a lack of discrimination or overgenerosity. However, the comparative study did not uphold the view that the provision of social benefits on the basis of needs does not seem to matter greatly for the level of support.

Support and legitimacy are denied to social programs whose beneficiaries are considered not to deserve them. Does that mean that support is granted to programs that are directed at those who merit the benefits? The high support for social security in Germany has been explained by the link between contributions and benefits (Wilson 1993). By contrast, the absence of a link between contributions and benefits in many social programs would account for the low support for welfare in Great Britain. It is then assumed that benefits targeted at those who deserve or merit them enjoy legitimacy. The comparative study of welfare legitimacy did not support these views. The merit of a social program increases support for such a program, but only in association with a wide range of other factors.

Titmuss (1974) has established a distinction between types of welfare state or, rather, between two poles in the development of the welfare state. The first type of welfare state is labeled residual; the other pole, institutional. The difference between them concerns the basis of access to welfare benefits: very selective in the residual type, universal in the other case. These two types also differ according to the degree of state involvement in the provision of such services. Moreover, the universal type redistributes income, while the residual does not, at least not to any great extent. Titmuss strongly advocated the more developed type of welfare, the universalist type, suggesting also more popular support for it. Such a view is upheld by Coughlin (1980), who attributes the high level of support, in a range of countries, for pension programs, health insurance, and family allowances to their universal character. In a rather similar perspective, Esping-Andersen (1990) seems to share the view, although not explicitly formulated, that social democratic welfare regimes are more legitimate and for this reason would enjoy more popular support; liberal regimes, less. This view is only weakly upheld by the comparative analysis.

A distinction has also been made between direct state provision of welfare services and benefits in the form of financial transfers. According to Alber

(1988), this constitutes one of the major differences between a Scandinavian type of welfare state and a Continental type. Do transfers and services generate a different level of support/ legitimacy? It has been found that the provision of services, rather than financial transfers, generates support.

The most popular social programs in Britain have been clearly identified: pensions, education, and health services. These services are directed, potentially at least, at the whole of the population: they "command mass support because they meet mass demands" (Taylor-Gooby 1985). Not only are populations in nations with a large social policy sector more supportive of welfare, but "heavy" social programs receive a stronger support (Ringen 1987). Or else: "Anti-welfare state sentiments over the past decade have generally been weakest where welfare spending has been heaviest, and vice-versa" (Esping-Andersen 1990: 33). These comments point to the size of welfare programs as a relevant factor. However, a large program (i.e., as measured by the proportion of GDP that it absorbs) does not necessarily spread widely. In the same way, universal welfare programs do not always mean large programs. The size, scope, and mode of access to benefits (e.g., universal access) that characterize a welfare program are best kept separate. They may stimulate different levels of support. For instance, no basis exists to believe that support for widespread services or benefits derives from their universal character, defined as mode of access.

It would seem that a high level of support is related to the widespread character of such services, what Alber (1988) has called their scope. A very high level of support is enjoyed by services that benefit the whole population, that is, have a wide scope. The widespread character of a program, as opposed to a narrower scope, occupies a crucial place in determining the level of support. The widespread character of a welfare program contributes significantly to generating support for it, while the narrow character of a welfare program strongly militates against a high level of support. The scope of social programs operates in both directions: a widespread social program upholds support, while the narrow scope of a program weakens this support.

How do we account, then, for the particularly high level of support for the welfare state that is registered in Ireland? A first explanation points to the level of economic development and prosperity: "We expect, therefore, that the inhabitants of nations which are less advanced and prosperous will express a more positive attitude to state intervention than those of the most prosperous nations" (Haller, Höllinger, and Raubal 1990: 34). Poorer countries tend to express more support for state involvement in welfare provision. However, some very rich countries also register a high level of support for welfare institutions, thus undermining such a relationship. It could then be contended that the welfare state in Ireland is strongly supported because the benefits and services that are provided by the state are widespread (i.e., they cover a wide range of people). Even unemployment benefits in Ireland are best defined as widespread, because of the number of people involved. This explanation may help clarify the nature of the link that seems to exist between the level of welfare support and the level of economic prosperity. If one makes the assumption that, in poorer countries, more people depend on welfare, then an indirect link is established between welfare support and the level of economic development.

THE STRATEGIES OF THE STATE IN THE WELFARE FIELD

It has been established that the state constitutes a crucial player in the welfare field. This central position is ensured by the fact that it practically finances all social policy programs: directly by spending public money and indirectly when contributions to the Social Fund are treated as another form of taxation. But the state does not rely only on economic resources. It controls in a direct way all income maintenance programs, in the sense that it has set them up and manages them on its own. It also exercises administrative control over such social services as education and health or over the provision of public housing, even if it does not itself run such services. The state then operates in the welfare field with formidable power resources. It also enjoys authority in the field, for it can present itself as the representative of the people against all particular interests and groups. This authority is rooted in representative procedures and institutions; it generates a reserve of legitimacy on which the state draws when needed, and this legitimacy contains the symbolic capital accumulated in the past.

The state strategically makes use of the relevant resources in the welfare field. But what exactly is it trying to achieve in doing so? What, in other words, is it endeavoring to gain through its involvement in the provision of welfare? The state, like every other agent, is concerned with maximizing the values that are useful to it. It aims at increasing its symbolic capital, to use Bourdieu's vocabulary, but also its power capital. Symbolic capital refers to that very special resource that makes the state an acceptable institution to the majority of the population and that justifies its action. It is equated with legitimacy, which manifests itself in the form of enduring approval and popular support for the institution. The increased power that the state hopes to produce for itself through its involvement in the welfare field constitutes a rather different kind of resource. This resource is utilized in the larger field of power relations, where the relations of force are set. The determination of these power relations depends on the level of pressure that is exercised in this global field. The level of pressure directly derives from the relations of power that are established in the diverse subfields, from the "capabilities" that can be mobilized. But at the same time that a capital of power is generated in the welfare field, the field of power sets the context within which the welfare game is being played.

The state enters the welfare field with a range of resources that we call economic, political, and symbolic capital, and it uses them strategically. It does so in ways that aim at generating additional resources of legitimacy and power. The stake for the state is to maximize the relevant resources and to produce more capital than it actually spends. It has to convert a set of resources into another set of resources in a way that ensures some gain. The following analysis focuses on these conversions and on the factors that determine the rate at which one kind of resource is converted into another.

The state is engaged in a delicate balancing act in which, through its involvement in the provision of welfare, it seeks to accumulate legitimacy, its symbolic capital. It does that mainly, in Habermas' vocabulary, through acts of compensation. It provides a range of social benefits and services that require a large volume of public money. Finance comes from taxation and social security contributions; extracting it may incur heavy costs and a potential loss of symbolic capital. The state must ensure that the costs of obtaining the necessary economic capital do not exceed the gains in legitimacy that are generated by its involvement in welfare provisions. The main stake for the state concerns the rate at which it transforms its economic capital into symbolic capital. It undertakes to maximize legitimacy (symbolic capital) at the lowest economic cost (economic capital). But the reverse side of this exchange also holds true: it must find ways of extracting the necessary economic capital at the lowest possible cost of symbolic capital. It has to reach a balance between reaping the symbolic advantages of its welfare involvement and containing costs, potentially unlimited, of providing social benefits. And this balance depends, at least to some extent, on circumstances.

The first relevant circumstance relates to the symbolic cost of extracting economic resources in the form of tax. Taxation is never popular, but the Irish pattern of taxation has been persistently criticized for its inequities. It is perceived as leaning heavily on some categories of people, particularly on employees. Some statistical evidence upholds the perception that the self-employed, particularly, farmers, find it relatively easy to evade taxation. Profit and capital gains often enjoy generous treatment. Despite such perceptions, the Irish state does not face intense or open opposition to the high level of taxation or its inequities. In 1979, a massive demonstration was held on the streets of Dublin in protest at the level of taxation for employees. But disapproval of, and hostility toward, taxation mainly take the form of widespread avoidance and evasion. The ability of the state to raise revenues from taxation (mainly direct taxation) remains quite severely constrained.

The use of economic resources for providing social benefits does not automatically produce approval. It depends on a range of features, such as the mode of access to social benefits, the coverage of social policy programs, and the level of benefits. The review of the factors determining popular support has pointed out those features of social policy programs that generate symbolic capital and those that do not. All means-tested programs attract little popular support. On the contrary, benefits given in the form of services enjoy a high level of legitimacy; benefits that primarily involve a financial transfer do not produce a similar high level of legitimacy. A similar comment applies to the scope of welfare programs: those programs that cover a large number of people are supported far more than those that are targeted at particular categories of people.

One could, of course, ask why the central authorities in all countries do not simply adopt a set of social policy programs that maximize their legitimacy? Once the factors determining the generation of symbolic capital have been identified, all countries would choose similar programs and produce a convergent welfare system. But the welfare system is predominantly shaped in the field of power, in which the major forces in society relate to each other. The modalities of organization and functioning of any social policy program create winners and losers, and maximizing legitimacy does not represent the overriding consideration for many of the players and is not the only relevant consideration for the state.

The state also participates in the welfare field with a capital of power at its disposal. The state holds administrative responsibility for the whole social security system, although it is not so directly involved in the management of social services such as education and health. It still bears most of the responsibility for the effective delivery of benefits and the quality and efficiency of such services. The quality of services, of course, depends on the amount of material resources invested in such services. It also hinges on the ability of the state to follow through with its schemes: its effectiveness and also its efficiency, which demand the display of its capacities.

Several considerations appear relevant in this context. The "caring" activity of the state generates legitimacy benefits only to the extent that the state is not held responsible for the problems that created the need for such welfare in the first place. If, for instance, the economic policy of the state is blamed for increasing mass unemployment, the welfare measures introduced in favor of the unemployed will not gain the state much symbolic benefit. For this reason, the state will endeavor to displace the focus of attention away from its own contribution to the problem or from its failure to reduce it. The provision of welfare benefits can prove counterproductive in other ways, as far as legitimacy is concerned. The conditions that are set for receiving welfare benefits often lead to stigmatization and create a great deal of resentment.

The production of symbolic capital depends on the evaluation that people make of the diverse facets of the welfare system. It constitutes the outcome of a judgment and is based on the values that are relied upon in this context. So which values is the Irish welfare system expected to uphold? Many commentators have analyzed the welfare system from the point of view of the equalization of living conditions that it is supposed to produce. The Irish welfare system is not organized in a way that ensures a significant redistribution of income. In any case, redistribution does not represent the rationale underlying the organization and functioning of the welfare system in Ireland. In fact, the latter contributes in a fairly direct way to the class structuration of Irish society. It offers alternative access to material resources for welfare recipients and opens another structure of economic opportunities for those who find employment within it.

The idea that welfare services contribute to the stratification of a society has been developed by Esping-Andersen (1990). This approach has been applied to

Ireland to show how some social categories are shaped and sometimes generated by public social policy (Breen et al. 1990). The Irish welfare system creates its own categories of interest around the access to, and the level of, welfare benefits and services. Relevant social services produce different categories of people, according to the conditions of access to such benefits. For instance, access to mortgage relief or to council housing clearly sets apart two categories of people, with very different interests. Different pension interests are also formed according to the kind of program, contributory or noncontributory, public or private, in which they participate. The welfare system does not simply reflect or follow the main lines of social division. For instance, the fact that employees in the private and in the public sector enjoy different pensions schemes and benefits reflects a deep division within Irish society, according to the modalities of participation in the labor market. But the way that the pension system as a whole operates greatly reinforces this line of social differentiation. The difference in welfare regimes associated with these two sectors contributes in a significant way to the structuration of Irish society. Besides various categories of welfare recipients, the welfare system produces diverse categories of welfare providers. Professional workers such as doctors, teachers, nurses, and social workers obtain material resources on the basis of their participation not to the market but to the public sector.

Although the state does not necessarily seek to reduce social inequalities, its action may still be animated by a principle of distributive justice. It would endeavor to ensure a distribution of income that, although unequal, can be deemed fair. After all, a major part of social security is based on the principle of insurance in which a link is made between contribution and benefit. But the Irish welfare system is not easily analyzed in terms of granting what people deserve or merit. David Rottman et al. (1982) have investigated the impact on socioeconomic groups of their relation to the state in terms of the balance of costs and benefits. Some redistribution occurs within the categories of employees. Those who enjoy a high income lose out most to the state, while those with a very low income gain from their relationship to the state. But this redistributive pattern does not include property-based groups. For instance, all categories of farmers benefit from their relationship to the state, even those with high incomes. This does not conform to the principle of distributive justice. To take a very different example, can the existence of a category of long-term unemployed living in poverty be interpreted as complying with the principle of distributive justice?

This brings up another basis for evaluating the welfare system: the extent to which it contributes to social integration. It does so, allegedly, by upholding a range of social rights and fostering a sense of citizenship. We have already commented on the fact that the Irish welfare system offers few universal benefits. Social policy programs in Ireland do not hinge on the notion of citizenship. Welfare in Ireland, far from promoting social integration, has retained a large category of socially assisted individuals living on the edge of poverty, strongly stigmatized, and generally excluded. To conclude on this theme, the welfare system in Ireland does not fare well in terms of the three main values that we have considered. The state generates little approval and legitimacy on such a basis.

Another general circumstance may determine the rate at which the state generates its symbolic capital. Some players seek to insulate the welfare field from the broader relations of force in society at large: those players enjoy a stronger position in the welfare field than in society and they yield more influence in the context of welfare. Their control over the welfare stakes is enhanced by a sheltered, differentiated welfare field, set apart from the wider struggle in which they count for little. Other social forces, more central to the core of power relations in society, occupy a rather marginal position within the welfare field. The differentiation of the welfare field diminishes their power within it. All this means that the degree of differentiation of the welfare field constitutes a major stake in its construction. Some forces aim at sheltering the welfare field from the broader context, at separating it from the larger struggles within the social formation. Other players would rather open the field to those social forces that command a greater strength in society at large than in the welfare field. The welfare state can be neither totally differentiated and acquire a separate dynamic nor totally absorbed by the field of power. One suspects that the state, in the Irish context, prefers a less autonomous welfare field: this allows it to limit its welfare effort (itself very costly in economic and consequently in symbolic capital) by pointing to the resistance of influential groups. It also manages to contain in this way the influence of the Catholic Church within the welfare field, without undermining the general support that it receives from it. In this way, the degree of differentiation of the welfare field constitutes a "circumstance" that determines the rate of conversion of symbolic capital.

The state operates in the welfare field with another resource, that of symbolic capital that derives from its authoritative position as a bearer of public power. Symbolic capital (its authority) can then be easily transformed into power capital. This conversion happens within the welfare field when the state uses its authority to commit public resources to social policy programs and deliver social benefits, despite obstacles and possibly against opposition. The state relies on its own legitimacy in order to assert its power in front of other players, but it also mobilizes the legitimacy that emanates from other players in the welfare field—more particularly, the Catholic Church, which yields considerable symbolic capital in this field—to increase its power capital. The power capital that the state succeeds in producing in the welfare field, on the basis of its authority and its ability to marshal the legitimacy of other players, is then used in the global field, among other things, to contain or decrease the influence of these forces.

CONCLUSION

In this chapter, the rationality of state activity in the field of welfare has been investigated. Welfare development in Ireland has not led, as anticipated on the basis of the relevant literature, to the greater involvement of local authorities. The welfare system has continued to develop along the lines that characterized it from the start: that of a high level of centralization. Social security programs remain firmly controlled by the state. A great deal of autonomy is nonetheless allowed to a range of voluntary organizations in the running of social services, such as education and health, but not to local authorities or agencies.

The caring role that the state has undertaken can be looked at from various angles. In this chapter, the state is treated as a rational agent, with its own orientations and interests, tightly enmeshed in a web of power relations between social forces. The state is mainly interested in securing and even increasing support for its activity. Its welfare functions are best analyzed in these terms. The approval for its welfare activity, which adds to the support that it receives from the mainstream of society, is based not on self-interest but on general values. To that extent, one may speak of legitimacy. It constitutes the resource that the state seeks to maximize through its welfare activity. The factors that determine the level of state legitimacy in its welfare function have been identified. Two factors seem crucial in this respect. Programs that are widespread, that is, that concern a large proportion of the population, are highly supported. Furthermore, social services, rather than financial transfers, enjoy a high level of legitimacy.

If the state is interested in converting the resources that it invests in the welfare field into legitimacy (and into power capital in a less direct way), how does it ensure a good rate of return and maximize its symbolic capital in the field? Some of the factors that determine this rate of conversion have been suggested. They relate to modalities of social policy programs, the basic values implicated in the welfare system, and the level of differentiation of the welfare field.

NOTES

1. Adapted from Peillon 1993.
2. Based on Peillon 1995.
3. Based on Peillon 1996.

4

Welfare and the Catholic Church

A link has been observed between Catholicism and welfare development. The comparative literature suggests that Catholicism represents a major force in welfare development but that it brings about a particular type of development: away from a reliance on universal social benefits. These ideas appear relevant to the study of welfare in Ireland. To what extent has the Catholic Church molded a distinctive welfare regime? The investigation is extended to cover the major orientations of the Irish Catholic Church toward social services and the welfare state in general.

The literature on comparative welfare has begun to emphasize the "Catholic factor." It has also been contended that a weak labor movement can be compensated for by a large Catholic constituency. A strong Catholic political representation has often operated as a substitute for the labor movement in the development of the welfare state. In other words, a society with a large Catholic population sometimes experiences a high level of welfare development, even with a weak labor movement. We need to investigate this idea further. John Stephens (1979: 100–101) has recorded a link between Catholicism and welfare spending. This relationship would be, in large part, accounted for by the commitment of the Catholic Church to the poor and the vulnerable. He suggests that such a link depends on the political context. It is mainly observed when a Catholic party, located at the center, possesses a substantive base among the organized working class.

Harold Wilensky (1981) has also taken into account the impact of Catholicism on welfare development. He measured the strength of the Catholic factor in terms of the electoral basis of Catholic parties. He concluded that the latter have a strong influence. Catholicism and welfare development, he declared, are linked through "corporatism." The social teaching of the church has, for a long time, revolved around corporatism, which was given as the solution to the contradictory alternatives of market capitalism and centralized socialism. Corporatist linkages are said to contribute to welfare effort. Wilensky also asserts that the more intense the competition between Catholic and Left parties, the more that Left parties in power will spend on welfare. His argument really concerns the way that the working class distributes its vote. Catholic parties further welfare development only to the extent that they attract a significant share of the working-class vote. This implies that a dominant left-wing orientation and Catholic parties strongly based in the popular classes form two different bases for welfare development.

Gøsta Esping-Andersen (1990) has also stressed the relevance of Catholicism for welfare development. He makes a distinction between the liberal, conservative, and social democratic welfare regimes. The corporatist regimes have typically been shaped by the Catholic Church. He refers to a subtype of conservative welfare regime as Catholic-authoritarian. Catholic parties in countries such as Holland, Italy, and Germany mobilize large sections of the working classes; they pursue welfare programs that are not drastically at variance with their socialist competitors. The relatively high level of decommodification found in Continental European countries is also related to a long tradition of conservative and Catholic reformism. In summary, Esping-Andersen maintains that there exists a clear correspondence between welfare regimes and the dominant political orientation. He concludes that the conservative welfare regime is fashioned by the influence of Catholicism (Catholic party strength). Universalist welfare regimes, on the other hand, depend on a strong social democratic movement.

Charles Ragin (1994) also points out the relevance of Catholicism for welfare development. Instead of relying on the electoral strength of Catholic political parties, he takes into consideration the percentage of the Catholic population as a measure of Catholic orientation. He uses a method that identifies the configurations of factors that accompany the development of types of welfare system. He manages to isolate the relative weight of the Catholic factor and reaches definite conclusions about the impact of Catholicism. He concludes that a high Catholic percentage of the population, combined with a lack of ethnic division or left-wing government, constitutes one of the configurations associated with the development of a corporatist welfare regime. Austria, France, Italy, and Belgium provide examples of such a situation. A low percentage of Catholic population belongs to the configuration of factors, which includes high GDP per capita and strong left-oriented cabinet, which produces a social democratic welfare regime. In Ragin's analysis, the Catholic factor does not operate on its own, but in a particular context and in combination with other factors.

Ireland may constitute a good case study for understanding how Catholicism shapes the welfare system of a country. It shows how the church has effectively stalled the emergence of universalist social benefits and services; how its concern with poverty has sustained a reliance on social assistance; how it has intervened in public debates in relation to social services but has had little impact on social security; how it has molded a welfare system that stood as an alternative to the universalist welfare principle: and how it could not ultimately uphold this alternative orientation. This chapter focuses on the goals that the Catholic Church in Ireland pursues in relation to welfare and the mechanisms through which it has participated to the elaboration of social policy and to what effect.

ANALYSIS OF THE CATHOLIC CHURCH IN IRELAND

The conventional story holds the view that the Irish Catholic Church was at first strongly opposed to the development of the welfare state, mainly because it feared the pervasive presence of the state. However, the magnitude of welfare needs led to an implicit change of policy, and the church soon urged the state to take up extensive welfare responsibilities. This interpretation of the link between Catholicism and welfare in Ireland is in serious need of revision. This chapter develops the view that Catholicism represented, from the start, a major force behind welfare development in Ireland. But, in keeping with Catholic social thinking, this development was channeled along a path that strongly contrasted with the social democratic orientation (based on universal social services). The Catholic Church was not engaged in a blockage of the welfare state but in directing social services in a particular direction. The extent to which it has succeeded in this endeavor is now investigated.

Very few systematic accounts of the link between the Catholic Church and social policy in Ireland, as opposed to loose commentaries or even historical narratives, have been put forward. For instance, how can we explain the quite extraordinary shift in the hierarchy's social policy in the early 1970s?

The standard analysis of the position of the Catholic Church in Ireland has long remained the work of John Whyte (1980). He examined the role that the Catholic Church has played in relation to public policy since the beginning of the Irish state and up to 1979. He concluded his analysis by rejecting two conventional ways of analyzing the nature of the relationship between church and state in Ireland. The first one simply views the Catholic Church as an interest group like any other. Whyte argued that the power exercised by the Church went beyond the influence that any organized group may seek to apply on the central powers. The bishops enjoy an authority of their own and see their duty as giving guidance to the state. They do not relate to the politicians in a way that resembles that of lobbyists. The second approach emphasizes the overwhelming influence of the Catholic Church on Irish society as a whole. Whyte accepts that Irish politicians heed bishops' statements and go a long way to avoid the opposition of the higher clergy. But he also contends that the Catholic Church does not exercise the kind of power that would transform Ireland into a theocratic state. The power of the hierarchy varies a great deal according to a range of factors. It exerts a definite influence over health, education, and personal morality. It wields little authority in sectors of policy such as social security and even less in relation to nationalist issues or economic policy. Officially, the Catholic Church does not seek to impose its teaching on the state and ensure that its moral tenets would become the law of the land. It states its views on the rights and wrongs of issues and argues its case; but it no longer expects its position to be reflected in legislation. For instance, the hierarchy considered that contraception was morally wrong, but in 1979 it officially accepted that the state legislated its introduction.

Having rejected these two approaches, Whyte puts forward his own model of the relations between state and church, which he views in terms of mutual adjustment. He constantly emphasizes the extensive consensus that exists between church and state. He points to the cordial nature of the relationship between bishops and ministers, even when disagreement occurred. All this implies that the Catholic Church does not have to exercise its influence over the central state. "Churchmen and statesmen were moulded by the same culture, educated at the same schools, quite often related to each other. In these circumstances the chances for conflict were cut to a minimum" (Whyte 1980: 366). The 1970s saw a great deal of change in Irish society and also in the position of the Catholic Church in Ireland. Even then, Whyte contended that the fundamental consensus remained, in that bishops and ministers were adjusting to the new situation in much the same way. If anything, the church engaged in a critique of the way that Irish society was developing and was particularly concerned with unemployment and poverty. This model of the relations between church and state in Ireland is best referred to as one of homogeneity and consensus. The mutual adjustment that takes place between bishops and ministers simply derives from the fact they both have their roots in the same culture. Adjustment without the exercise of power proves possible as long as the culture from which such people emerge remains homogeneous: what happens to this model when culture itself is split, when this homogeneity is shattered, and people's experiences of the new social conditions diverge considerably? This story unfolded after Whyte's writing, in the 1980s and 1990s.

Liam Ryan (1979) has put forward a different model of the relations between church, state, and society. He contended that the Catholic Church was adopting a new, different role: that of the "conscience of society." What does that mean? The main process seems to involve for the church a disengagement from the structure of society, a deinstitutionalization, so to speak, and the assumption of a critical attitude toward the way that Irish society is organized and operates. The church is more and more denouncing existing injustices, discriminations, and inequalities. The church has long included, as least as part of its teaching and activity, a prophetic orientation. Part of this orientation remains the anticipation of the ills to come, of the trends that must be corrected if serious problems are to be avoided. The critique of the relentless progress of the liberal economy in Ireland, with its widespread consequences, prompted bishops for practically the whole of the twentieth century to warn their followers against the new ways and denounce the consequences of such trends. But such episcopal and clerical pronouncements were, by and large, formulated in the language of morality; they urged believers to show vigilance and resist temptations offered by the new world. Social problems were still defined in moralistic and individualistic terms: now social problems, what are perceived as the ills of society, are defined in structural and collective terms. They have become moral problems of a very different kind, and these problems cannot be solved simply by moral exhortations.

But the model of the church as the conscience of society required another, fundamental transformation. This voice should no longer originate from an institutional church, deeply implicated in the structure of power of this society, in fact, an essential pillar of the established society. If the church is to become an "institution of social criticism," it can no longer operate as an institution of power within this society. In the words of Liam Ryan, the church had now to use the power of persuasion rather than dogmatic command; its credibility depended on the wisdom of its words rather than on the dignity of its office. When this institutional disengagement is effectuated, the Catholic Church remains concerned with public morality. But public morality is no longer defined in terms of what corresponds to the creed of the church or, even worst, to the self-interest of the church as an institution. The intervention of the church in public affairs no longer seeks to impose the Catholic credo on the whole population. Public morality is equated with the collective good, the good of society in general. This assumes that the Catholic system of beliefs provides the basis for a universalist critique of Irish society, that the Catholic creed determines right and wrong not only for Catholics but for everybody: Catholicism does not advocate a particular system of beliefs but upholds universal values. The principles at the core of the Catholic creed should be adopted not because they are Catholic but because they sustain the common good.

This passage from particularism to universalism presents many difficulties and dangers. It may involve a deception, in which a particular ideology or creed is offered as universal. Unable to impose its views, the effectiveness of its intervention now depends on its ability to argue convincingly that it defends the public good. This analysis of the role of the Catholic Church in Irish society suggests a trend; it does not imply that the Catholic Church has fully assumed this new role and relinquished its use of power. I also imagine that this analysis possesses an element of advocacy: it recommends that the church embrace with greater determination such an orientation.

The last twenty years have not indicated in a clear way which path the Catholic Church intends to follow. The Catholic Church, or at least some agencies within it, has become a significant voice of social criticism. But rather than the disembedded or disembodied voice of collective consciousness, such a voice is deeply rooted in an apparatus of power. Furthermore, this transformation has not, as such, been chosen. Many factors and mechanisms are forcing the church to alter the way that it relates to Irish society and to the Irish state. The church is moving away from the exercise of institutional power, in part, because this institutional power has been seriously eroded. The dignity of the priestly office no longer allows the church to be heard, simply because the priestly office has lost a great deal of its dignity. Could the power and self-interest of the church still drive this transformation? The erosion of its institutional resources would simply prompt a greater reliance on symbolic resources.

Tony Fahey (1998) has recently returned to the issue of the changing mode of involvement of the Catholic Church with social policy. He establishes a clear distinction between two periods of times. In the first one, the church exercised a deep and practical influence on social policy, mainly because it ran most social services: schools, hospitals, orphanages, and assistance to the poor. But it did not put forward new ideas or develop original thinking. In fact, according to Tony Fahey, the social teaching of the church was characterized by an apparent lack of social conscience, by a failure to acknowledge the stark inequalities that existed in Irish society. Until the 1970s, the Catholic Church concentrated its activity on providing social services, but it did not articulate a clear social teaching. Tony Fahey explains this dramatic change in terms of factors internal to the Catholic Church: Vatican II and the development of liberation theology mainly but also a long-term decline in religious vocations that slowly generated a shortage of personnel. After the 1960s, the church faced difficulties in providing social services, but it displayed a greater commitment to social justice and made "an option for the poor": "The pre-1960s pattern of strong social provision and weak social thought has been reversed in the decades since. Catholic social provision has declined in the face of a rapid fall in the numbers of religious, but Catholic social thought has become more assertive, sharp-edged and committed to the cause of social justice" (Fahey 1998: 427). Such an analysis portrays an institutionally entrenched Catholic Church that, for various reasons, chooses to connect in a different way with social policy.

Fahey states that the primary purpose of social service provision for the Catholic Church was to disseminate and safeguard the faith, not to combat social inequality or reform society. One is presented here with the scenario of a church that, once institutionally self-preserving and entrenched, opted at one stage to act in a predominantly conscientious way. "This was so largely because social service provision was a means rather than an end for the Catholic Church—it was an instrument for the dissemination of the faith, not a field of endeavour which was worth pursuing in its own right" (Fahey 1998: 417). Why, then, did social service provision come to be considered a worthwhile field of endeavor? Why did the Catholic Church cease to treat social service provision as a means for the dissemination of the faith? The language here is probably too loose, for the Catholic Church in Ireland could not have been concerned with the "dissemination of the Catholic faith." The faith was well disseminated in Ireland, with little scope for further progress. But the church had, nonetheless, to reproduce itself: to ensure that believers remained believers, to enforce the practical rules attached to the faith, to protect the institutional position of the church, which facilitates the socialization of people as Catholics; to institutionalize rules that conform to Catholic creed. The reproduction of the Catholic Church in that sense is never ensured. One may suggest that its changing relation to social policy is accounted for by the changing conditions of its reproduction. This idea is elaborated in the final part of this chapter, after we have established the main social policy orientations of the Catholic Church in Ireland.

The claim has been made that the Catholic Church has not been very successful in shaping the welfare system in Ireland or, more precisely, that the Irish welfare system is not deeply imbued with Catholic values. Mary Daly (1999) compares social policy in Ireland and Germany and contends that the German welfare system upholds Catholic values to a greater extent than does Irish welfare.

She reaches this conclusion on the basis of the support provided to the family by social policy programs. Only families requiring assistance receive significant support in Ireland, while the German welfare system offers more sustained, consistent, and across-the-board support. Furthermore, the protection of the material interests of the weakest categories, to which the Catholic Church is committed on the basis of its teaching, did not lead to the upholding of social rights in Ireland: it continued to rely on social assistance. The author concludes that the Irish Catholic Church, although influential in social policy making, failed to fashion it according to the core value of Catholic social teaching. The welfare system in Ireland was deeply marked by a traditional Catholicism, which operated mainly at the political level and displayed little of the social Catholicism that one finds in Germany. The power of the Catholic Church in Ireland has paradoxically not been conducive to the development of a welfare system permeated by Catholic values.

THE SOCIAL TEACHING OF THE CATHOLIC CHURCH

The social policy of the Catholic Church has been articulated by the bishops themselves in several pastorals. But the policy implications of such pastorals have been developed by a commission of the hierarchy, the Council for Social Welfare. More recently, a distinctive voice has emerged from the religious orders and mainly from the Conference of Religious in Ireland (CORI). Numerous religious orders, besides the diocesan clergy, perform a range of social services (such as education, nursing, social work) that are considered important for the church. These religious orders have been required, by the Vatican, to come together at the national level and form an organization composed of superiors or representatives of these orders. They work out their views on a range of relevant issues and are consulted when need be. They have of late become an alternative voice within the Catholic Church, particularly on social matters.

In the following pages, the position of the church is presented and discussed in its own terms, without reference to the actual practice that derives from such a social teaching. The discourse of the Catholic Church is centered on a fundamental value that can be formulated as simply the value of human life and the absolute need to uphold the dignity of human beings. Several objectives are implied by such a fundamental value. "One of the foremost duties of Christians in society is to work for conditions in which all the children of the nation will be guaranteed equality of dignity and opportunity" (Irish Episcopal Conference 1975: 20). The church takes the high moral ground and calls for an equalization of social conditions, particularly for the removal of gross inequalities within the community. This redistribution of income is best achieved through progressive taxation and welfare benefits. The church does not have clear ideas concerning how much inequality is justified or tolerable. "Gross" inequalities refer to excessive inequalities, to the presence of a large group of poor people in the midst of plenty. The church does not promote an equal society but, more modestly, a less unequal society. It calls for equalization rather than for equality. This idea of equality is itself constantly blurred by a systematic reference to equity, and the two terms are sometimes used indiscriminately.

A similar slippage is observed when equality is defined mainly in terms of access and opportunity. Such a formulation of equality is associated with a liberal approach, for which inequality becomes justified when all possess the same chances of attaining the desired goals: "Steps, therefore, that make for increasing equality in access to opportunity and to public services and benefits are of high social and economic value" (Council for Social Welfare 1976: 21). But equality is mainly seen in terms of income redistribution; church statements address at length the necessity of taxation, even of a high level of taxation to sustain the capacity of the state to provide welfare benefits and services. The burden of taxation must be shared equitably, that is, paid by all on the basis of their ability to pay (Council for Social Welfare 1980: 9).

The church is concerned with meeting the particular needs of the most vulnerable in society. This, of course, requires some redistribution of wealth; but it is also based on another fundamental Christian value, solidarity. Society has an obligation to help those who cannot cope on their own. Christians should play an active role in seeking improvements for those whose income is seriously below what is needed to live with dignity in Ireland today (Council for Social Welfare 1989: 35). Particularly, they must enforce society's responsibility toward those who are unemployed, protect their standard of living, and help them improve their lot. "So too, in our own time, unemployment takes its place alongside other wrongs as a denial of the dignity of the person made in God's image. This reverence for the human person is the foundation of the Christian's preferential option for the poor" (Irish Catholic Bishops' Conference 1996: 15). The "haves" are required to act out their moral duty of looking after the "haves-not." This represents the religious basis of social solidarity, and it constitutes a commitment that falls far short of equality. The practice of solidarity should lead to a decrease of social inequality, not to its eradication. In relation to the poor, the Catholic Church seeks to uphold two of its fundamental values: equality and solidarity, which both derive from the dignity invested in human beings. In that sense, a tension exists in the upholding of these two values, and solidarity takes precedence over equality in the Catholic ethic.

It is also out of concern for human dignity that the church expresses criticism about the way that those who depend on social assistance are treated. The manner in which unemployed people receive payment is condemned: the delays in payment, the long queues that they endure, the abrupt treatment that they sometimes suffer (Council for Social Welfare 1989: 49). The church sympathizes with the deep sense of frustration experienced by those who depend on welfare and the feeling of being demeaned that derives from rigid and insensitive procedures (Council for Social Welfare 1996: 11). It strongly denounces any attempt at introducing conditions for obtaining welfare benefits: "It is, frankly, intolerable, and a totally misguided foundation on which to build the type of workforce needed in both parts of Ireland, that individuals should have to take part in particular training, not because of any expectation that it will lead to a job, but simply because they may lose their social welfare entitlement if they do not" (Council for Social Welfare 1989: 52). Generally speaking, those who have to rely on social assistance should not be considered passive recipients; their active participation in the administration of the various schemes should be encouraged.

It could be contended that the church has always exercised "an option for the poor." But the language sustaining this commitment has changed significantly. In the past, this "option for the poor" led to charity, to a personal commitment to improve the living conditions of those in material need. This personal responsibility has not disappeared, and pastoral letters emphasize the Christian duty of individuals in their communities to work toward that end: "We urge every parish and Christian community to show creativity and determination in bringing together people from every walk of life to develop a truly inclusive community where the rights of unemployed people are fully respected" (Irish Catholic Bishops' Conference 1996: 28). Christians are now encouraged to exercise a political duty, exhorted to put pressure on society, to force the state to assume its responsibility toward the poor. Individuals still matter, but tackling poverty is beyond the capacity of any individual or even voluntary association. Only the state possesses the resources and power to address this problem. For this reason, the language of the church has shifted from moral prescription, directed at individuals, to social critique. The main problems faced by Ireland, most crucially those of unemployment and poverty, are now perceived as the product of the very structure of Irish society, of the way it is organized and functions.

The fundamental dignity of humanity, on which hinges so much of the social teaching of the Catholic Church, is mainly upheld through work. Every individual's capacity for work should find its appropriate use. Even property is now justified in terms of "serving labor": "Our Church's social teaching is also aware of the link between the ownership of property and the exercise of human work. It holds that ownership carries with it a moral obligation. The nature of that obligation is clear: 'the only legitimate title' to the possession of the means of production 'is that they should serve labour'" (Irish Catholic Bishops' Conference 1996: 18). Society robs an individual of his or her dignity when this capacity to work is not allowed to be exercised. This dignity is partially restored when unemployed people are granted a sufficient income. Furthermore, work must be justly rewarded and provide a fair wage. All this does not mean that the Catholic Church has turned materialist and rates social worth according to income. Far from it. The church denounces what it perceives as the increased materialism of advanced societies, which, in its own words, "has not improved us as a people" (Irish Episcopal Conference 1983: 12). It remains that human dignity is fulfilled through work that allows for an adequate standard of living and a meaningful participation in society.

This option for the poor is rooted in an obligation to care for others and in the solidarity that links people together. This solidarity expresses itself principally within family and community. Communal bonds are mobilized in the struggle against all those social problems that bring suffering. A particular emphasis is placed on rural communities, which are considered to be threatened by economic development. The bishops' calls for special measures to protect and foster rural communities express, in large part, the high value that has traditionally been placed on a rural way of life in Ireland. But concern is also shown for those communities that have become pockets of unemployment and poverty and experience severe social segregation. They must be helped in their effort to solve these disadvantages and associated problems (Council for Social Welfare 1989). The appeal for a regeneration of such communities can easily be interpreted as a hankering after an idealized past. One gets a similar sense of looking back to the past, when the church closely links social policy with the upholding of the family unit: "In our view the over-riding aim of the social services should be to strengthen family units and to develop them into truly self-sustained entitities. This can only be achieved by comprehensive services administered by caring local communities" (Council for Social Welfare 1972). This theme has reappeared more recently but in a more defensive way: to ensure that social security provisions do not operate in a way that militates against stable family units. A similar attempt at protecting the institutional basis of the church is made with its defense of the involvement of voluntary organizations. But voluntary agencies, mainly religious organizations, are seen as complementing, rather than being a substitute for, public services. These themes of community, family, and voluntary organization no longer occupy a central place in the public statements of the Irish Catholic Church.

The final element of social teaching and, in a sense, the most dramatic one relates to rights. Rights refer to the entitlements associated with being a citizen, an individual member of society. They are defined in universal terms; such entitlements uphold human dignity, which is placed at the core of Catholic social teaching. Welfare payments must not be considered an act of charity but moral and legal entitlements; one should then speak of a right to income support, of a right to a just wage and to security for workers and their families (Irish Episcopal Conference 1996: 17). Support for some kind of guaranteed minimum income was mooted as early as 1972, but it was put forward as a means-tested Family Income Supplement (Council for Social Welfare 1972: 12). One observes in this context a curious blurring of this language of rights, for entitlements as of right are directed at those people who badly need support. The next comment has a curious ring about it: "[T]he individual who can establish his need can claim the benefit as of right" (Council for Social Welfare 1972: 14). Despite a language of rights, it is proposed that such welfare recipients will receive their benefits on the basis of their needs, duly means-tested. It would seem that such an approach still belongs to the liberal mode, although the church urges generosity in social assistance. It bears little relation to social policy based on rights, when every citizen or, even better, every resident is entitled to the same range of social services and benefits. This principle forms the basis of the social democratic welfare system. The church up till the end of the 1960s primarily sought to ensure that the welfare system in Ireland did not follow the social democratic road, and it proved very effective in this respect. It is then not without some irony that, a few decades later, the Catholic Church is articulating a social democratic discourse of rights in order to bolster what remains a liberal welfare regime of social assistance.

Besides this support for a generous social assistance, the Catholic Church has also endorsed the extensive social insurance framework. But it did not shape it in any fundamental way. It has, however, pressed for the extension of the social security net, particularly to farmers and the self-employed. Furthermore, the Catholic Church expressed its approval of the central tenet of the *Report of the Commission for Social Welfare*, that social welfare provision in Ireland should rely on improved and extensive social insurance, while social assistance would merely complement it (Council for Social Welfare 1992: 10). The then minister for social welfare was criticized for undermining the social insurance system when he tried to dissociate contributions and entitlements (Council for Social Welfare 1992: 9). The Council for Social Justice, the body appointed by the hierarchy to consider social issues and devise social policy orientations that conform to Catholic values and principles, promotes a social welfare system based on social insurance. But it also advocates that social assistance should offer benefits that match those of social insurance. It favors a common level of payment for assistance and insurance.

The final and crucial dimension of the Irish welfare system that we need to consider relates to the provision of social services, mainly health services and education and, to a lesser extent, personal social services. The Catholic Church has traditionally provided these services and has struck some kind of accommodation with public authorities. So, where does the Catholic Church stand in relation to this aspect of social welfare, and how does it relate to its practice? The same values are invoked in this context as were identified for social security. "In its Submission the Council argued for equity as a core value in healthcare: it saw this as deriving from the Christian emphasis on the innate dignity and equality of all people" (Council for Social Welfare 1990: 2). Furthermore, the provision of health care should both reflect and promote social solidarity and responsibility rather than deepen divisions (Council for Social Welfare 1990: 1).

In relation to health, the church is mainly concerned with offering equal access to health services. This concern relates to both the speed of access to health care and the quality of this care. The health system in Ireland is based on a dualism of private and public health care. The problem of access does not arise for general practice, as those who belong to the low-income category enjoy a medical card that entitles them to visit a doctor of their choice and to free drugs; about a third of the Irish population obtains this medical card. The other two-thirds have to pay for the services of general practictioners, and no private insurance covers them against such expenses (except for the possibility of tax allowances if the expenditure exceeds a certain amount). Everybody is entitled to free hospitalization in public hospitals, but consultant fees are charged to those beyond an income ceiling. In practice, a third of the population is insured against the cost of hospitalization: the issue of inequity emerges in this context. Those who rely on the public health services often face long queues, not incurred by private patients. The conditions under which care is provided also lead to the realistic suspicion that private patients are better treated, even if they do not necessarily receive better medical care. The church is very critical of state policy that encourages a strong private health sector, financed through voluntary health insurance. This, it is claimed, generates a public residual sector that remains underfunded and provides second-rate care (Council for Social Welfare 1987: 5). It is asserted, with some historical basis: "The general experience in such situations has been that 'a service for the poor is a poor service'" (Council for Social Welfare 1987: 8). The inequity of a two-tiered health system is confounded by the fact that private health care is heavily subsidized by the state.

The church advocates a unified health service, very much along the lines of the National Health Service in Britain, paid from general taxation: "The Council fully supports the Commission's conclusion that the attainment of an 'equitable, comprehensive and cost effective' system can best be achieved through a model which is essentially publicly funded and regulated" (Council for Social Welfare 1990: 3). It emphasizes that the attainment of equity in this context depends on "adequate levels of care" as much as on the equality of access to such services (Council for Social Welfare 1990: 13). The commission goes one step further and advocates the possibility of positive discrimination, which will compensate for the unequal conditions of access, such as geographical distance. The church proposes that the Irish health services be organized along universal lines of free treatment at the point of use. People would contribute to the cost of such services according to their ability to pay, that is, through general taxation (Council for Social Welfare 1990: 5). This call for a universally based health service appears all the more significant in that the church has waged and won a long and mighty battle on this very issue. If the Irish health service is presently two-tiered, the responsibility must be principally born by the church itself. The powerful coalition of interests that has produced such a health system is now gone. But a nagging question remains, never referred to in this new discourse of the Catholic Church on the health services, concerning the administration and financing of hospitals in Ireland, the majority of which are still under the control of religious orders. One is told at length that the health services (meaning mainly hospitals) must be generously funded out of general taxation. This sorts out who will pay but not who will own, control, or administer the hospitals. Is the church thinking of a kind of deal in which the state pays, and the church continues to manage the service? Such a suggestion is not so far-fetched, as it has already been operating partially in the health services and has formed the basis for educational provision in Ireland. One would then end up with an interesting hybrid of a health service characterized by "private universalism"! The Catholic Church has taken the moral high ground in advocating the primacy of equity, but it has so far avoided saying anything authoritative about the control of hospitals. It continues to be involved in the running of hospitals that care for private patients. The practice of agencies within the church does not always conform to its core discourse.

A rather similar analysis applies to the church's discourse on education. It hinges on the denunciation of inequalities of access to education and suggests a range of financial measures that could encourage the participation of low-income categories: mainly, subsidies to parents and sufficient funding to schools to stop the practice of asking for voluntary subscriptions. Third-level education appears particularly inequitable in this respect. Recourse is made to a language of the right of the child to education. The universalist principle is then invoked in relation to education (Council for Social Welfare 1993: 3). The Catholic Church strongly endorsed equal access to all levels of education, but the issue remains of who manages the schools. One returns here to the privatized universalism, which was mentioned earlier, in which the state ensures access for all to education by financing the costs of such services, while the service itself is delivered on their own terms by voluntary organizations. Universal access to education is seen as compatible with a particularist, religiously based education. After all, a tension persists between state and church in relation to the contents of education.

It may be useful at this stage to recapitulate the main ideas implied in the discourse of the Catholic Church on social policy matters, to identify the main principles at the core of the church's social teaching.

1. The most fundamental policy orientation relates to the church's commitment to social insurance: people should insure themselves against social contingencies and even be obliged to do so. This crucial recommendation of the *Report of the Commission on Social Welfare* received the unambiguous support of the church. This policy orientation is easily missed, for, in practice, the church has never been involved in the provision of social security, which is entirely operated by the central state.

2. This support for mainstream social policy is accompanied by a discourse that advocates a commitment to, and generosity toward, the poor and vulnerable. The value of equality is invoked in this context, although what equality actually means for the church is not that easily fathomed. The distinction between equity and equality has become blurred, and greater equity, rather than equality, is called for. How far the process of equalization is supposed to proceed is never clarified. Another ambivalence exists in its language of rights and its upholding of social assistance: the church appears to contend that poor people have a right to be assisted by the state. This is not saying much, for the language of rights is used to argue for a generous social assistance, not a universalist social security. This ambiguity creates a space that allows for an accommodation between radical statements and a practical acceptance of the heavy reliance of the Irish welfare system on social assistance. The language is radical because it has moved from moral prescriptions directed at individuals, to a call for altering the structure of society that generates deep social divisions and social exclusion.

3. The Catholic Church is now championing universal health and educational services, the very policy that it once so forcefully rejected: services should be freely accessible by all and paid through progressive general taxation. But this radical rhetoric is not necessarily matched by radical practice, for the issue of the control of hospitals and schools is not addressed in such a discourse. This leaves room for the continuation and possible extension of the institutional arrangement that has developed in education, where free and state-paid access goes with a private control of such services. We have referred to such a setup as private universalism. On the other hand, the church may well have decided that it no longer possesses the necessary manpower to continue and manage such services, that the struggle to retain an institutional control over such services is already lost. In this case, the ambiguity would resolve itself, although the church shows few signs of wanting to relax its control over education.

4. Some themes still linger from the past: the focus on the family as the most relevant unit of welfare, the importance of community, the reliance on voluntary organizations. These themes have been relegated to a secondary position, mainly because the Catholic Church has accepted that the welfare system is necessarily dominated by the state. But the issue of the welfare mix is very much alive, and the church has not really engaged into a debate about the most appropriate links between the diverse elements of the welfare system: market, family, community, voluntary organizations, and state.

The Catholic Church relies on very distinct principles in its advocacy of social policy. It calls for generous assistance to the poor, compulsory social insurance, and universal social services. A fruitful tension may develop between these three dimensions, and a certain amount of ambivalence presides over their coexistence. Over the last thirty years, the social teaching of the church has changed considerably, though not perhaps as radically as the rhetoric suggests. Rather, the discourse has been altered and radicalized, and the implications of core values have been quite systematically followed through, but not necessarily to the final level of practice. Its language turned radical when it had no practical implication for the church. With only residual involvement in the provision of social assistance, the church started to analyze poverty and unemployment in structural terms. It also urged the state to display more generosity, to effectuate a more significant redistribution of income in favor of the poor. The loosening of the church's institutional control over social services leads to a more radical discourse, hardly translated into a different practice. Rather than engaging in strategies that support its institutional base, it would seem that the church has more to gain from adopting a critical discourse. Its best strategy now is not to behave in a strategic way.

This strategy has been adopted, in a more determined manner, by the Conference of Religious in Ireland. The hierarchy enunciates the official social teaching of the Catholic Church in Ireland and takes precedence, but the church speaks with many voices. One such voice has emerged quite recently to articulate a distinctive social policy. It is closely associated with the Conference of Major Religious Superiors (CMRS), which in 1994 was renamed the Conference of Religious in Ireland (CORI). It constitutes a statutory body within the Catholic Church for the religious orders. The Education Commission, the Healthcare Commission, and the Justice Commission have put forward fairly clear views on social policy.

The Justice Commission has formulated social policy orientations that it claims to be rooted in core Christian values. The fundamental value in this respect is given as the upholding of human dignity, which implies a right to work and to receive a sufficient income. Community is also valued as the most natural place for upholding this human dignity. CORI adds values that have not featured in explicit Catholic social teaching before: participation is emphasized and the idea of sustainability is invoked. The reference to these two values may be interpreted as an attempt to update Catholic social teaching in a way that promotes democracy, social inclusion, and a balanced relationship with the environment.

CORI, through its Justice Commission, relies on the social democratic language of rights, and particularly social rights. It has put forward the idea of a "basic income." In this scheme, everybody is granted a wage by the state, without conditions, that guarantees a minimum standard of living to all. Such a policy would eradicate poverty at one stroke and recognize the value of all kinds of labor (mainly caring at home or working for voluntary organizations) that are not nowadays financially rewarded. Such a basic income is ultimately justified by the fact that everybody is entitled to enjoy a minimum standard of living; a basic income provides an effective way of ensuring such an entitlement. People are free to participate in the labor force and generate additional income. They will pay tax on such an income, without any allowance. Without entering into a technical discussion about such a scheme, suffice it to say that it represents an interesting and original proposal and that it would overcome many difficulties associated with the existing welfare system. The opponents of such a scheme point to its high cost and claim that it possibly constitutes a disincentive to work. The point is, however, that CORI advocates an income maintenance program that is unambiguously based on the existence of rights. This differs from the mix of social assistance and social insurance that is supported by the church, albeit with a touch of social democratic rhetoric about rights.

We have already noted that the church is not really involved, in a practical way, in the financing and administration of social security in Ireland. It invokes general principles, without practical implications for itself. It does not have to heed the realism of such shemes or display its awareness of the main forces shaping such a social security system. It can, in other words, assume a highly principled attitude, articulate its view ex cathedra, and uphold radical policy orientations. This approach has been adopted by CORI. Such a prophetic mode of policy intervention appears to contradict, in some way, the values of participation and inclusion that it champions: policy is formulated without involving or consulting the social categories targeted by these policies. But this unequivocal "option for the poor" generates definite benefits. Defending the excluded and standing up for those who have no voice allow the Catholic Church to perform a new role in which it is seen to occupy the high moral ground and act in accordance with its value commitment.

This legitimacy was recognized by the state when CORI was included in the so-called fourth pillar in the negotiations for the national agreement. Various organizations, including CORI, were invited to participate in this process. They exercise some influence, as the approval of this fourth pillar of social partnership is required. CORI has become the representative of the excluded; this raises by itself an interesting paradox. As the organization of the religious orders in Ireland, neither poor nor excluded themselves, it acts as the patron of the poor and vulnerable. It claims to speak for them or at least to defend their interests. Its commitment to a program of equalization and the assertion of their social rights express these interests in social policy terms. In doing so, it upholds a policy in which the excluded do not actually participate in a direct way in the process of consultation and decision making, one in which they are represented by powerful patrons. But the symbolic benefits of such an arrangement appear considerable for the church.

Religious orders own and manage schools, hospitals, orphanages, and so on; this constitutes their institutional base. They are located in an objective position within the welfare field, and their vested interest is easily identified. In relation to education, they are mainly concerned with access to education, particularly for the poorer sections in Irish society and other disadvantaged groups. They demand more public money to be invested in schools. But CORI also stresses the necessity of a change in the way that schools are run: a move away from a hierarchical management of schools toward a more collegiate one. It advocates the development of a close partnership between school, family, and community. But it remains silent on the question of who controls schools. However, the agency organizing the religious orders is willing to contemplate fundamental changes in the administration of schools: "The principles of partnership imply levels of participation and democracy which cannot be sustained by existing structures" (Conference of Major Religious Superiors, Education Commission 1992: 27). CORI has even hinted at the possibility of a phased withdrawal of religious orders from education.

CORI also argues for a shift from hospital-based medicine to community care, which, in a sense, diverges from their institutional power base. However, the Healthcare Commission stresses the importance of family and community in caring, for instance, for older people. It invokes the principle of subsidiarity, which has long been used by the church to resist "state encroachment." Religious orders envisage a continuing role for their voluntary organizations in this context. They also call for a range of measures that imply increased public financial support. One is falling back here on the well-rehearsed formula of social services provided and administered by voluntary organizations but paid for by the state.

CORI's voice is distinctive. It advocates a policy that does not fully correspond to that developed and upheld by the hierarchy. Its policy orientations are not constrained by other considerations or socioeconomic realism. It can take risks; some of its policies will be adopted, and others will be discarded. In championing consistently greater care for the poor and the disadvantaged and pressing for greater equality and inclusion, it has distanced itself from its institutional power base. CORI has been recognized by society at large as the main spokesperson for these categories. It is now reaping the benefits of such a policy shift, benefits that no longer enhance its institutional influence but remain largely symbolic. The legitimacy that derives from its "option for the poor" is becoming the most crucial resource of the Catholic Church.

THE CATHOLIC CHURCH IN THE WELFARE FIELD

Tom Inglis, in the revised version of his *Moral Monopoly* (1998), has made explicit the theoretical framework that organizes his analysis. Bourdieu's concept of field occupies a significant place in this framework. Inglis argues that the Catholic Church generates and controls what he calls religious capital, which he presents as a subcategory of cultural capital in Ireland: this capital is attained when individuals behave according to the ways set out by the church. Individuals who possess such a religious capital can trade it for other resources. The acquisition of social capital (being well known, well connected, and well respected) depended, to a large extent, on the ownership of religious capital. Attending mass on Sundays represented a key strategy in maintaining social capital. Religious capital helped in the accumulation and trading of symbolic capital, which, in Ireland, centered on the power of the church to legitimate or "bless" those who engaged in approved practices.

The aim of Inglis' study can be formulated in two different ways, although they represent the two faces of the same coin. It endeavors to understand the way that the Catholic Church has shaped the lives of Irish people, and it aims to fathom how the church has produced and maintained its power within Irish society. The author develops the view that the Catholic Church has maintained its power by engendering a particular type of individual. The power of the church depends on the production of individuals who adhere at a deep level to Catholic values, norms and practice.

The power of the church rests on the adherence of its followers to its beliefs, norms and practices. This adherence is ensured by the production of a religious habitus but also by the production of a religious capital. This power of being obeyed has secured for the church a monopoly over morality, over the definition of what is right and wrong. The monopoly of the church over morality is immediately translated into a monopoly over the shaping of a Catholic habitus. Pierre Bourdieu, when studying the mechanisms through which an institution maintains itself, speaks of reproduction; he has written several books on the way that social structures reproduce themselves. The reproduction of the Catholic Church hinges on generating the kind of resources, of capital necessary for such a task: economic, political, social, and also symbolic capital, and this requires control over relevant institutions through which the followers of the faith are formed. Tom Inglis also records the increasing difficulty that the church has in reproducing itself, as an organization placed in a key position within Irish society. It is failing to attract sufficient personnel; the legal framework in which it operates sustains its position of power less and less; its control over a multitude of agencies and institutions is slipping away; it is experiencing internal doubt and questioning. Every one of these occurrences undermines its hold over morality, its capacity to produce a strong Catholic habitus, maintain religious capital as central to social life, and consequently accumulate other forms of capital. The reproduction of the Catholic Church is clearly threatened in Ireland by the decreasing value of its religious capital.

The social teaching of the church can be analyzed using such a framework. The central idea in Bourdieu's model would point to the fact that the Catholic Church endeavors to reproduce itself: as an organization constituted around religious norms and commanding the obedience of a large number of followers. The church acts in a way that sustains its continuing existence, and it does that on the basis of crucial resources. This reproduction of the Catholic Church ultimately depends on its ability to mold individuals, to produce what Bourdieu would call a Catholic habitus. The institutional control of schools and hospitals, the provision of personal social services, and the monitoring of religious norms and practices through confession and pastoral work all contribute to such a task. Traditionally, the reproduction of the church has hinged on its institutional control, which facilitated access to individuals. It now relies less and less on its institutional basis. The loss of institutional control must be compensated for by increased legitimacy. The welfare field now represents the main area of activity where the church can generate this legitimacy, this symbolic capital. The church relies on a range of resources, or capital, in order to function in the welfare field and it converts these resources into the type of capital that it finds most valuable. So we need to answer three questions in order to account for the orientation and activity of the Catholic Church in social policy:

1.   What resources are available to the church in order to act in the welfare field?
2.   Which resource does it seek to generate there?
3.   How is such a conversion effectuated?

The church operates in the welfare field with a formidable range of capital. It occupies a strategic position in this field through the control that it exercises over the delivery of health and educational services. Most schools and numerous hospitals are run by individuals who, as priests or members of religious orders, are subjected to the direct authority of the church. We may call this form of power capital power control. The Catholic Church also enjoys a high level of legitimacy when it deals with questions of social policy. It claims authority to speak on matters of education and morality dealing with health and human reproduction, and it has succeeded in presenting itself as the voice of the underprivileged, the poor, the excluded. For a long time, this claim has not been challenged, certainly not by those in positions of political authority. An erosion of this historical status quo between state and church has recently been observed. The latter can still count on a high level of symbolic capital when it operates within the welfare field, although a declining one. Finally, power may indicate the capacity of agents in the field to have access to individuals in order to mold their behavior. This form of power capital, quite specific to the church, is central to the activity that takes place within the welfare field; we call it power access. This evokes the work of Michel Foucault on the constitution of the individual as subject.

An illustration of what is involved here is given once more by Tom Inglis (1998). He is mainly concerned with analyzing the strategies that have been used by the Catholic Church to reproduce the Catholic faith and ensure conformity to its teaching. In doing so, he offers an insight into the way that the church reaches individuals, how it shaped and "normalized" individual behavior. Most significant in this context is the process through which the church "familialized" social relations. The author points to the transformation of houses into homes, which were turned into private space (Inglis 1998: 187, 193). This process coalesced around the alliance between the mother and the priest. "It was through the school that priests, nuns and brothers reached into the home....Family life began to revolve around the school timetable. It introduced a whole cycle of discipline into the family....Children had to be got up and out to school. Children were inspected for cleanliness." The church has relied on the mother to promote such a "familializing" strategy, in which individual interests were subordinated to those of the family. This goal was upheld by mothers for their own reasons: they pursued a strategy of enhancing their power within the familial unit and raising their prestige within the community. The point is not only that the Catholic Church succeeded in civilizing and moralizing people by its caring functions of education, health, and social welfare, but that it achieved its aim through access to the familial setting, facilitated by its welfare functions. This capacity to reach individuals and mold their behavior around selected norms must be treated as an important power capital. It represents a resource that places the Catholic Church in a strong position within the welfare field; by forging a Catholic habitus from the inside, it ensures a quasi-automatic compliance with its policy orientations.

Finally, one should not neglect the social capital of the church. Social capital refers to the networks of support and relationships that can be mobilized. The clergy itself may be viewed as a very effective network that operates in two ways. The first activation of this configuration of networks is effectuated through the various ways that priests have of relating to, and supporting, each other. Solidarity and friendship have been shaped by seminarian schooling and are sustained by regular gatherings. Diocesan solidarities are also actively cultivated. It must be remembered that most priests find themselves in positions of influence and make use of their positions for this purpose. This configuration of networks may also be activated in a hierarchical way. When needed, the bishops mobilize their clergy. The social capital of the church refers, perhaps more significantly, to groups and associations that revolve around the church. Even the Sunday mass gatherings generate such a social capital. They become a resource that is used in support of the church's position, within and outside the welfare field.

The Catholic Church enters the welfare field with a high level of both symbolic and power capital. In the past, the reproduction of the Catholic Church ultimately rested on its institutional basis. The church was, above all, interested in converting the legitimacy that it enjoyed into institutional power in the welfare field. The conditions for church reproduction have altered considerably. The church now prefers to accumulate its symbolic capital and to strengthen its overall position, to a great extent, independently of its institutional power. The welfare field is nowadays the main area where it can sustain and enhance its symbolic capital, and it does so mainly by promoting its caring image. This does not mean that it does not endeavor to guarantee its control over the delivery of a range of social services in which it has historically played a central part. But such a control has become far less crucial. Its institutional basis has not lost significance for its reproduction; the shaping of individuals as Catholics still requires deep penetration of civil society on the basis of its institutional presence. The latter allows the church to activate a large network of voluntary associations and, more essentially, to obtain access to families and individuals through the services that it provides.

It may be useful at this point to outline the main conversions of capital in which the Church is involved in the welfare field:

- Institutional power (power control in the present framework) has traditionally been converted into access capital. But this conversion requires the backing of some legitimacy, which has recently been undermined by a range of scandals about orphanages and reformatory and boarding schools run by the church.
- This capital control is not automatically transformed into legitimacy. It does so only to the extent that welfare services supplied by the church are in high demand. This demand rests on the production of a habitus that puts a high value on education given in Catholic schools and on health care delivered in Catholic hospitals.
- The legitimacy of the church confirms the control that it exercises over a range of institutions. At the very least, this symbolic capital offers some protection against damaging institutional erosion. For this reason, legitimacy becomes the most crucial resource of the Catholic Church, a resource that is nowadays mainly generated in the welfare field. But this control continues to depend on the ability of the church to mobilize a wide range of economic resources and recruit sufficient manpower.
- A similar statement applies to the conversion of symbolic capital into access capital. This conversion is not effectuated in a direct way and requires the existence of a strong institutional basis.

It then appears that, in the welfare field, the Catholic Church is more and more intent on generating symbolic capital. It uses this resource, in a broader context, for containing its institutional erosion and ensuring the production of a Catholic habitus, at least among a significant minority.

The welfare field forms the main basis of social activity for the church, the place where it enjoys some leeway in its strategic conversion of resources. But this implies that the Irish welfare field remains highly differentiated from society. It means that the configuration of forces active in the welfare field does not correspond to the configuration of forces acting within the social formation as a whole. The main difference concerns the weight of the Catholic Church within the welfare field, a weight that it does not possess in the social formation as a whole. One should also note the strong presence of the professional providers of social services. On the other hand, important forces in the social formation do not enter the welfare field. The Catholic Church has, as a result of what one may call a historical compromise, been allowed to retain a central position within the welfare field. This has mainly taken the form of control over educational and health services. The church has also been conceded authority to speak on social matters, and its voice is considered seriously. It would gain very little from a fuller inclusion of welfare within the social formation, for it cannot hope to occupy a central position in the broader field. For this reason, the church has a vested interest in sheltering the welfare field from its broader context, in separating it from the larger struggles within the social formation. Its influence is directly linked with the high level of differentiation of the welfare field. Within the welfare field, it generates resources that it needs to mobilize in the broader social formation. But the development of a welfare corporatism is undermining this differentiation. The integration of some Catholic agencies in the partnership hardly compensates for it.

CONCLUSION

Bourdieu's model, in a sense, supersedes the three analyses that were presented at the beginning of this chapter. Whyte's study pointed to the mutual adjustment that took place at an early stage between the political elite and the Catholic bishops. Such a consensus was made possible by the fact that these two groups shared very deep roots in the Irish agrarian culture. But, in this perspective, welfare is seen as merely reflecting and extending a consensual network. It denies social policy as a distinctive domain of activity. Ryan anticipated that the Catholic Church was moving away from the institutional play of influence. He advocated for the church a new role, that of the conscience of society. But one did not get an analysis of the reasons and the mechanisms through which this shift in the position of the Catholic Church was to take place. Fahey gives some historical reasons for the shift, which he views from a slightly different angle: from an emphasis on the provision of services, to a commitment to social justice. The reasons given for this shift appear internal to the church and hardly relate to the structure of Irish society and the way that the Church is placed within it. Each of these analyses gives a partial picture; each points to a specific aspect of the way that the Catholic Church relates to social policy. But the issues addressed by these analyses are accounted for only when reshaped within Bourdieu's model of the welfare field.

The church has, for a long time, constituted a major force determining public social policy, and in that context it has developed a close relationship with the state. It commanded such a dominant position only because it possessed resources that in the Irish context proved strategic. It had, over a long period, developed a range of social services in a private capacity and retained control over them. Some of these services were seen as absolutely crucial to the reproduction of a strong Catholic Church in Ireland: schools in which new generations of believers were socialized but also all caring institutions that allowed for the exercise of a "pastoral power." The church also enjoyed a high level of legitimacy in social matters, and the political class banked on church approval, at least in those areas that, like social policy, were perceived as relevant for religious concerns. The church possessed resources that the state could not disregard, and this placed it in a strong position. The state did not have the economic resources necessary to create a secular system of schools, hospitals, or a range of personal social services. It would not risk the loss of legitimacy in front of a church that, to a large extent, commanded the obedience of its followers in moral and social matters.

The church itself depends on state resources. It requires public money to run the institutions that it controls. More importantly perhaps, the church needs the seal of the state: its schools, hospitals, and various social services had to be included in the public sphere. Only the state can grant the legitimacy that derives from being a public institution. Religiously based institutions became public institutions, but without losing their religious character and, more essentially, with remaining under the control of church authorities. The dominant position of the Catholic Church in Ireland was, in the past, entirely accounted for by these flows of resources exchanged between church and state. In such a context, the church retained absolute control over the conditions of its reproduction, in a way that protected its entrenched position. This situation corresponded to the mutual adjustment between state and church that has been analyzed by John Whyte. The conversions of capital created a positive game in which both main players in the welfare field were gaining.

Liam Ryan has recorded the slow move of the Catholic Church away from a reliance on institutional power. But this transformation is explained by a change of mind by the church itself. Tony Fahey adopts a similar view, while explaining this shift in terms of a range of contingent factors. The control over schools and hospitals, he argues, is slipping away because of a lack of personnel. The relevance of the church for social policy has also been largely eroded, as the welfare system now develops around a system of social security in which the church has no stake and about which it had little to say. The obedience of church followers to church teaching has become more selective, even in relation to personal morality and social matters. This was demonstrated by the widespread adoption of contraceptive practices by Catholic women. Faced with declining control over social policy institutions and weakening legitimizing power, the Catholic Church "reinvented itself"; it no longer relied on its institutional position.

The Catholic Church endeavors to increase the kind of resources that would strengthen its position in the welfare field: the legitimacy that derives from caring for vulnerable groups in society or, better still, to become their voice and their representative in front of the state. Through its "option for the poor," the church appears as the unselfish carer of all those who cannot look after themselves. It claims a new legitimacy and occupies on this basis a central place in the making of social policy. The Catholic Church is experiencing a very deep, internal tension between the two strategies for generating legitimacy: the institutional road of mobilizing the obedience of followers versus the prestige that derives from a commitment to the poor and the vulnerable. The state still needs the economic capital of the church, in the form of all these educational and health institutions, although less and less so, and it continues to pay for their running. The legitimacy that is granted by the church to public policy programs, practices, and institutions still matters in many ways; it now represents a less crucial resource for politicians and government, but it remains significant. The legitimizing power of the church is less embedded in its institutional basis and more in its association with the poor and the marginal. The Conference of Religious Organisations has for this reason been included in the fourth pillar of partnership: this organization is seen as a useful representative of the disadvantaged and a relevant participant in the negotiations that take place at the national level to decide upon the economic and social policy of the state. The latter continues to draw on the symbolic power of the church, but a symbolic power that is now generated not in the name of Catholic orthodoxy and interests but on the basis of a commitment to social justice. This fundamental policy shift is rooted in the objective position of the Catholic Church in the welfare field, that is, in the conditions that determine its reproduction.

Bourdieu's model offers a sustained account of the change in the Catholic Church's social policy. Instead of focusing on the contingent effect of ad hoc factors or even stressing purely voluntary change, it allows for a systematic sociological analysis. It does so by analyzing the resources on which the Catholic Church relies in order to operate in the welfare field and the way that these resources are transformed into the capital that it seeks to maximize.

5

Other Forces in the Field

The state and the Catholic Church have contributed in a crucial way to the shaping of the Irish welfare system. But they have not done so on their own. Other forces operate in the welfare field, although the list of significant players remains quite limited. In this chapter, the position of these other significant groups is investigated. The trade union movement has progressively developed its social policy orientation. Welfare matters do not constitute a central concern for employers, but they are, nonetheless, implicated in them, if only as contributors to social insurance. The feminist movement has, from the 1970s, imposed its presence in the field and has endeavored to reshape social services in a way that relates more closely to women's needs.

Entry into the welfare field requires a minimal amount of relevant resources, what Bourdieu calls capital. The capital that is possessed by these three social forces (the trade union movement, employers, and women's movement) is a power capital; it corresponds to the capacity to mobilize people in the political system and exercise influence, or else this power derives from control over politically strategic resources. This chapter analyzes the dynamic generated in the welfare field by these three social forces.

THE TRADE UNIONS AND SOCIAL POLICY

In the 1940s and 1950s, the trade union movement in Ireland displayed a limited interest in welfare issues and in the development of a welfare system. The trade unions saw themselves as engaged in the more important question of industrial bargaining: setting wage levels and defining conditions of work. The shortage of social housing had become an issue in the late 1940s, and a call was made in the Conference of the Irish Trade Union Congress (ITUC) for erecting prefabricated houses. Health issues occupied quite a significant place in the ITUC activities in the early 1950s, mainly because of the controversy about the

Mother and Child Scheme which was forcefully opposed by the Catholic hierarchy. Social security questions were referred to, from time to time, in annual conferences. The ITUC supported the introduction of a social insurance scheme in 1953, however limited it may have been. With Northern Ireland as the main point of reference, Congress sought social security entitlements that were enjoyed by Northern Irish workers. But it responded to social policy development in a piecemeal manner and did not marshal a great deal of energy in expounding and promoting the social security regime that it favored.

Social policy moved slowly to a central position in the concerns of the Irish Congress of Trade Unions.[1] This centrality reached its peak in the 1990s with the adoption of the concept of a "social wage." On top of the income that they obtain from employment, the standard of living of workers also depends on services and benefits provided by the state. Social policy moved even more to the central stage with the development, during the 1980s and particularly during the 1990s, of "corporatist bargaining." This kind of bargaining involves a trade-off between the main economic groups and the state. It implies, most of the time, an acceptance of moderate wage increases by the trade union movement in exchange for improved social benefits. Nowadays, the latter constitute a key element of industrial bargaining and economic policy.

The second main feature of Congress' social policy over the last half century relates to its constant call for extension of benefits, particularly of coverage. This applies most clearly to health services. Congress has consistently pressed for free and universal access to hospital services. It has repeatedly denounced the two-tiered nature of hospital services, with different conditions for public and private patients. This call for extended coverage also encompasses all schemes of income maintenance. Congress has promoted the development of social insurance first for manual workers, then to all employees, and finally, more recently, to the self-employed and part-time workers.

All this does not mean that the Irish trade union movement was backing the kind of universalist welfare system that social democratic parties and the labor movement in Europe have fostered and often achieved. It has, in fact, opted for an insurance scheme, with benefits linked to income and contribution. Furthermore, Congress has displayed a certain ambivalence in relation to the abolition of separate occupational schemes. It apparently challenged the occupational fragmentation of welfare schemes, particularly those of employees in the public and private sectors. Public sector workers benefit from a special and possibly privileged social security regime. Nevertheless, Congress expressed its opposition in 1988/1989 to the uniformization of social security schemes, if this meant a loss of income or social benefits for public sector workers. The weight of public sector unions within Congress mostly accounts for this ambivalence. All this implies that the trade union movement is advocating a comprehensive social security system, but not a universalist one. It seeks to include within a social insurance network as many social categories as possible. But welfare benefits are not enjoyed as of right; people obtain benefits only to the extent that they contribute. The main policy goal remains a reduction in the number of people receiving social assistance and an increase in the number of those who are insured. Even in relation to social services, Congress only partially defends the introduction of universal services. It has never challenged, for instance, the assistance-based scheme of medical cards, which allows about a third of the population free access to the service of general practitioners.

Since the 1970s, the trade union movement has focused more closely on welfare issues. This can, in part, be accounted for by Ireland's entry into the European Community. It found out more about welfare benefits enjoyed in other European countries and realized that, in some countries, social benefits contribute significantly to the standard of living of the employees. The point of reference had shifted away from the British welfare system, which, not particularly generous, relies quite heavily on means tests and social assistance. From the 1970s, Congress called for the Irish welfare system to be developed to the level of other European countries.

The growing commitment of the trade union movement to social policy issues has never really translated into militant action. Delegates to the annual conferences in the 1950s regularly complained about the lack of commitment of Congress and its leadership to social policy. Such issues never led to mass mobilization or industrial action. Pressure was exercised through submissions to the relevant ministers in letters and direct representations. Congress also participates in the formulation of social policy through its involvement in the National Economic and Social Council (NESC). The latter represents a good example of the kind of corporatist decision making through which the welfare system is advancing. This procedure became the main form of policy making in Ireland in the late 1980s and particularly in the 1990s. This takes the form of national agreements in which the representatives of the main socioeconomic forces negotiate and arrive at a common policy. This program typically involves a trade-off between economic and social issues. Nowadays, the trade union movement influences the development of the Irish welfare system not through the exercise of political pressure but through negotiating directly with the state and other partners.

Donal Nevin (1994), a former president of the ITCU, has defined the main social policy orientation of the trade unions in rather similar terms. He emphasizes that social welfare development occupied a secondary place in Congress's activity. Strong internal resistance made it quite difficult for the trade union movement to work toward a uniform and equalizing welfare regime. But social policy came to occupy a central place in the concerns of Congress, so much so that in the early 1990s it adopted the concept of a social wage. It has been calculated that, on average, social benefits contribute to about one-third of gross earnings.

These trends appear in a sharper light when we focus on the different programs. For a long time, unions were content to deal with not very consequential aspects of income maintenance schemes. Congress constantly demanded increases in welfare benefits. It also strove to remove anomalies; for instance, young people and married women were required in the early 1960s to pay a full contribution, while they enjoyed only reduced benefits. The trade union movement has, from an early time, called for a comprehensive regime of social security. But such a comprehensive system developed only slowly. Congress endeavored to remove the income ceiling. In 1969, it actively sought the extension of the social insurance scheme to all employees, without income limitation. Then, the trade unions campaigned for the abolition of the distinction between insurance schemes for public and private sector employees, although it ran into difficulties in this respect. In the next stage, Congress pressed for the extension of social insurance contributions to the self-employed. In 1991, social insurance was broadened to part-time workers and to those working in irregular employment. Its commitment to extend social insurance was seriously tested in relation to what can be considered the privileged social security regime of public sector employees. Its effort at overcoming the segmentation of social security between private and public sectors proved quite ambivalent. In 1988, for instance, it opposed the extension of Pay-Related Social Insurance to public services workers.

This commitment to social insurance was balanced, from the early 1970s, by the more universalist proposal of a basic minimum payment for all. It was proposed that those who depend on welfare benefits, either on the basis of social insurance or social assistance, should receive a minimum income, that is, a minimum standard of living. Congress has also pressed for an equalization of welfare regimes for men and women employees.

Workers are directly concerned with old age or retirement pensions, and the trade unions developed a policy on this question at an early stage. In 1959, Congress called for a reduction of the pensionable age to sixty-five. It has also constantly demanded an increase in the level of pensions. But, perhaps more significantly, it declared itself in favor of contributory pensions related to income. This implied that both contributions and benefits would vary according to pay levels. It supported a system of social insurance that would guarantee that benefits remain proportional to contributions and income. It so doing, it upheld income differences between occupational groups. Years later, in 1993, the insurance principle of public pensions was reasserted with a call for a greater difference between contributory and noncontributory pensions. This demand figured on the list of priorities in the late 1970s and was reactivated more recently.

In relation to pensions, Congress has endeavored to bring more and more categories of people into pension schemes. Very few employees actually enjoyed pensions, besides the means-tested pensions. In 1964, Congress argued that state and semistate agencies should, by law, set up a pension scheme for all their employees. This represented an attempt to include manual workers in the pension schemes of nonmanual workers in the public sector. Then, Congress pressed for a uniform pension scheme that would cover all categories of workers. This pension scheme would encompass all employees, manual and nonmanual workers in both private and public sectors. It envisaged the creation of a national pension fund under state control; this fund would unify all existing pension schemes. Later, it strove to bring in self-employed workers and various categories of workers. But the separation between private and public sectors has remained a troublesome issue. A conflict developed within Congress on this very issue about the level of contribution and the entitlements of public sector employees.

Congress had at an earlier stage called for the introduction of a general compulsory health insurance scheme, covering hospital care and drugs. In the 1970s, Congress clearly opted for a comprehensive hospital service. In 1976, it pressed for an abolition of income limit eligibility, at least for manual workers. In 1979, it opposed the creation of three categories of eligibility to health services and sought a hospital service that would be freely accessible to all. It became more and more critical of the dual nature of hospital care, one for public patients and another for private patients. However, this universalist orientation possessed clear limits and related exclusively to hospital care. Congress never seriously challenged the medical card scheme, which is enjoyed by the poorer third of the population. Already in 1960, Congress had opposed the introduction of objective means tests for access to free General Medical Services, implicitly placing such access at the discretion of health authorities. It was in that sense bolstering a discretionary procedure, as opposed to one based on objective standards. Local politics at that time was characterized by a high level of clientelism and patronage; such a policy orientation was not encouraging a clear definition of welfare entitlements. It also favored a scheme that would allow a choice of doctors for patients entitled to free medical services. But it never really took up this issue of medical cards, which really contradicts its policy of promoting a comprehensive health system.

Congress upheld a clear universalist orientation in relation to education. It was mainly concerned with ensuring greater educational opportunities. It demanded better services in primary schools. This inevitably meant increased public resources to reduce the pupil–teacher ratio and also special facilities for schools in underprivileged areas. In relation to secondary education, it supported the introduction of free education in the late 1960s. At a later stage, it backed up the introduction and development of community schools. In 1990, it even declared its support for a comprehensive, multidenominational school system. The issue of equal opportunities appears most acute at the third level. Its policy answer in this respect focuses on the provision of adequate grants to students, and it accepts that such grants must be means-tested.

The trade union movement has consistently emphasized the development of scientific and technical education. This issue makes sense when set in the context of an educational system that was, and continues to be controlled by religious denominations and that stressed the value of "humanities." The whole educational system seemed to be geared, up to the 1960s, to train the professions: doctors, lawyers, teachers, and so on. Not only did it neglect a more technical and even scientific formation, but technical secondary schools were viewed as second-rate, while scientific subjects did not figure prominently in the secondary school curriculum. The trade union movement clearly sided with those who insisted on the role of technical and scientific education for socioeconomic development. Congress considered that a greater emphasis on technical and scientific education at school would open access to working-class children. Regional technical colleges created a technically oriented third-level education; they facilitated in no insignificant way the access of low-income categories to third-level education.

Congress has quite consistently pressed for the development of an educational system that would be accessible to all, at all levels.

The main social policy orientations of the trade union movement have been briefly reviewed. We have established that the ICTU constitutes a significant actor in the welfare field. How can the action of Congress be analyzed in terms of Bourdieu's model? In other words, what resources does this actor possess in order to operate in the welfare field? What does it want to achieve? We need to answer these three questions.

Trade unions uphold the interests of their members, who nowadays benefit from many social policy advantages. For this reason, they show great interest in, and concern about, welfare matters. Trade unions operate in the welfare field on the basis of their capacity to mobilize their members and apply pressure on the political center. Social benefits and services directly contribute to the standard of living of employees; for this reason, they constitute a stake in the political game that is played between the major forces in society for the distribution of wealth. The mobilizing capacity of trade unions makes up a power (political) capital that is used for maximizing welfare benefits and services. This resource, by and large, reflects the position of this socioeconomic category in the structure of Irish society as a whole.

Trade unions operate effectively within the welfare field because they bring with them a power (political) capital. They represent the vast majority of employees, who form a large welfare constituency. They employ this power capital in order, in the first instance, to amass symbolic capital, to increase their legitimacy as representatives of employees, as the ultimate defense and guarantee of the standards of living of their members. In that sense, the trade union movement transforms its political capital into a symbolic one. It does so for its own advantage. But its political and symbolic capital is ultimately mobilized to broaden the range of social benefits, to improve the level and quality of welfare services and to facilitate access to them. In other words, it endeavors to maximize the economic capital that accrues to its members. It uses its political capital to accumulate economic capital, although this endeavor also enhances its legitimacy.

Trade unions find it difficult to function in the welfare field. Instead, they bargain for trade-offs in which productivity increases are exchanged for welfare advantages. For this reason, the Irish Congress of Trade Unions does not press for a greater differentiation and autonomy of the welfare field: it would rather open this field to those social forces that , like itself, maneuver best in society at large.

The action of the trade union movement has been analyzed in terms of the social benefits that may be enjoyed by the employees whom Congress represents. But, besides the consumers of welfare, one also needs to take into account the providers of social services, who are grouped in professional organizations and even in trade unions. How does Boudieu's model apply to them? In their activity, the associations of professional providers of social services, such as medical doctors and teachers, are, to a large extent, confined to the welfare field. They rely on two types of capital. First, they claim expertise in their field, and their claim is backed up by a range of academic and professional credentials; they possess the accredited knowledge and competence to perform their professional role. This corresponds to what Bourdieu calls cultural capital. But the use of this cultural capital is also regulated by professional organizations. It is assumed and expected that they perform their task not for their own benefit but for the benefit of their clients. The respect and deference shown to them depend on such requirements being fulfilled. They deliver their services according to an ethical code that gives precedence to the quality of their services and the welfare of their clients over all other considerations. They generate in this way a symbolic capital that they convert into economic capital. Some professional categories exercise a great deal of influence on, and even control over, the way that such services are organized and delivered. They enjoy in this way some power (control) capital, which they utilize as a resource in the welfare field.

The strategy of the professional associations involved in the provision of social services appears quite straightforward. In order to operate in the field, they rely on the fact that they alone can provide the services that are required, that their expertise is socially sanctioned. Their cultural capital is easily transformed into symbolic capital. The possession of this double cultural/symbolic capital allows them, first of all, to exercise some control over the delivery of such services and sometimes a direct involvement in their management. But, more essentially, this cultural capital is used to obtain a high level of economic return. Professional providers exchange their cultural capital, backed up by power (control) capital, for economic capital. All the crucial moments in the history of the Irish welfare state have brought this stake to the fore.

The rate at which this cultural capital is converted into economic capital is determined by several factors. First, one has to take into account the mediating effect of another type of capital, professional control over the delivery of such services. When professionals are directly involved in the administration and running of the service, they exchange their cultural capital at a higher rate. The ability of such groups to engage in strategies of professional closure constitutes another important factor. When professional bodies set the conditions of entry, certify the expertise received and regulate professional practices, they enhance the bargaining power of the profession. Medical professions have been far more successful than teachers, for instance, in this strategy of closure. Finally, the possibility of entering into alliances with other agents in the field changes the conditions of exchange. Both the medical and the teaching professions have, from time to time, turned to the Catholic Church for support, which has usually been granted and has secured them a higher economic return.

WELFARE AND THE FEMINIST MOVEMENT

Welfare issues have been placed squarely at the heart of feminist activity, in its various forms. The Irish women's liberation movement in the early 1970s put forward the following demands: equal pay, equality before the law, equal education, legalization of contraception, and justice for deserted wives, unmarried mothers, and widows (Mahon 1987: 58). Three of these demands relate directly to welfare. Even the demand for gender equality before the law points to the many forms of gender discrimination that exist within the welfare system. In a similar way, the First Commission on the Status of Women placed welfare issues high on the agenda in its drive for gender equality: differential access for women to welfare benefits; child allowances that are paid to the "breadwinner"; the precarious situation of widows, deserted, wives and unmarried mothers; gender stereotyping in education.

However, despite the long list of demands, most of the energy of the women's movement has been absorbed by what one may call reproductive issues. These refer mainly to contraception and abortion and highlight the core feminist values and aims of women's autonomy and control over the female body. Feminist groups have also been active in the provision of services to various categories of women. Good progress has been made, if not in eliminating, at least in reducing gender discriminations in relation to welfare benefits. But the action of the feminist movement does not seem to have contributed in a crucial way to achieving such results. The issue has been taken up by the European Commission, and a systematic policy of gender equality in this context has been imposed on Irish governments by the European Community. Irish authorities have responded with a great deal of reluctance but have had to comply in the end. This demand from the women's movement had to be turned into mainstream European policy before it succeeded.

The success of the women's movement in relation to welfare is, for this reason, mixed. It achieved considerable success in areas where it invested a great deal of energy and resources. Some of the discrimination faced by women in welfare terms was removed, but this should hardly be seen as the successful outcome of their action. In other areas, such as women's poverty, the women's movement did not display a high level of commitment and mobilization. It was also confronted with more formidable constraints, which cannot be reduced to inequality between men and women.

Gender Discriminations in Welfare

The Irish welfare system has historically been constructed on the basis of a gender bias; it was from the start designed to sustain the family unit. It rests on an ideology of familism, which upholds the view that the responsibility of looking after the material needs of wife and children rests on the husband, while women assume responsibility for caring within the family. This has also been referred to as the male breadwinner model. In such a perspective, welfare claims are made for the family as a whole. Social policy programs aim at maintaining the male breadwinner family unit; they also intervene when support is required in order to compensate for its temporary or permanent collapse. In such an ideology of familism, welfare expenditure is meant to assist the caring mother and her children. Support is granted either on the basis of the husband's participation to the labor force or else, if the husband does not or cannot fulfill his function, to alleviate acute need and destitution. In both cases, the married woman enjoys no independent right to welfare benefits. Her claims depend on the rights of the husband, which have to be established by his insurance contributions or else on a plea of poverty, but not as of right.

Such a male breadwinner model has been central in shaping the Irish welfare system. The Irish Constitution of 1936 placed a great deal of emphasis on the protection of the family. The state is meant to ensure that mothers are not obliged by economic necessity to engage in labor to the neglect of their duties in the home (Conroy Jackson 1993). This provided the ideological and legal underpinning for organizing the welfare system on the basis of such a view of the family: one in which the husband/father works outside the home, while the wife/mother takes care of the family. She depends on her husband for ensuring the economic well-being of herself and her children. The fundamental inequality of men and women in relation to social benefits derives from this basic premise of the welfare state in Ireland.

Social policy benefits are tailored to secure minimal living conditions for the family unit and to protect the family in case of serious difficulty experienced by the breadwinner: unemployment, disease, death, and so on. Married women staying at home, close to half a million, have access to social benefits, such as pensions, not in their own right but only as wives and mothers. As dependents of their husbands, they enjoy no protection other than the one that derives from their legal relationship to an insured husband. The methods for payment of welfare benefits confirmed women's subordinate status within the home. Up till 1985, the father, rather than the mother, collected supplementary allowances and benefits for dependent children.

Married women in the labor force, who numbered close to a quarter of a million in 1991, are entitled to social security benefits in their own right. However, before 1986, they did not receive equal benefits. A lower rate of benefit applied to married women, compared to men, in relation to unemployment, sickness, or invalidity pension. They could claim unemployment benefits for a shorter period than men and single women. The vast majority of married women were debarred from obtaining unemployment assistance; this benefit was paid, after means testing, to those who were no longer covered by unemployment insurance. Married women could not claim unemployment assistance, and for this reason they were not allowed to participate in state-sponsored employment schemes.

With Directive 79/EEC on Sex Equality, the European Community committed itself to the principle of equal treatment for men and women in social security matters. The Irish government took more than fifteen years to implement this EC Directive, as granting equal welfare benefits to married women required fundamental changes in the very structure of social welfare. The Social Welfare Act (no. 2) of 1985 put into effect the relevant legislation for Ireland. It equalized the rates of benefit payable to married women for unemployment, disability, invalidity, and occupational injuries. It also introduced a similar duration of benefits for men and women. It admitted married women to the unemployment assistance scheme, subject to means testing. Finally, it revised the conditions governing the payment for adult and child dependents. Generally speaking, the implementation of this equalization policy did not quite match its spirit. Welfare entitlements continued to be denied on the basis of answers to questions about child care and domestic responsibilities. Entitlements to unemployment benefits, for example, were frequently refused to women with children because they were assessed for "availability for work." They were asked questions such as "who will mind the children" and "who will cook the dinner"; men were, of course, never queried about such matters.

Working married women are entitled to social security benefits on the same terms as those applied to married men and single women. But the removal of unequal access to social benefits does not mean equalization in practice. Social insurance schemes often lead to married women's not receiving the same level of benefits. This derives from the conditions of participation of women in the labour force. The reliance on part-time work and the interruptions of employment for familial reasons translate into lower social benefits for women. In Ireland, as in most countries relying on social insurance, women do not fare equally in relation to social welfare, even if they enjoy similar formal entitlements.

A range of women's benefits has been introduced since the late 1960s and early 1970s, directed at deserted wives, prisoners' wives, and unmarried mothers. They were all social assistance payments, with the exception of the deserted wife's benefit, which was automatically granted. In 1973, a social welfare allowance was started for unmarried mothers. It constituted, for all practical purposes, an allowance for housework and child care. But claimants could not register for unemployment or take up employment. For that reason, they did not accumulate a contribution record for social security benefits. They were also prohibited from cohabiting with a male partner, contributing further to their isolation as a special category of social welfare recipients. In 1990, a new social security measure for lone parents was brought in that streamlined six different social welfare schemes; it initiated a single, unified lone-parent social welfare allowance, available to women and men in the categories covered. The Second Commission on the Status of Women (1993) went one step further and advocated the individualization of all welfare benefits.

There is some debate about the interpretation to be given to the benefits and services that have been granted to those women whose situation does not conform to the conventional familial status. Such benefits are seen by some as concessions that in no way support the alternative forms of family and remain firmly within a familist framework (McLaughlin and Yeates 1999). Others are more inclined to view the social programs directed at women in nontraditional families as a significant deviation from the breadwinner model (Daly 1999).

Social Services for Women

One of the main concerns of the feminist movement has, from the start, related to reproductive issues, which have crystallized around the availability of contraceptive devices and, at a later stage, the question of abortion. At stake was the control of the reproductive function, or who controls women's bodies in their reproductive function. A great deal of the feminist movement activity aimed at asserting the autonomy of women in this context, in terms of their individual choice and also, perhaps more essentially, in terms of the mores and the legal system through which the reproductive function is regulated in a way that does not always uphold women's autonomy. A major aim in the first years of the Irish women liberation movement concerned the availability of contraception (Smyth 1988: 336). The so-called contraception train, organized by the Contraception Action Campaign (CAC), represents one of the most highly symbolic acts of the original feminist groups, through which it became well established in the public sphere; participants to this action, on their way from Belfast, distributed condoms to passers-by on their arrival in Dublin. This illegal action attracted a great deal of media interest. But the focus on contraceptive issues did not meet unanimity within the movement; two founder members had originally disagreed with its inclusion in its aims, especially for unmarried mothers. Following the contraceptive train action in 1971, a founding member resigned. The action was not limited to a campaign for changing the law of the land. It also took the more practical and immediate form of setting up a network of women's clinics. The Fertility Guidance Clinic, supported by the International Planned Parenthood Association, opened in Dublin in 1969. It was followed a year later by a Family Planning Rights group. "Because of a loophole in the law, the clinic could dispense contraceptives freely, at the same time requesting 'donations' from its clients" (Mahon 1987: 63). The feminist movement was initiating a move toward the establishment of special agencies and organizations that provided women with services relevant to them.

Not until 1979 did the Health (Family Planning) Act make contraceptives legally available, albeit in a limited way. The focus then turned to the question of abortion, a far more controversial issue even among women. A Woman's Right to Choose Group (WRCG) was formed, advocating the possibility of abortion. Their action unfolded in a context in which the liberal agenda, mainly developed around the contraceptive issue but also around the looming battle over divorce, was being challenged by a gathering of organizations. The protracted battle largely revolved around the delivery of services in women's clinics. Services such as counseling on pregnancies and referrals to clinics outside Irish jurisdiction were targeted by the Pro-Life Amendment Campaign (PLAC) and subjected to obdurate legal battles.

In order to ensure women's control over their reproductive functions and consequently over their bodies, the women's movement chose a course of action that had a significant impact on welfare in Ireland. The strategy of setting up agencies to cater to the specific needs of women or particular categories of women is not limited to the provision of contraceptive clinics or, later, to diverse forms of counseling and referral on reproductive issues. In the early 1970s, elements within the feminist movement moved toward self-help and single-issue groups (Smyth 1988: 336); they initiated services not yet available to women. One could mention an early manifestation of this orientation with the creation in 1960 of the National Association of Widows in Ireland (NAWI). This organization, representative of widows, was active mainly in the areas of social welfare and taxation. It sought to protect women against poverty but also campaigned for adequate financial provision for single parents; it even called for the creation of state-funded child-care centers. But the feminist movement as such bore a more direct responsibility for the creation of a range of agencies that offer specialized services for women (Connolly 1997). A number of self-help groups sprang up; they were involved in lobbying for their particular concern, but, more essentially, they were providing a range of services to their members and to women in general.

Cherish was created in 1970 through a newspaper advertisement. An organization of single mothers, it was set up with a dual purpose. First, it lobbied for the provision of an unmarried mother's allowance, which was actually granted in 1973, and, generally speaking endeavored to improve the lot of unmarried mothers. But it also functioned as a self-help organization that provided a range of services to single parents: day care, accommodations if necessary, legal advice, and so on. Cherish managed to bring to the fore the issue of single parenthood, which had been largely denied as a serious problem in Ireland (Smyth 1988: 337).

Action, Information, and Motivation (AIM) started in 1972 and performed a range of functions. It sought legal reforms for women and campaigned for the Social Welfare Act of 1974, which transferred the legal rights of the children's allowance from the father to the mother. It pressed for the introduction of the Family Supplementary Welfare Allowance in 1975 and the Family Law (Maintenance of Spouses and Children) Act of 1976. It also operated as an information and advice center for women. The Dublin AIM group founded the Irish Women's Aid Committee in 1974, which inaugurated the first hostel for battered wives in Ireland. Additional shelters for deserted wives and women victims of domestic violence were thereafter opened by AIM groups throughout the country (Mahon 1987: 60). While Women's Aid addressed the problem of domestic violence, the Rape Crisis Centre was set up in 1977 as a service dealing with women who had been victims of sexual violence. The Association for Deserted and Alone Parents (ADAPT) started in 1973 to campaign for a better treatment for deserted wives.

All these initiatives, which emerged from within the women's movement, added to the development of a shadow welfare system. They identified services not delivered by the state and simply took responsibility for them. Their action represented a radical critique of a welfare system generated by men; it meant that such a welfare regime did not meet some fundamental needs of women. But, crucially, the setting up of such groups and self-help agencies met a fundamental requirement of the movement: that of women's controlling the delivery of services aimed at women. Of course, running an effective service costs money. It requires a level of resources not available to such groups, once the pioneering stage has passed. Typically, such groups turned to the state in order to secure funding. The provision of funds and premises by the state for centers managed by women became at an early stage a demand of the women's movement. These organizations obtained funding from public sources, mainly in the form of discretionary subsidies from relevant ministerial departments. Some of the services were, at least in part, taken over by the Health Boards. But the tension remains between the need for state funding and the determination of these groups to retain control over the services that they provide. The feminist movement was falling back to the model that had long operated in Ireland in health and education. The state pays, while a voluntary organization administers the service. The feminist movement seems in this way to adopt the kind of accommodation that has historically been struck between church and state in Ireland. But does such an arrangement correspond to the relative strength of the state and the women's movement? So far, the state has supported these groups and services, but without long-term commitment. Although short-term solutions have the knack of lasting a long time in Ireland, this model of public finance with administration by voluntary organizations has so far not been fully institutionalized in this context.

A similar issue has emerged in relation to poverty, which was not a central concern of the feminist movement, mainly because it did not relate to the direct experience of the participants. "Women from low income communities have not been significantly involved in the women's movement in Ireland. It is only in the very recent past that women from such communities are themselves mobilising around issues that affect their lives" (Daly 1989: 127). But the focus on what has been referred to as the feminization of poverty has moved this issue to a more central position. It is, indeed, contended that women are more likely to experience poverty. Women depend on welfare benefits to a greater extent: they live longer and make up a higher proportion of pensioners and the great majority of single-parent families are headed by a woman (Millar, Leeper, and Davies 1992). Social insurance also militates against women, as they find it difficult to accumulate the necessary level of contributions. Furthermore, they receive lower pay than men and often work part-time. Finally, it is contended that the distribution of income within the family opens the possibility of women's being poor within a well-off household.

Studies have been undertaken to measure these features empirically. Generally speaking, it was not found that women were more at risk of becoming poor. A roughy similar proportion of men and women could be classified as poor. An exception must be made for single-parent families, with widowed or single mothers facing a greater risk of poverty (Nolan and Callan 1994: 184). The idea of hidden poverty was not supported either. It seems that income is broadly shared within families, even if husbands often enjoy a higher level of personal money than their wives. But this does not appear sufficient to produce poverty within families.

Poverty has been included on the agenda of the women's movement mainly with the development of local women's groups. In 1989, 98 of the 160 women's groups were operating at the local community level (Daly 1989: 101). These groups have often been initiated by professional workers. They are set up in communities considered deprived and are meant as a strategy to overcome poverty by encouraging social contact, imparting information and skills, developing positive self-images, contributing to group development, delivering counseling services, or, more practically, running crèche facilities. Many of these groups have been funded by a special scheme of the Department of Welfare. In 1990, 199 groups benefited from the Scheme of Grants for Locally Based Women's Groups. The figure increased to 333 in 1992. This represents an attempt to find a way of overcoming women's poverty through the provision of a range of services and structures controlled by women but largely paid for by the state. One observes here again the strategy of establishing parallel welfare services and structures. The effectiveness of such parallel institutions in overcoming poverty remains to be established.

Women in the Welfare Field

Women figure prominently as beneficiaries and as providers of social policy programs. They also constitute a force operating within the welfare field. What resources allow the women's movement to enter the welfare field and operate effectively within it? Like trade unions, the feminist movement relies on its power (political) capital: it possesses a high capacity to mobilize members, to put pressure on political agents, and, in a general way, to uphold the threat of possible trouble. The political capital of the feminist movement is utilized to maximize economic capital, by ensuring the public financing of a range of women's agencies, by pressing for a recasting of the way welfare benefits are redistributed, and by demanding more generous benefits. The feminist movement in Ireland has succeeded in imposing new caring functions on the state, such as the protection of battered wives, counseling for sexual abuse and rape, and family planning and contraception. Some of these functions have emerged around agencies that have been set up by women and remain largely under their control. However, the state is urged to contribute to the financing of such services. The control that women's agencies exercise over the provision of some services produces another resource for them. They hold some power (control) capital, albeit a small amount, as the state now depends on such agencies to deliver these services and would find it difficult to bypass them.

However, it seems that the women's movement does not convert its resources, mainly its political capital, into material and power control capital at an advantageous rate. Its mobilizing power appears on the decrease, and, as we have seen, the main welfare gains for women originated outside Ireland. Furthermore, the state has taken responsibility for some of the services relevant to women. Many family-planning functions are now assumed by Health Boards or have been integrated into normal medical services. One observes, most of the time, a dualism between state-controlled and women-controlled services. This dualism, in which the state takes over some of the services initiated by women, implies that the state erodes the position of women-controlled agencies and, in a sense, weakens the determination of the state to subsidize services provided outside its control.

THE QUALIFIED SUPPORT OF EMPLOYERS

Employers have found it quite difficult to speak with a unified and coherent voice. The Federation of Irish Industries was initiated in 1932 and underwent several changes. The effective representation of employers became a crucial issue in the late 1960s, and it was proposed to revamp the organization. But the proposal was not implemented, and, instead, two organizations were created. The

Confederation of Irish Industry (CII) represented industrialists, while another organization, the Federation of Irish Employers (soon to be renamed the Federated Union of Employers) upheld the interests of employers in wage negotiations and industrial relations. This arrangement lasted from 1969 to 1992, when the Irish Business and Employers Confederation (IBEC) was formed through the merger of CII and the Federated Union of Employers (FUE).

Generally speaking, employers have not that much to say about welfare matters, which do not constitute a central concern. For instance, no special committee dealt with social policy matters in the structure of the CII. Social policy issues were sometimes raised under various headings and mainly in the context of taxation and public expenditure or manpower policies. But some kind of social policy was, nonetheless, elaborated by employers, mainly in response to unfolding events or decisions made by the government of the day. These themes were sometimes referred to by the chairman in his address to their annual conference. The *Annual Report* gives some indication of what was said or done under this heading. Weekly newsletters also comment on various aspects of social policy. In 1996, a systematic statement on social policy matters was proffered by employers. IBEC published a policy document entitled *Social Policy in a Competitive Economy*. It examines in some detail relevant aspects of the welfare system and formulates a clear position on behalf of employers. Most of the views put across in this document had already been aired in various publications of this and previous organizations. But this policy document goes further and indicates in a more sustained way employers' thinking on welfare issues. The present analysis focuses on this document, but it also relies on diverse publications, such as annual reports, newsletters, and brochures dealing with specialized topics. This approach provides a sense of the way that employers' social policy has evolved, while presenting a coherent overview of their position.

Limiting the Welfare State

Employers, through their representative organization, are at pains to emphasize their support for the provision of social protection. They accept that people aspire to improved social services, as well as better living conditions; they acknowledge that high levels of investment are needed to protect those who are socially disadvantaged. Employers declare themselves generally supportive of welfare provision, but, as the saying goes, the devil is in the detail. Employers find many occasions for qualifying their statements of support.

Employers' hostility toward their financial contribution to social insurance is repeatedly stated in all public statements and publications. The annual president's speech and the budget submissions repeatedly raise the question of Pay Related Social Insurance (PRSI) contributions, which employers have to pay for each of their employees. The point is made over and over again that such PRSI contributions should be significantly reduced, as they add to the cost of labor and undermine the competitiveness of the Irish economy. For this reason, employers' organizations have lobbied intensively against increasing the ceiling for the employer's contribution. Yearly submissions to the budget stubbornly return to this question. A wide range of measures, some of them quite eccentric, is put forward in order to deal with this issue. They have proposed a decrease in social insurance contributions and suggested that the loss of revenue be balanced by increased direct taxation (*CII Newsletter*, August 19, 1980). At one stage, they put forward the idea of a selective reduction of social contributions for labor-intensive manufacturing firms (*CII Newsletter*, January 13, 1981). They have even mooted the idea that a PRSI relief for these labor-intensive firms should be offset by a Social Welfare Charge of 2 percent levied on public sector employees (*CII Newsletter*, January 17, 1984). They have demanded that employer's PRSI should not be charged for one year in respect of additional employees (*CII Newsletter*, November 11, 1986). They view this social insurance contribution as a tax on employment and a particularly obnoxious one, which significantly adds to the cost of labor. Employers bitterly complain about the shift that has taken place in the financing of social insurance. They have seen the relative share of the state contributions to the Social Insurance Fund fall to practically nothing, while their own relative share has increased to about two-thirds.

Employers' views on social policy derive quite directly from what they see as the requirements of the economy, that is, of continuous wealth creation. All their public statements on this issue revolve around that theme for as long as they have expressed a view on the question. Only a thriving and competitive economy creates the possibility of adequate social protection. Social expenditure adds to the cost of labor, directly in the form of the PRSI but also in the form of a high level of public expenditure, which inevitably translates into high levels of taxation. In a sense, this represents the critical angle from which employers qualify their general and principled acceptance of the welfare state. They repeatedly assert the need to curtail public expenditure.

In order to achieve that, they advocate a range of measures. First of all, they call for a general reduction of wastage, which they consider to be inherent to the way that the public sector operates. But when the chips are down and despite their principled support for social protection, employers envisage a significant trimming of the Irish welfare system. First, welfare benefits in Ireland are deemed too generous, and indeed they contend that the definition of poverty in use remains far too loose, as it would include 80 percent of the world's population. Social expenditure has run ahead of wealth creation and must be cut back (*CII Newsletter*, October 12, 1982). Second, they consider the public provision of a broad range of services to be wasteful. This occurs because of the lack of incentive to curtail the consumption of services that cost nothing to those who avail themselves of it (*CII Newletter*, October 12, 1982). Health and education are clearly targeted here, and it is even suggested that charges be introduced for some of these public services (*CII Newsletter*, November 30, 1982). When pressed, employers advocate a reduction of social services. For instance, they countenanced at one stage a reduction of hospital beds, as well as a shift from public to private provision of health services. They favor the development of private hospitals and reliance on private health insurance (*CII Newsletter*, July 29, 1986).

But the reduction of public expenditure should mainly rely, according to the employers, on a more selective targeting of social benefits: "[P]articular regard must be had to maintaining social cohesion and protecting and providing opportunities for the socially disadvantaged" (IBEC 1996: 3). It is clearly stated, here as elsewhere, that the welfare system is meant for the socially disadvantaged. The Irish welfare system has been based, at least in part and for some time now, on social insurance. No statement from the representatives of the employers or any document from their organization makes reference to this principle of social insurance. Social contributions from both employees and employers are treated as another form of taxation. Employers have never acknowledged that the welfare sytem in Ireland attempts to offer social security on an insurance basis; people pay their social contributions when they are working and receive benefits when they unemployed, sick, or simply retired. This has nothing to do with being disadvantaged. Although this kind of social security is meant to include everybody, Irish employers write and talk about social policy as if they were thinking of social assistance, targeted as tightly as possible. They keep the liberal welfare regime as their point of reference, a regime that is meant to take care of the very poor. They contend that state aid is indiscriminate (*CII Newsletter*, October 12, 1982).

This issue relates to employers' interests in another way. Anxious to ensure a fluid labor market, they view some welfare benefits as inimical to the achievement of such a goal. They express many reservations about unemployment benefits. IBEC, by and large, accepts that a core of long-term unemployed will not benefit from the upturn of economic conditions and that special measures are required for them. It acknowledges the existence of an unemployable category, permanently dependent on the welfare state, and seems content to leave the public authorities to deal with this issue of social exclusion. But social benefits may create a disincentive to work: "The level of social welfare payments and secondary benefits is therefore effectively placing a floor on the wage at which people will accept employment" (*IBEC News*, July 1996). IBEC also suggests a shortening of the duration of unemployment benefits (*IBEC News*, December 1996).

Although in favor of all schemes that aim to provide training for the young unemployed, IBEC envisages a robust approach to this question. Early school-leavers or young unemployed should be obliged to take up training or work-experience opportunities and be penalized if they do not. One is back to the old theme of the impact of the welfare system on work incentive and the fostering of dependency. In its comments on the 1999 budget, IBEC welcomed the Employment Action Plan, which encourages unemployed people to go back to work by training them. It also favors the education and employment opportunities offered to those under twenty-five, chiefly when the application of this scheme forces a significant number of bogus unemployed claimants to sign off the registry. IBEC consistently argues for tighter control of welfare abuse. It singles out short-term sickness benefits, which, because of their tax-free status, have become a clear disincentive to work. Claimants should be referred for medical checks, and, generally speaking, claims need to be more systematically investigated and fraud curtailed.

Employers mainly complain about the level of public expenditure and lament the inability of public authorities to reduce the tax burden. Remarkably, most of the demands made by employers imply additional public expenditure. This applies, for instance, to education and the call for the provision of educational infrastructure that is required by economic development. IBEC overcomes this apparent contradiction between its demand for a decrease of public expenditure and its demand for an increase of particular types of state expenditure by redefining expenditure that they consider necessary as investment rather than cost. The same views seem to be held in relation to child-care facilities, which the state is asked to finance, at least in part.

Employers express their hostility toward the diverse EU programs, which are meant to offer protection to employees. They are concerned about the introduction of further legislation at the European level and denounce the overregulation of the labor market. Numerous rules and regulations have been introduced either to comply with European policy or, more simply, to follow the general trend in other European countries. For instance, employers do not find helpful the new legislation on part-time work. They also complain about a basic lack of consultation.

IBEC rejects the necessity of further European harmonization. It gives three main reasons to resist this trend toward increased social protection for employees. One relates to the relatively backward nature of the Irish economy: Ireland cannot afford the level of protection that is enjoyed by more developed and more established industrial countries: "At European level, the government needs to secure recognition for the fact that we remain a less advantaged country whose problems of peripherality and degree of economic development make the pace of progress on social policy issues a critical matter" (*IBEC Annual Review* 1994–1995: 4). Furthermore, this increased regulation deviates from the trend, as some of these older industrial countries are striving to bring more flexibility into their work practices. Finally, Ireland's economic success has, to a large extent, depended on attracting international companies, and too tight a regulation of employment would undermine this attractiveness. Employers are, of course, acutely aware of the fact that the relative strength of unions and employers differs radically at a European level and within Ireland. They maintain that the balance that has been achieved in Ireland should not be interfered with from outside: "In addition, as the Social Dialogue is working well, any tinkering with the process must have the support of the current Social Partners" (*IBEC News*, March 1996). Independently of the relative position of Ireland within Europe, they also view the EU social policy as counterproductive in any case, for it erodes the competitiveness of the European economy worldwide.

Education and Training

Employers have shown a great deal of interest in the educational system and have articulated clear views on this topic. Education recurs as a concern of employers. For a long time, they have felt dissatisfied with education in Ireland, particularly with the weak position of science and technology at school. But their hostility toward the educational system runs deeper. Not only do they seek more relevant courses, with a greater emphasis on language skills, art and design courses, computer courses, and science and technology, but they are looking for a closer link between school and industry. The administration of schools and universities should be made more accountable. The industrial ethos needs to be introduced and fostered in schools at an early stage. This requires a transformation of the syllabus, and they consider that the organizations representative of industry should have a say in the determination of school syllabus (*CII Newsletter*, February 3, September 1, 1981).

Concern about educational and training matters has considerably increased in the light of recent economic development and its accompanying labor shortages. IBEC stresses the need to invest in the education and training of the workforce. It even acknowledges some shortcomings of employers in this respect. Their lack of participation in the training process implies that they do not quite get the labor force that they require. They emphasize the need for greater investment and also for taking more responsibility for the development of the workforce. The formation of an independent, employer-led training body is even envisaged. They state their commitment in the future to play a strong leadership role in determining the direction of training in employment. Nevertheless, the state is asked to bear a higher share of the cost of training initiatives.

Nowadays, IBEC places great emphasis on the flexibility and adaptability of the labor force as a crucial factor in economic development. Today's economy necessitates not only a highly skilled labor force but also a very flexible one. IBEC turns once more toward education to generate a labor force with all these qualities. The educational system must now produce workers with up-to-date knowledge, skills, and technological know-how but also good interpersonal skills, teamwork abilities, initiative and flexibility as well as accepting continuous, lifelong learning. It has moved from the rigid position that criticized the educational system for its failure to produce the precise skills required by the economy at the time. Employers have adopted a more enlightened attitude toward education and no longer expect definite skills and knowledge from the educational system, as this skill and knowledge become rapidly dated. Flexibility is now the key word, and in that sense employers find themselves more in tune with the ethos of educators, who have long resisted too narrow a formation in favor of a broader education that nurtures ongoing intellectual development and fosters an ability to adapt quickly to very different situations. "IBEC has emphasised the need to develop a broadly based education system on which more specialist knowledge and skills can be built at a later stage and as the need arises" (IBEC 1996: 21). This does not mean, however, that employers have ceased to push for a greater emphasis at school on technology, engineering, science, computer skills, and better language skills. In their submission to the Higher Education Authority, they strongly advocated increased investment in the third-level sector, with a particular effort for promoting research and development and enhancing marketable skills.

Equality in the Workforce

In quite a stunning statement, employers proclaim their support for equality: "There are good economic and social reasons for supporting the principle of equality in economic and social life" (IBEC 1996: 26). This statement is somewhat mitigated by the way that they define equality. They are referring to the lack of discrimination on the basis of gender, age, religion, race, disability, and so on. They reassert that all individuals are entitled to, and should be guaranteed, full and active participation in employment and economic life. But they warn that this support for equality does not extend to an "equality of condition": "IBEC believes that the idea of building a society which guarantees equality of wealth, income, working conditions, power and privileges is inimical to the views and aspirations of most people in society and is incompatible with a market economy" (IBEC 1996: 27). Even their support for the more benign type of equality is qualified. For instance, gender equality will not be achieved by the introduction of quotas or through any legal measure or compulsion. They claim that this equalization will occur slowly as part of a drastic change in attitudes. Employers are nonetheless encouraged to introduce measures that facilitate the participation of women in the labor force: flexible hours, part-time employment, career breaks, and so on. Equality will be attained mainly by the adoption of such facilitative measures on a voluntary basis. In fact, IBEC warns against the danger of overregulation in this area of discrimination and equality. Very little remains of their principled support for equality, as they have managed to dismiss just about every policy measure that would promote such equality. This aspiration toward equality implies nothing other than the promise of the employers' goodwill. It simply means that the self-interest of employers nowadays demands that they draw equally on the whole labor force.

The issue of child-care facilities comes to the fore in this context. IBEC supports schemes to assist employers to get involved in the provision of child-care services for their employees. It looks toward a higher level of participation of women in the labor force as a way of relieving labor bottlenecks. But it sees other advantages in adequate provision of child-care facilities: to prevent early school-leaving and social exclusion, to set child-care services on a more formal basis, and to eliminate the unfair competition from the black economy. Employers assert that the primary responsibility for developing child-care services must rest on the state. They mainly recommend the use of tax breaks for parents to pay for the care of their young children and for a range of allowances and tax relief to help the development of child-care facilities. They also ask the state to take responsibility for the formation of child-care trainees through the training agency Foras Áiseanna Saothair (FÁS).

Employers adopt a very pragmatic approach to the welfare system in Ireland. They do not put forward general values or principles according to which welfare provisions should be shaped. But it is not difficult to discover the kind of welfare system that they favor: one in which social benefits are clearly targeted to the "poor and the disadvantaged." They seem to uphold a version of the residual or liberal welfare regime. Within that framework, employers may at times express their welcome for increases in social benefits. Generally speaking, they profess a principled support for welfare provision while all the time pressing for a trimming and containment of social expenditure.

As already noted, social policy occupies a secondary place, albeit a growing one, in employers' concerns. This social category, despite its dominant position in the structure of Irish society, does not constitute a major actor in the welfare field. It, nonetheless, operates within it and relies on a capital of political power in order to do so. This capital does not derive from any mobilizing power but from its control over core economic resources, such as investment and employment. The necessity of economic development greatly enhances the political value of these resources. Furthermore, employers enjoy another relevant resource: they have the benefit of a fairly easy and direct access to politicians through various social networks. This represents part of their social capital.

Employers mobilize their political and social capital in order to contain their material contributions to welfare. Their goal remains largely negative: they seek not to maximize material resources but to avoid high levels of social contribution. This strategy manifests itself quite clearly in their hostility toward Pay Related Social Insurance (PRSI) contributions and in their relentless critique of the high level of public expenditure and taxation. But they also press for more public expenditure on services that they consider beneficial for economic development. Besides material capital, employers endeavor to increase, in a selective way, their control capital. Once more, this takes the negative form of minimizing state regulation of the labor market. More positively, employers call for greater accountability for educational agencies and greater participation in the determination of the school syllabus.

CONCLUSION

The three agents in the welfare field analyzed in this chapter are engaged in a straightforward and rather similar strategy: converting political capital into material capital. This contrasts with the complex and multidimensional conversions that the state and the Catholic Church effectuate.

The activity of the trade union movement in the welfare field follows a simple logic of transforming its political capital into material capital. This material capital takes the form of better social services and increased social benefits. Such conversion, if successful, of course, adds to the symbolic capital of trade unions; they can realistically present themselves as defending the living standards of the working population and of the most vulnerable among them.

The women's movement has also used its mobilizing power to generate more social benefits for women. But it has mainly contributed to the development of a parallel welfare system comprising a range of services relevant to women and administered by them. It has striven to convert its mobilizing capacity into resources for these parallel services, as well as ensuring its continuing control over such services.

Employers operate in the welfare field on the basis of a different kind of political capital. Their economic resources, those of investment and employment creation, are easily transformed into political capital. The latter is actually enhanced by the close association that employers enjoy with the political elite. They bring into play this double capital mainly to curtail or at least contain the level of social expenditure that they incur. But they also endeavor to increase their participation and involvement in education and training.

NOTE

1. The Irish Congress of Trade Unions (ICTU) was created in 1959 and brought together the two competing federations of the Irish Trade Unions Congress (Irish TUC) and the Congress of Irish Unions.

Part II

The Dynamic of the Irish

Welfare System

6

Welfare and State Autonomy

The development of the welfare state in Ireland has not been studied in any detail. The different accounts of welfare development available in the relevant literature have not been applied in a sustained way to the Irish context. An article by O'Connell and Rottman (1992) provides an exception to this statement. In this piece of work, the authors reject the conventional explanations of welfare development. They contend that industrial development and welfare effort are not closely related in Ireland. They also point to the fragmentation of the trade unions and the electoral weakness of the labor movement; on that basis, they dismiss the social democratic account of welfare development. The two explanations are rather succinctly discarded, and the authors do not dwell at length on such perspectives. Instead, they uphold a state-centered approach. The latter reacts against the tendency to account for state activity in terms of external constraints and sociological determinisms, in which the state is perceived as an instrument controlled and used by other forces.

Two versions of this call "for bringing the state back in" can be identified (Skocpol 1985). The stronger version assumes that the state constitutes a major force in society and that it is self-determining. State activity is not explained by external processes and constraints, which are rooted in society; on the contrary, the state possesses its own goals and is able to shape society. The weaker version of the state-centered approach recognizes that the state forms a significant force in society, but not necessarily a predominant one. The state is, nonetheless, presented as self-determining. O'Connell and Rottman work within this weaker version: "But our state-centred interpretation is contingent on three other variables that constrain the autonomy of the state: political system characteristics; class structure and mobilisation; and the capacities of other interest groups" (O'Connell and Rottman 1992: 231). The state-centered approach is then used as a framework for interpreting welfare development in Ireland. The state is considered to have had an important autonomous impact on welfare development, although not an exclusive one. But the autonomous contribution of the state to the development of the Irish welfare state is asserted rather than demonstrated. This chapter undertakes such a demonstration. To what extent has the state contributed in an autonomous way to the shaping of the Irish welfare system?

Eric Nordlinger (1981) has made a strong claim for what he calls the state-centered approach. He forcefully argues that state activity is not adequately accounted for by external, social determinisms that weigh on this institution. The emphasis is firmly set on the state's ability to act on its own. The notion of autonomy is used in a mainly symbolic way to signify that the state cannot be reduced to the constraints that bear upon it, that it constitutes an agency able to define and achieve its own goals: "Look at least as much to the state as to civil society to understand what the democratic state does in the making of public policy and why it does so; the democratic state is frequently autonomous in translating its own preferences into authoritative actions" (Nordlinger 1981: 203).

Nordlinger identifies three different types of state autonomy. In the first type, the state realizes its preferences against the opposition of other social actors that hold different preferences. In the second type, the state holds preferences that differ from those of other social actors but manages to change the preference of these actors. In the third type of state autonomy, state preferences correspond to those of social actors, and the state realizes its preferences without facing opposition. In this case, one observes convergent preferences from the very start. This constitutes, to say the least, a weak type of autonomy.

The empirical test used in this chapter derives directly from the classification of state autonomy put forward by Nordlinger. It focuses on the fit or lack of it between state and societal preferences, meaning here the respective preferences of the main relevant forces in society. State and societal preferences can be either divergent or nondivergent. The term "nondivergent" encompasses convergent preferences, compatible ones, or even indifference. "To discuss state autonomy under conditions of divergence and nondivergence all that needs to be established is that considerable variations in the fit between state and societal preferences exist, that there are numerous instances of divergence and nondivergence" (Nordlinger 1981: 31).

Such an exclusive reliance on preferences creates some difficulties. It totally bypasses the issue of the determination of such preferences: how do social agents come to have their preferences? Statements of preference participate in strategies in which agents are engaged. They already take into account the preferences of other actors. For this very reason, preferences do not necessarily remain stable. Nevertheless, the preferences formulated provide the most reliable indication of the goals pursued by the various agents. Furthermore, the empirical test on which this analysis relies simply records the divergence or nondivergence between preferences; it throws absolutely no light on the processes involved, on the way the policy outcome is achieved.

The test of state autonomy involves relating state preferences and societal preferences. The latter refer to the preferences, divergent in all likelihood, of various private actors. In the context of welfare development on which we focus, state autonomy is upheld when:

- the way welfare develops corresponds to state preferences, despite opposition from other forces (type I);
- the state manages to alter the pattern of preferences in society, from divergent to nondivergent preferences (type II);
- the state realizes its preferences, which also correspond to the preferences of the main forces in the welfare field (type III).

The state is not autonomous if its preferences are determined by other forces or if welfare institutions develop in a way that does not correspond to state preferences.

SOCIAL SERVICES

The constellation of forces that are active and influential changes according to each sector of the welfare system. In the educational field, the state, the Catholic Church, and teachers' organizations have played the major role. The church and medical doctors have, along with the state, shaped the health services. The state, trade unions, and, to a lesser extent, employers occupy the key positions for elaborating the diverse schemes of income maintenance. This chapter focuses on the degree of autonomy enjoyed by state agencies in expanding the welfare system in Ireland. It is conventionally asserted that the prominence of the Catholic Church in this field has denied any autonomy to the state: "Until relatively recently, one of the more notable features of the Irish society has been the pre-eminence of Catholic social teaching" (Curry 1993: 10). On the other hand, the main interest groups would have played only a limited role. Nevertheless, "[t]he trade union movement was more united from the beginning of the 1960s that it had been since the end of the war and it also began to place emphasis on the need for improvement of social services" (Maguire 1986: 250). While the trade unions pressed for an extension of welfare services and an increase in welfare benefits, "[t]he main business organisations, by contrast, have repeatedly called for reductions in the levels of public expenditure and taxation and have criticised what they perceived as the ad hoc expansion of social programmes....high levels of taxation and social transfers create disincentives for employment" (Maguire 1986: 363). More recently, the women's movement has made its mark on the Irish welfare system.

A far more controlled analysis of the relative weight of the agencies involved in the development of the welfare system in Ireland is required if one is to move beyond loose commentaries. We must also allow for the possibility that the level of state autonomy varies according to the area of social policy considered. The following analysis focuses on important moments in the development of the Irish welfare system. For each selected moment, the preferences of the main groups or agencies involved are recorded. Such preferences are defined as divergent or nondivergent in relation to the final policy outcome.

Health Services

The health services in Ireland have had a tormented history. Some of the most dramatic and revealing events in the life of independent Ireland have taken place in this context. We may start our considerations with the Health Act 1947, which attracted strong criticism from the Catholic hierarchy and the medical profession. Their criticisms hinged on what they saw as the unjustifiable extension of the role of government. But the conflict between state and church did not come to a head, as the bill was withdrawn in order to test its constitutional validity.

The opposition hardened for the next round of health policy making, when a proposal emerged, based on the Health Act 1947, for a Mother and Child Scheme (1951). It introduced free maternity care for all expectant mothers and free medical care for all children up to the age of sixteen. The new minister for health was intent on setting up a full public health service; for him, the Mother and Child Scheme represented a step in this direction. From the very start, the Catholic bishops and diverse religious bodies objected to the compulsory nature of medical inspection in schools. This inspection and referral to health authorities did not accord with the views of the Catholic hierarchy, which saw them as an intrusion in family prerogatives. The bishops also objected in strong terms to the right of health authorities to educate women in regard to motherhood and children in regard to health. Public education concerned with body matters—and with reproduction, more particularly—was not acceptable. No guarantee existed that such an education would correspond to the church's views and rules on such matters. The bishops were also opposed to the provision of a free service for those able to pay for it (Whyte 1980).

Medical doctors demanded that free medical care be made dependent on a means test. They were, of course, concerned about the prospect of a shrinking pool of private patients. "The medical profession opposed the scheme because it did not want a comprehensive state health service, preferring instead a mix of public and private" (Curry 1993: 114). On the other hand, the main confederation of trade unions at that time in the Republic, the Irish Trade Unions Congress, called for an early implementation of the scheme (Irish Trade Unions Congress 1950–1951). The direct confrontation that ensued between the state, on the one hand, and a coalition of church and medical associations, on the other, led to the resignation of the minister for health and the withdrawal of this piece of legislation.

The policy outcome did not correspond to the preferences of the ministerial department involved. We have to ignore, for the time being, the fact that the government as a whole did not fully support the minister for health and had divided loyalties. The preferences of the Catholic Church and those of the medical professions corresponded to the policy outcome. The issue was not very high on the agenda of the ITUC at that stage, but its policy preferences really diverged from the policy outcome. In conclusion, the preferences of the main state agency involved were not realized in the face of opposition by the Catholic Church and the medical practitioners and despite the support of the ITUC. This represents a clear case of lack of state autonomy.

But the story does not stop there. The resignation of the minister for health over the Mother and Child Scheme was soon followed by a general election and a change of government. The new minister for health had been the main force behind the promotion of the 1947 Health Act; he took up from there and set out to introduce relevant legislation. The Health Act 1953 extended eligibility to public hospital services to 85 percent of the population; only the 15 percent in the high-income category would have to pay for their own hospital services. The act created a rather awkward scheme involving three categories of eligibility, based on means tests. The idea of a comprehensive and free health service for all children under sixteen was simply abandoned. The extension of public general medical services had formed a major policy orientation of the Department of Health, but that program was never again put on the agenda. Although the extension of the already watered-down Mother and Child Scheme was promised at that time, the promise was never fulfilled.

Different interpretations of the Health Act of 1953 have been given. For some, this act did not greatly differ in its main principles from the one that had been rejected in 1951 (Whyte 1980; Maguire 1986). The political skill of the new government ensured the smooth passage of a rather similar piece of legislation. In the other interpretation, the new bill took into account the opposition of the Catholic hierarchy and removed everything to which they strongly objected (Barrington 1987). Most of the compromise and accommodation had come from the department. One may add that the ITUC welcomed the bill as offering some improvement, while at the same time pointing out shortcomings such as the continuing reliance on dispensaries and the lack of a comprehensive health service. The outcome conforms to the preferences of all relevant agents or, rather, there is no actual divergence between them. This lack of divergence could mean support, relative indifference, or even strategic, rather than enthusiastic, acceptance. In any case, this situation of consensus corresponds to Nordlinger's type III of state autonomy.

The Health Act 1970 had an easier passage in the Dáil. It was preceded by a White Paper in 1966 that proposed significant developments in the health field. It did not envisage any significant extension of services, only an extension to the middle-income group of assistance toward drug costs. But it proposed to eliminate the dispensary network of public health and to replace it with a choice of doctor in general medical services. Not only did it press for the cooperation and coordination of county hospitals, but it created new health boards for the administration of health services on a regional basis. This effectively removed health from the direct responsibility of local authorities.

These measures received the approval of the medical profession and the Catholic Church. The Department of Health had entered into an alliance of interests, and this alliance ensured a trouble-free adoption of this scheme. Some questions were raised about aspects of the proposed reorganization of health services. How were they going to be financed in the long term? How were health and hospital services going to be regionalized? A major question remained to be resolved, and it proved troublesome. How were doctors going to be paid in the proposed choice-of-doctor scheme? The doctors themselves demanded payment for each service rendered, while the department did not want to enter into a scheme in which expenditures were controlled only with great difficulty. It favored a capitation fee paid for each patient registered with a doctor. After lengthy and protracted negotiations, the department conceded a "fee-per-item" mode of payment, with control for potential abuses. ITUC expressed its support for the scheme as a step in the right direction, and the right direction meant for it a comprehensive health service, without means tests and open to all. This, of course, it never got, even when the Catholic Church started asking for it. Such a configuration of preferences corresponds to type III of Nordlinger's state autonomy.

In 1973, the minister for health decided to introduce free public hospital services for all. In practice, he was removing the income ceiling for such social benefits. The representative organizations of hospital consultants, the Irish Medical Association and the Medical Union, asked the minister for health not to abolish the income ceiling for health benefits, at least until agreement had been reached on a national contract for consultants. They claimed that the removal of the income ceiling would increase the load of hospital services at a time when they were already under severe pressure. It also meant, more realistically, that consultants were very worried about the removal from their clientele of close to 300,000 private patients who contributed significantly to their income. Faced with such opposition, the minister received the support of the ICTU, which urged him to widen eligibility for hospital and outpatient services. In August 1973, the minister declared his intention to introduce full eligibility for all employees to hospital services. The Catholic hierarchy's Council for Social Welfare quickly welcomed health services for all, a far cry, indeed, from the position taken by the hierarchy less than twenty years earlier. The relations between the Ministry of Health and the medical professions became quite tense and the negotiations for consultant contracts were postponed on several occasions. Confronted with the noncooperation of consultants and with their rejection of diverse proposed compromises, the minister had little option but to withdraw the Health Services (Limited Eligibility) Regulations 1974 (*Dáil Report* 1974).

Several years later, another minister for health put forward the Health Contribution Bill, 1978, which extended the pay-related scheme of health benefits contributions. The bill was implementing the free hospitalization scheme for all, but with some restrictions. Those with an income above the ceiling for social security contributions had to pay for consultant fees and maternity treatment. The bill was taking on board the consultants' main objection to the previous piece of legislation. We observe here, as in 1953, the reversal of Nordlinger's type III autonomy: the constellation of forces within civil society successfully alters state preferences to make them congruent with their own. This represents a clear case of nonautonomy for the state.

In the field of health services, the state realized its preferences only when in tune with other agencies in the field. It actually changed its preferences in a way that made them nondivergent. The fact that the Catholic Church did not prefer a particular policy was not sufficient to stop this policy, although a strongly expressed opposition did suffice at an early stage. But the church did not carry through its preference in the free hospitalization scheme. Consultants' opposition to it ensured its downfall and its replacement by a scheme more compatible with their interest. Overall, the state enjoyed a low level of autonomy in the health field: it was not able to realize its preferences in two cases, and it altered its preferences in two other cases and achieved its goals in another case only because they also corresponded to the preferences of all other forces.

Education

For a long time, few players were involved in shaping education. At the highest level, only the Catholic Church and state carry weight, and the church has exercised an effective veto on central issues. It has played, and continues to play, a central part, mainly because it directly manages most primary schools and controls most secondary schools through religious orders. But the Catholic Church has also placed education very high on its agenda. Ensuring a Catholic education to Catholic children has been defined as a priority, as the main rationale of church policy, and this meant education in schools controlled by Catholic clerics. The church refers in this context to the Catholic hierarchy, but also to the various organizations of managers and heads of secondary schools. Although these church agencies did not always press for the same policy, the hierarchy always took precedence when it mattered.

The teachers' unions for primary and secondary education occupy a central place in the educational field. A very deep rivalry separates the two unions for secondary schooling (Association of Secondary School Teachers and Teacher's Union of Ireland), as they organize teachers in different types of schools. This antagonism has led teachers in secondary schools to adopt a policy of upholding the denominational character of secondary schools and defending their independence from the state. In this respect, they have allied themselves with the school managers and with the churches.

For a long time, too, the state did not take a very active part in the educational field. "Up to then (1960s) the Department seemed content to leave the control of the system to the three main interest groups, the church, teachers' unions and parents" (Curry 1993: 110). However, in 1966, the minister for education proposed to introduce free secondary education. There was no particular or pressing demand for such a policy, and the move took everybody by surprise. I rely here on the analysis of this episode developed by Séamas Ó Buachalla (1988). The managerial bodies of secondary schools (fourteen such bodies in 1985) declared their opposition to this policy of free secondary education for all. The managerial body for Protestant schools, the Secondary Education Committee, stressed that such a policy did not meet their needs as a religious minority. It had already created a new structure in Protestant secondary education, which met their specific needs, and it had achieved that through discussion and diplomacy. The managers of secondary Catholic schools expressed opposition to the scheme and put pressure on the

Department of Education to negotiate with them. The minister for education had not consulted them prior to announcing his proposal. But he had consulted the Catholic hierarchy; the latter did not display great enthusiasm for the policy but found it difficult to oppose, as popular opinion was very much behind the minister.

The teachers were, through their trade unions, mainly concerned with working conditions and wages and did not form a major force in shaping educational development. If anything, teachers in secondary schools tended to uphold the denominational and independent character of their schools: they were broadly aligned with school managers. At this stage, parents did not have an organized voice.

One observes in relation to the 1967 Free Education Act another case of type III state autonomy. However, if one looks more closely, the case for state autonomy is stronger than in previous instances. A state agency, the Department of Education, initiated a policy that was resisted by the religious orders in charge of secondary schools. However, if the Catholic Church did not support it, it did not oppose it either. The issue was not high on the agenda of teachers' organizations, although they would hardly obstruct such a move. Even the ICTU expressed its support for free secondary schooling, after the event. The ITCU Conference congratulated the minister for implementing such a policy. Although the state was not entirely united on this issue, it was able to carry through its policy because it did not face opposition, but ambivalence and passivity from other forces. It demonstrated in this context its capacity for autonomous action. The preference of the state appeared sufficient, but only in the absence of determined opposition by the Catholic Church.

From the middle of the 1960s, the state became an active force shaping the educational system. The change from a passive to an active presence in this domain had been prompted by the realization that the educational system was not adapted to the requirements of industrial development. The state soon promoted the idea of comprehensive schooling, which would put an end to the division between secondary and vocational schools, increase the status of technical education, provide a less denominational education, and facilitate the rationalization of the school system. The introduction of comprehensive education did not proceed very far. It was soon replaced by the idea of "community schools." Such schools would demand the cooperation and, possibly, amalgamation of secondary and vocational schools in each locality, as an alternative to separate secondary and vocational schools. A *Community School Document* was made public in November 1970, which formulated the policy orientations of the Department of Education in this context. Religious orders declared themselves hostile to this proposal and denounced the amalgamation as a mechanism to push them out of secondary education. At first, the Catholic hierarchy expressed strong reservations but soon declared its will to cooperate, granted that it be given guarantees about the religious and moral formation of Catholic children, who were going to form the vast majority of pupils in such schools. The Association of Secondary Teachers of Ireland (ASTI) adopted a defensive position. It aligned itself with Catholic managers and indicated its concern at the possibility of state control over secondary schools. It also feared the loss of status for secondary school teachers, in comparison with teachers in vocational schools.

In 1971, the Department of Education published proposals for the management of community schools. They represented a fairly drastic change of heart by the Department of Education, for they granted the trustees of secondary schools the power to nominate four out of six members of the Board of Management. This undermined the central thrust of the community school idea, away from a multidenominational education and away also from a broad representation of all relevant interests in the local community. The 1974 Draft Deed of Trust again modified this scheme. The Catholic management insisted on retaining a majority on the board and was adamant about having reserved places on the teaching staff. At this stage, the ASTI had accepted the community school idea but complained bitterly about the lack of teachers' representation on the schools' board and objected to the "faith and morals clause." The Conference of Major Religious Schools strongly resisted the statutory representation of teachers on the board at first but soon relented, provided that the trustees' representatives held the majority; they still insisted on reserved teaching places for members of religious orders.

The ICTU welcomed the introduction of community schools. This type of school was perceived as responding to the main concerns of the unions in this domain. They were bridging the gap between secondary and vocational schooling. In so doing, they were raising the status of technical and scientific education. They also carried the promise of better access to education for working-class children. Finally, the ICTU saw this new type of school as part of a move towards nondenominational schooling, which it welcomed. On all these counts, it was going to be disappointed.

If one wishes to formalize the community school issue (1970–1981) in terms of preferences, the following picture emerges:

- The preferences of the Department of Education were formulated in the original document (1970), but the main goals had not been achieved at the end of the process. The preferences of the Department of Education did not conform to the policy outcome.
- The secondary school teachers showed little enthusiasm for the whole idea. They resented their failure to obtain representation on the boards of management. At the same time, they did not reject the scheme absolutely; in fact, teachers in vocational schools were relatively supportive.
- Originally, the Catholic Church was opposed to the whole idea, but it soon obtained concessions that in its eyes guaranteed the Catholic character of such schools and its capacity to exercise a determinant influence within them. To a large extent, the outcome represented a compromise that it was willing to accept, but not necessarily with great enthusiasm.
- The ICTU had consistently called for greater recognition of technical/ vocational education, and the idea of community schooling was pushing in that direction. At the same time, it did not favor a denominational type of education. Overall, the trade unions did not express strong views on this issue.

This sequence of events in relation to the introduction of the community schools raises some interesting questions of a general nature. First of all, it points to the difficulty of deciding what the preferences of the state are (in this case, the Department of Education). Initial statements have been taken as an expression of preferences, but it was soon subjected to the intense pressure of powerful groups. The final policy proposals differed greatly from what was indicated at the beginning. Did state preferences refer to the goals that the state formulated initially or to those that it stated after negotiations and pressure? Furthermore, all the major actors in the field modified their views and consequently their preferences while the issue remained alive. The hierarchy and the Catholic schools' management did not always speak with one voice, and the latter was far more hostile to the idea than the hierarchy, but both changed their policy as the situation evolved. The Association of Secondary School Teachers experienced a similar change of heart and, in fact, moved from a strategic alliance with the church to a fairly straightforward conflict on the issue of teachers' representation. These changes have to do with strategic positioning in a fluctuating situation, but they underline the fact that preferences are defined within a particular situation, not in an absolute way.

Nevertheless, the two situations with which we have dealt point to very different conclusions about state autonomy in the educational field. In the case of the introduction of free secondary education, the state took the initiative within a context of consensus. In the community school case, the state failed to realize its preferences when confronted with the strong opposition of the Catholic Church. It adopted a policy that could be reconciled with the preferences of the latter.

INCOME MAINTENANCE

The situation for income maintenance schemes differs greatly from such social services as health and education. Income maintenance programs involve financial transfers: unemployment benefits, health insurance, pensions, family allowances, and so on. We may start with the Social Welfare Act (1952), for it constitutes a significant landmark in the development of the Irish welfare state. It set up a compulsory insurance scheme for all employees in respect of disability, unemployment, and widowhood. It mainly brought together all the various schemes already in existence and coordinated them. It strengthened the insurance principle, as opposed to assistance, as the basis for social benefits. It offered coverage to all employees and provided flat-rate benefits for flat-rate contributions. Not only employees (below a certain limit for nonmanual workers) but employers and the state were also asked to contribute to the scheme. Finally, a contributory pension was introduced for men at seventy years of age and women at sixty-five years.

The main characteristic of this act relates to the fact that it generated little controversy. The minister for social welfare sent a copy of the proposed act to each Catholic bishop, but he received very few responses from them. The bishops do not seem to have developed a collective opinion on the question. Some clerical voices were heard formulating objections to the scheme, once more playing on the theme of state intrusion leading to totalitarianism. Even the criticisms of Bishop Dignan, who was the author of a national welfare project based on social insurance but independent of the state, did not carry great weight. His main objection was directed at the fact that the scheme excluded the large groups of self-employed and small business. But this did not add up to church opposition: its general indifference placed it in the nondivergent category. One observes here another case of type III autonomy in Nordlinger's classification.

The Social Welfare (Pay Related Benefits) Acts of 1973 introduced pay-related benefits in addition to the existing flat-rate benefits for social unemployment and sickness. This development was welcomed by the ICTU. It objected to two provisions, which were removed after consultation with the minister. It also called for the welfare insurance scheme to be extended to all workers, along with a call for a general pension scheme and the elimination of the distinction between private and public sector workers. The act was passed with little controversy. Only the employers (Federated Union of Employers) complained that social welfare schemes were becoming too costly. They demanded that consultation take place between the state, employers, and employees before major policy changes were launched (*Irish Times*, July 5, 1973). This just about amounted to divergent preferences.

Another Social Welfare Act (1973) removed the income ceiling for compulsory social insurance contributions and benefits. This implied that all employees would participate in the scheme of social security, independently of income level. This measure was passed without opposition, although some serious difficulties emerged in relation to the application of the measure to health insurance and health services.

The Social Welfare Act of 1988 extended social insurance to the self-employed. The Green Paper on the extension of social insurance to the self-employed pointed to the absence of a representative voice for the self-employed. "Part of the difficulty in identifying the needs of the self-employed in the matter of social security stems from the absence of any clear-cut indication as to their aspirations in this area" (Department of Social Welfare 1978: 24). Very diverse occupations are included in this employment status. Farmers form the bulk of the self-employed in Ireland, about two-thirds. They are well organized, and it would be surprising if they did not have any view on this issue. Professional workers and many in the retailing business also belong to this category of self-employed. One suspects that many self-employed do not consider their participation in a state social insurance scheme as of any benefit to them; they have already made their own provisions for contingencies or old age.

The prospect of extending the social insurance scheme did not meet with great enthusiasm from farmers. The discussion and negotiation for such an extension were conducted in the context of preparing a submission to the National Pension Board. Both farmers' organizations, the Irish Farmers' Association (IFA) and the Irish Creamery Milk Suppliers' Association (ICMSA), represented the self-employed on the board committee. They refused to sign the report on the extension of PRSI to the self-employed, mainly because the report recommended that the self-employed pay the employee and the employer's contributions, that is, 7.5 percent of their annual income. They themselves thought it unfair to ask them to pay more than 3 percent, which corresponds to the employee's contribution. The IFA also expressed a more general objection to the proposal: it claimed that the Pensions Board was seeking to put the responsibility on the state to provide pensions for all citizens, regardless of income, when it would be more appropriate to encourage citizens to arrange privately for their own pensions (*Irish Farmers Journal*, January 16, 1988). They were arguing for the possibility of opting out of the scheme for those who could show that they were already providing for such a benefit on a private basis. They found very few allies in this stance, as the state was granting pensions to many farmers on a noncontributory basis. In fact, the farmers had conceded the principle of such an extension and were already negotiating for the conditions under which they would participate in the scheme.

The small retailers, grouped in the Retail Grocery Dairy and Allied Trades' Association (RGDATA), also responded to the Green Paper on the extension of social insurance to the self-employed. They put forward a strong claim to be included in a scheme of social protection. "Many self-employed were forced, for their own protection, to procure personal cover for themselves, and one would think that this expediency was not born out of a sense of independence inherent in their way of life or their ability or inability to pay, but purely and simply because of the absence of any comprehensive scheme that would incorporate them" (*Retail News*, January 1979). At the same time, they did not seem able to identify a common ground for all shopkeepers. They expressed their favorable attitude toward such an extension in general terms but remained unclear concerning the modalities of their inclusion.

Other groups in society have called for such an extension of social insurance. In 1972, the Commission on the Status of Women urged the introduction of a compulsory widows' and orphans' pension scheme for all those outside the existing compulsory insurance categories. They were, in all likelihood, concerned with the welfare position of the wives of self-employed people. The ICTU approved this extension of social insurance to self-employed, a measure that it had advocated beforehand. It had already declared, on several occasions, its support for a comprehensive social security scheme. Many farmers were receiving old age pensions without contributing to the payment for such a benefit. Noncontributory pensions are means-tested but paid for out of general taxation. The contribution of the self-employed, particularly farmers, would then redress the balance; they would enjoy a benefit for which they had contributed. This call for the compulsory contribution of self-employed to social insurance became part of the agreed policy orientation in the Programme for National Recovery.

The church had, as far back as 1972, called for such an extension of social insurance. This policy preference was formulated in *A Statement on Social Policy* (1972), elaborated by the hierarchy's Council for Social Welfare. It was further reiterated in *Planning for Social Development. What Needs to Be Done* (1976).

The state acted within a broad consensus on the extension of the Social Insurance Fund to the self-employed. But there was strong opposition from the self-employed, and particularly from the farmers, to the rate of contribution. The outcome in this context represented a compromise, with the self-employed being asked to pay not the employer-plus-employee contribution (altogether 7.5 percent of income), but the employee contribution in the first year, gradually rising to 5 percent of their income in subsequent years.

SOME CONCLUSIONS

Several general conclusions can be drawn from the analysis of the eleven cases considered.

- All the cases of significant development in the field of social security display a rather similar configuration of preferences. The state acts in a context of consensus or near consensus. The Catholic Church does not have a high profile in this field and hardly represents a force within it. This contrasts with the social service fields of health and education. This relative lack of interest in social security, apart, of course, from its concern for poverty, means that social security is animated by a very specific dynamic.
- All this implies that the state enjoys a different level of autonomy in these three welfare subfields: very little state autonomy in health, a rather mixed picture for education, and a great deal of autonomy in relation to social security.
- Another general conclusion needs to be drawn from the previous analysis. Nordlinger is anxious to establish the reality of state autonomy, and he presents it as something absolute. Our analysis has shown that state autonomy can vary a great deal, depending on the configurations of forces in which it is involved and according to the interest that it has invested in the field. In this context, state autonomy becomes a variable.
- We have recorded no case of type I and type II state autonomy. It must be noted that all the observed cases of state autonomy correspond to Nordlinger's type III. This, as we have seen, is at best ambiguous: the state realizes its preferences, which correspond to the preferences of all the major forces in the field. But such a situation does not guarantee state autonomy, for the state could be forced "to realize its preferences" by all the relevant forces (not even envisaging the possibility of these forces determining the preferences of the state). Nordlinger chooses to interpret this kind of situation as indicating state autonomy. It seems that such situations need to be analyzed more closely, in order to decide one way or another. We were able to reach a definite conclusion in relation to the introduction of free secondary education. But the conclusion is not always as straightforward as that.

Overall, the case for state autonomy in the welfare field is not strongly supported by our analysis. This means that welfare development in Ireland has not been shaped by the state as a distinctive force. We are also in a position to reach some conclusions about the impact of the organized working class on welfare development. Two different indicators of the strength of the working class are conventionally used in this context: the electoral strength of the leftist parties, associated with their participation in government, and the strength of the trade union movement. Although weak in electoral terms, the political Left has, nonetheless, exercised power on a regular basis, although always as a minor partner in a coalition.

The strength of the trade union movement depends on its capacity for mobilization and its internal coherence. The Irish working class is quite effectively organized, and most categories of workers are included in the unified body of the ICTU. Has the presence of a relatively strong, although not radical, trade union movement had an impact on the Irish welfare system? The policy preferences of the ICTU were never realized in the health field when they stood against the preferences of the Catholic Church or of doctors; only when they coincided with those of the other major players in the field did they see their policy preferences realized. A similar consensus was established in policy developments within education. For instance, Congress remained ambiguous toward the final proposal for community schools, but it did not, as such, oppose it. The situation appears even more straightforward in relation to income maintenance: the preferences of Congress were always realized, but in a context of consensus. From this systematic pattern, one concludes that Congress has not constituted a driving force in welfare growth. It failed to have its preferences realized when opposed by other significant forces. But it was considered significant enough to figure in the configuration of forces that have shaped the welfare system in Ireland and pushed it along. Even if the "social democratic" explanation is not upheld in the Irish context, the trade unions cannot be discounted in the explanation of welfare development.

7

The Welfare Mix

A wide range of mechanisms and agencies, besides the state, is involved in welfare systems. The latter differ according to the mix of their major elements: the state, the informal sector, the voluntary sector, and market mechanisms. This mix should not necessarily be seen in terms of opposition between the state and the so-called private sector, for they interact in complex ways.

The welfare state comes to the fore when market mechanisms fail: when employed people become unemployed, when healthy workers experience ill health, and so on. In such circumstances, those who do not or cannot participate in the market avail themselves of a range of social benefits. But market mechanisms also operate within the welfare system to provide services and benefits to some categories of people. Market mechanisms remain very marginal within the Irish welfare state. A small number of private schools offer their services to fee-paying pupils, and private pension schemes are developing (Fanning 1999). Market mechanisms appear more significant in relation to health under two different, but closely related, forms. About a third of the population pays for health insurance, and this allows these people to be treated in private hospitals. Up till very recently, health insurance was provided through a semistate, non-profitmaking body. But it now faces the competition of private and commercial institutions.

A great deal of welfare is supplied by what is referred to as the informal sector. Rarely acknowledged as such, it basically includes family members and informal networks of help. It predominantly depends on the work of women, and we have already come across this issue in the context of the feminist analysis of welfare. In that sense, the welfare state constitutes a structure that closely involves the state, the family, and the labor market. A large amount of care is performed, often on an unpaid basis, by women who do not participate in the labour market. The informal sector predominates in support for elderly people and also, to a lesser extent, in the care of chronically ill or disabled individuals.

The attempt at restructuring the welfare state has revolved, at least to some extent, around the relationship between this informal sector and the state. The state is often urged to assume direct responsibility for the care of children, the elderly, the sick, and the disabled. The state can achieve such a goal by organizing day-care services or at least by subsidizing such care. This would free women from their caring responsibility and allow them to seek gainful employment. But it can also employ family members to look after relatives. Most countries have adopted a policy of remunerating carers in the informal sector. Allowances may be given to the disabled or the elderly to allow them to hire a carer, or else carers are directly paid an allowance or even contracted by state agencies to supply such services.

The informal sector forms the basis on which many such welfare services in Ireland are provided. But it remains informal, never formally brought into the operation of social policy. However, pressure is growing for the state to take into account some of the functions performed by the informal sector. This mainly takes the form of a payment to carers for their services. It also manifests itself in the form of demands for providing services or at least financial incentives for a range of services. This concerns, for instance, child care; the growing participation of married women in the labor force has placed the issue very much in the fore of social policy in Ireland. The informal sector will have to be brought into the formal sector, at least to some extent.

The study of the welfare system has long neglected the role of the voluntary sector in the provision of social benefits. A very wide range of tasks is often undertaken by voluntary workers: caring for old people and animating preschool groups, fund-raising, collecting secondhand clothes, driving a minibus, running charity shops, or even counseling (e.g., Samaritans). Only recently has a clearer picture of this voluntary sector emerged in the Irish context. Historically, the state has been marginalized in some sectors of the Irish welfare system. The Catholic Church has long enjoyed a very prominent position in relation to education and health. It is also linked with a large number of organizations providing personal social services. Most residential homes for handicapped people or children, for instance, were run by institutions linked with the church. The question of the welfare mix in Ireland, in a situation of weak market mechanisms and a marginalized informal sector, boils down to the nature of the relation between statutory agencies and the voluntary sector.

Even within this context, the picture appears complex. One cannot talk of a particular type of welfare mix according to which the Irish welfare system would be organized. It is, in fact, possible to identify four different types of relation between state and voluntary organizations. The first involves the link that has historically evolved between church and state; it has been analyzed in Chapter 4. The second type of connection has developed more recently; some people give the National Understanding of 1979 as the start of what will be called "welfare corporatism." The state and the main social partners negotiate and agree on a socioeconomic program that encompasses social policy measures. The state and selected voluntary organizations, together, decide on the kind of social policy that should prevail. A rather different welfare mix is observed in relation to personal social services: an informal mix, in which the state simply finances the operation of a range of organizations. Finally, a more structured connection between statutory and voluntary agencies has developed in the context of so-called partnership programs. These different welfare mixes are examined in the present chapter. But the question remains open, as the nature of the relations between public and private agencies is now part of a debate that is conducted around *A Green Paper on the Community and Voluntary Sector and Its Relationship with the State* (Department of Social Welfare 1997). This document is analyzed in the last part of this chapter, with a view to determine the likely shape of the welfare mix to come in Ireland.

CORPORATIST SOCIAL POLICY

Many Western European societies in the 1960s and 1970s turned to corporatism to manage the problems of the industrial society. By corporatism is simply meant the fact that representatives of the major interest groups participate, in a statutory or even in a regular way, in the making of relevant public policy decisions or the administration of public services. This coming together of private groups and central public authorities represents the mark of corporatism. Most European societies have adopted such corporatist features, albeit to very different degrees. But, in the early 1980s, they, to a large extent, moved away from corporatist decision making, even if such corporatist features remain part of their structure and traditions. Curiously, Ireland has developed pronounced corporatist features only lately; these corporatist features became more emphatic in the 1980s and even more so in the 1990s. But this corporatist orientation has proceeded further. Not only has such policy framework been elaborated and agreed upon by representatives of the major socioeconomic forces and the state, but it has connected, in an explicit social contract, economic and social objectives. Social policy has been brought into the corporatist framework, along with economic policy.

In the late 1950s, some attempts at planning were instigated, and several tripartite institutions were created. The regular and quasi-institutionalized consultative process between central public authorities and the representatives of the major socioeconomic groups was established in the 1960s. The representatives of dominant interest groups also belonged to various institutional bodies, as of right. Foremost among them was the National Economic and Social Council (NESC), which advised the government on matters of economic and social policy. Employers, trade unions, and farmers were equally represented in the council.

National wage agreements dominated the field of industrial relations from the early 1970s. They have progressively assumed the form of tripartite negotiations. At first, the state participated in these negotiations as an employer, anxious to ensure low pay increases. In 1976, it took a more active part in the negotiations and threatened to impose a statutory wage policy in order to obtain wage moderation. In 1977, the government offered tax concessions in exchange for moderate wage increases. For the first time, it was linking its budgetary policy and its wage policy in a way that allowed dominant interest groups to decide on budgetary policy. In 1979, the state proposed an explicit trade-off between wage moderation and social policy measures concerned with employment, social services, social security, and youth training. In so doing, the government was negotiating its social policy within a corporatist context.

The representatives of the major social forces in Ireland have come together more closely to agree on a coherent policy framework to which they commit themselves: the National Understandings of 1979 and 1980 have been followed more recently by the Programme for National Recovery (1987–1990), the Programme for Economic and Social Progress (1991–1993), the Programme for Competitiveness and Work (1994–96), Partnership 2000 (1997–2000), and the Programme for Prosperity and Fairness (2000–2003). In all these cases, the general thrust of development is defined, and goals are agreed upon. Such agreements were made between employers, the trade union movement, and farmers' organizations, along with the central power represented by governmental ministers or higher civil servants. The corporatist arrangement of Partnership 2000 was widened to include a fourth pillar.

Not only has the range of policy covered by national agreements been widened to include all relevant economic and social policy orientations, but the range of "social partners" has itself been extended. The National and Social Forum (NESF), created in 1993, brought together representatives not only of employers, trade unions, and farmers but also of political parties and voluntary organizations in the welfare sector. The forum emphasized the need for a more inclusive partnership approach, and its recommendations were implemented in the negotiation for Partnership 2000. A fourth pillar was also introduced, besides the employers, the trade unions, and the farmers. This fourth pillar was meant to represent and articulate the views of social categories that did not participate in the previous corporatist process of decision making. This community and voluntary sector comprises several constituencies: organizations representative of women, the unemployed, the disadvantaged, youth, the elderly, and people with disability.

Mishra (1990) has made a distinction between what he labels the "differentiated welfare state" and the "integrated welfare state." They are said to differ in the way that public economic policy and social policy are related to each other. In the case of the integrated welfare state, social objectives and economic objectives are closely and explicitly connected. One is not talking here of a link or even an implicit bargaining between economic policy and social policy, but a recognition and institutionalization of such a relationship. This situation corresponds broadly to what J.S. O'Connor (1988) has called "democratic corporatism." Strongly organized interest groups closely interact with a centralized government (and this feature makes it corporatist). But it is also characterized by a blurring of the distinction between public and private spheres, as well as of the boundaries of economic and social policy. Or rather, social policy is absorbed into general economic policy; it becomes part of a general contract between the state and the major socioeconomic partners. O'Connor sees this corporatist democracy as a continuation of the kind of compromise that has taken place between labor and the capitalist class in advanced capitalist societies. Moderation in wage claims and restrained strike activity are compensated for by advances in social welfare benefits (Marks 1985-1986).

Ireland has clearly moved toward an integrated welfare state, in which the agreement that is struck between social partners involves a trade-off between economic and social objectives. In the Programme for Economic and Social Progress (PESP 1990–1993), a quarter of the rather long document dealt with welfare-related issues. It committed social partners to protect the value of welfare payments against inflation and even increase their level to that recommended by the Commission on Social Welfare (1986). It further pledged an extension of social insurance coverage, an increase in child income support, a widening of the scope of occupational pensions, a more coherent delivery of social services, and a closer integration of the voluntary sector. The PESP also formulated clear policy orientations in relation to health services, with the intention of developing community-based services, ensuring access to hospital services, devolving greater executive policy to appropriate agencies in the health field, elaborating a "patient charter," and also promoting women's health services. In relation to education, the document focused on the participation of children with educational and social disadvantages and proposed a number of measures to address the problem. It also set up a pilot program for addressing the issue of long-term unemployment. Rather similar policy orientations were formulated in the Programme for Competitiveness and Work (1994–1996).

Partnership 2000 constitutes the outcome of another corporatist decision making. It formulates an explicit social policy orientation, with an action program for greater social inclusion: an antipoverty strategy; reforms of tax and welfare to improve the incentive for, and reward from, work; measures to address educational disadvantages; and consolidation of the local partnership approach. But the corporatist framework has been enlarged, and the voluntary sector—or rather selected organizations within it—participates in the process and monitors the implementation of the agreed program. The programs that have been agreed upon by the social partners for more than a decade now cover a wide range of economic and social policy. They relate to welfare payments, health provision, education, policy toward the unemployed, and so on. They balance economic and social policy goals in a trade-off that involves a whole package.

THE VOLUNTARY SECTOR

Reviewing the development of the voluntary sector in Ireland, Ruddle and O'Connor (1993) have emphasized the charitable tradition, which has been closely associated with religious orders. It originated, apparently, in the early nineteenth century, with the setting up of voluntary hospitals and the growth of charities as well as relief-giving agencies. In the twentieth century, voluntary organizations started to run residential homes for children and for adults with physical and mental disabilities. They also became involved in child care and the care of the elderly. This, of course, does not take into account the fact that one particular type of voluntary organization, the Catholic Church, has remained central to the provision of health and educational services.

Voluntary effort plays its greatest role in the field of personal social services (Powell and Guerin 1997: 102). In their study of voluntary organizations, Faughnan and Kelleher (1990) have found that the largest number of organizations deals with people with disabilities (26 percent). This is followed by local community groups (13 percent), homelessness (11 percent), unemployed people (11 percent), and women and single parents (9 percent). Organizations dealing with the elderly and with young people represent, each, 7 per cent of the total sample. Travelers, people with addiction problems, and so on, form the remainder.

The Characteristics of the Voluntary Sector

The Faughnan-Kelleher study (1990) gives a detailed portrait of the voluntary sector in this field. It clearly underlines the close link between many such associations and the churches: 57 percent of organizations in the study indicated some kind of religious involvement. This may mean that a member of a religious order or a diocesan priest founded the organization, that the organization is directed by a cleric, that a religious order appoints the management group, or that the diocese or the religious order supplies the premises of the organization. At the same time, the role of religious personnel in this field is changing. R. Gilligan has, in fact, remarked on the declining involvement of religious orders in some areas, such as child care: "[C]hild care is also marginalised within the Church system" (Gilligan 1993: 2). The church responded relatively late to youth homelessness. HOPE, the first organization for homeless people, was started by a German electrician, shocked by what he saw on the streets of Dublin. The Catholic Social Service Conference (CSSC) now runs an emergency hostel for homeless boys. The church never offered services for the victims of child sexual abuse. The Department of Health has located two assessment units in religious-run children's hospitals—Temple Street and Crumlin—but they were not actually initiated and are not run by the church. Most of the services related to drug abuse do not implicate the church, although some individual priests have been active in the field. Members of religious orders involved in this field are associated with organizations that operate outside the traditional confines of the church: Sister Stanilaus founded Focus Point, Peter McVerry, S.J., provides accommodations and support for rootless and vulnerable young people; and Frank Brady, S.J., played a key role in the formation of the drug agency Ana Liffey Project.

Pauline Faughnan and Patricia Kelleher have pointed out the great diversity of voluntary organizations, particularly in terms of their main activity. Nearly two-thirds of such organizations are involved in providing resources or services to some categories of people. The provision of residential care or accommodations accounts for the largest number of organizations. The great majority of voluntary organizations offer services as a complement to the state. But, in some cases, voluntary organizations constitute the dominant providers of basic services: this applies mainly to residential care for children and also care for the mentally handicapped. In this case, one observes the pattern, traditional in Ireland, of services financed by the state and run by voluntary organizations. Far behind, one finds local development associations (13 percent), then representative or umbrella organizations (9 percent), and finally campaigning or advocacy ones (7 percent). The voluntary sector is frequently presented as flexible and innovative, in contrast with a state sector, which appears cautious and operates according to rigid rules and regulations. But this study invalidates such a view: lack of flexibility, absence of consultation with clients, and reluctance to learn from experience on the ground apparently characterize the voluntary sector. The activity of such organizations remains quite routine, and it is not clear that the voluntary sector manages to reach out to people whom the state sector cannot reach.

Funding represents an important aspect of the relationship between voluntary organizations and the state. The survey reveals that over half the organizations obtain the bulk of their income from public sources. The actual finance derives from the Exchequer, lottery funding, and European Community programs. One-fifth of the organizations in the study depended totally on temporary employment schemes for all of their staff resources. A wide variety of statutory agencies finances voluntary organizations. The main funders are the Health Boards, which support community care and special hospital programs. In 1989, they were funding 730 organizations to the tune of IR£18 million (about US$20 million). Three-quarters of that money was used to provide services to children, youth, and handicapped people. The Training Authority FÁS contributes in a significant way to the funding of around one-quarter of the organizations: it is mainly concerned with training and temporary employment programs. The Departments of Education, Health, Justice, and Social Welfare are also involved in the funding of voluntary organizations.

Different statutory agencies fund voluntary organizations differently, without a uniform pattern. Funding arrangements remain, to a large extent, ad hoc and discretionary. Each organization negotiates with the relevant agency, without a clear framework or explicit criteria. For this reason, such funding is characterized not only by uncertainty but also by long-term insecurity: grants have to be renegotiated every year. The actual mechanisms of funding also differ considerably: "[S]ome organisations received a block grant, others an agreed proportion of overall expenditure, others grant aid based on per capita payments, while for some a system of deficit financing was in operation" (Faughnan and Kelleher 1990: 48). This lack of uniformity or coherence often means that public funding does not meet the financial requirements of such organizations. All groups engaged in these arrangements with public agencies express their dissatisfaction with the funding. They remain very ambivalent, however, about the prospect of formalized funding arrangements.

Another aspect of the relations between voluntary organizations and the state concerns the absence of a clear policy framework. This implies that the place and the role of voluntary organizations are not really worked out. The voluntary sector is not allowed to play a part in policy elaboration, and no formal structure facilitates its participation. Long-established organizations state that they enjoy easy access to politicians and public officials, but this access remains personalized. Beside this personalized access to relevant public figures, voluntary organizations have to rely on the normal mechanisms of lobbying from the outside: written submissions, delegations, tabling of motions in the Dáil and at the local government level. But no formal mechanism exists that would facilitate the involvement of the voluntary sector in the policy-making process.

The Voluntary Sector under Scrutiny

Voluntary organizations express dissatisfaction with statutory agencies or, rather, with the way that they are made to participate in the welfare state. They regret the absence of formal recognition of the voluntary sector and the lack of consultation mechanisms. Some argue that voluntary organizations are making up for the failure of state services, that they substitute for them. It is even contended, particularly by the Catholic Church, that the voluntary sector has for far too long subsidized the state and has hidden the real costs of some social services (Gilligan 1993: 35). The funding arrangements make their life particularly difficult. They also bemoan the fact that the state does not seem to have developed clear, overall policies, and the diverse statutory agencies do not operate in a coordinated way. But the voluntary sector is not itself beyond criticism, and the reliance on voluntary organizations creates a range of problems:

- The voluntary sector often fails to sustain long-term activities. The involvement of volunteers proves erratic and inconsistent.
- It also relies on people who are, by and large, untrained and not supported by other relevant services or experts. Voluntary organizations often do not possess adequate resources and expertise. They do not reach the necessary professional standards, in a time of rapidly changing needs and work practices. This lack of professionalism is, in part, related to the dominance of the church in the field, if, as it has been asserted, "central to a Christian ethos are the limiting concepts of voluntarism and charity, the former implying goodwill rather than professionalism/qualifications, and the latter which majors on doing things for people rather than with people" (Sweeney 1990: 185).
- Voluntary organizations lack accountability toward funding agencies and clients. Funding does not depend on an evaluation of the services that are publicly financed. This lack of accountability also refers to the fact that voluntary organizations are

organized in ways that rarely encourage or facilitate the participation of either volunteers or consumers of their services. They are usually run by an "elite," and they themselves state that they experience difficulties in promoting participation.

- The quality of their services is not guaranteed, and the recipients of such services rarely enjoy access to complaint procedures. Some organizations may even select their clients. For instance, "some of the voluntary organisations involved [in child care] have submitted to us that they could not cope with children who would seriously disrupt the running of the home and cause strain for those already cared for there" (Gilligan 1993: 22).
- They do not, and probably cannot, supply a uniform service across the board.

We can now outline the nature of the welfare mix in this particular sector of personal welfare services. The voluntary sector rarely operates on its own. It often complements the work of statutory agencies, but it may also function in those areas that public agencies reach only with great difficulty. The connection between voluntary organizations and the state has never been formalized or put on a solid footing. This precariousness is manifested in the funding arrangements but also in the lack of formal consultation with voluntary organizations. The label "welfare pluralism" has been used to refer to the arrangement of "administration of services by voluntary organisations where finance is provided by the state. The state and voluntary organisations in this model are expected to play different but interdependent roles in providing social services" (Powell and Guerin 1997: 134). But two setups need to be distinguished. In education and, to some extent, in the health services, services are provided by voluntary organizations (mainly the churches) and, by and large, paid for by the state. This setup is totally institutionalized. The welfare mix in personal social services does not share this high level of institutionalization.

Numerous calls have been made to reorganize the relationship between statutory agencies and voluntary organizations on a contractual basis. It is proposed that selected licensed organizations be financed to deliver services that clearly specify conditions and quality of services. The introduction of explicit and detailed contracts should overcome most of the problems that characterize the present arrangement. Service providers become accountable, and the selectivity of some services is negated. In exchange, voluntary organizations enjoy secure funding; they are also more closely integrated in a planned framework of services.

Only a small proportion of voluntary organizations favors formalized or contractual funding relationships (Faughnan and Kelleher 1990). Instead, they express concern about retaining their identity and autonomy. They are eager to protect their ability to engage in campaigns of advocacy and to innovate in the provision of social services. They want to uphold their own ethos and orientation.

PARTNERSHIP

The welfare mix that dominated the provision of social services in Ireland has progressively made way for a new arrangement. A range of factors has contributed to this transformation. The failure of the state to reduce long-term unemployment or the concentration of poverty in certain areas may have facilitated such a move. Most programs of community development have involved European funding, which often requires some form of local participation. Partnership at the national level, in which the main socioeconomic forces negotiate a comprehensive programme of development, had been deemed successful and possibly worth extending to regional or local policy making. In other words, partnership as a way of managing social problems became the flavor of the decade. Partnership "is premised on the ability of various social and economic agencies to transcend their differences and to combine forces in favour of a joint strategy" (Walsh 1994: 71). Partnership formalizes the participation of voluntary organizations in public administration.

O'Cinneide and Walsh (1990) have identified four separate strategies of community development that have been relied upon in Ireland. In the 1960s, local organizations ran a variety of community-based social services, coordinated by social services councils. Community Development Co-operatives sprang up in many rural areas but had declined by the 1980s. Then, community development became closely associated with antipoverty projects and also with employment and training programs. The idea of partnership emerged in the context of the last two strategies.

Community Development and Partnership

The main channel of this partnership has been community development, with a particular focus on poverty and unemployment. In this context, it is considered that poor people, instead of being subjected to the action of external agencies, should participate in the process of overcoming their own disadvantaged condition. Instead of statutory or even voluntary agencies providing services or offering benefits to them, these people should be actively engaged in the process. One notes a certain ambiguity as to the reasons that poor people are urged to engage in the process of surmounting their own poverty.

The first reason given for the participation of the disadvantaged remains instrumental. The state does not achieve its goals without the active participation of the groups that are targeted. It will fail to overcome the marginalization of those communities if it does not mobilize them. Their social integration demands that they themselves change attitudes, acquire skills, feel engaged as citizens, and so on. Community development is based on the view that the people themselves can do something about their own situation. Unemployment, particularly long-term unemployment, is dealt with through enhancing employment prospects or even by creating self-employment through diverse schemes. It is assumed that the solution to the problem, at least to some extent, lies within communities themselves.

Alternatively, community development relies on a political act in order to have an impact on the level of poverty: poor people and communities organize themselves and defend their interests. Only then will they be able to transform the distribution of power and income in Irish society. For this reason, community development involves consciousness-raising and empowerment. This implies that these social categories define their needs and exert collective pressure on relevant public agencies. But in order to attain such goals, these people require a considerable amount of help in the form of training, resources, relevant experience, services, and so on. "Community development is an important mechanism for tackling poverty primarily because it involves poor people in identifying their needs and engaging in collective action to pursue collective interests" (Cullen 1989: 28).

Various programs have been established to deal with disadvantaged areas. All these programs involve some kind of partnership between statutory agencies and voluntary organizations. It must be noted that poverty and unemployment do not represent the only issue for which the partnership structure has been used. The LEADER program endeavors to promote rural development through a partnership between voluntary and statutory organizations. It relies on the same idea of encouraging and mobilizing the energy and initiative of people in order to solve their own problems.

The first elements of this partnership idea were put in place with the nine projects of the Second European Programme to Combat Poverty (1985–1989). The basic relationship between voluntary and statutory agencies remained one of funding. Diverse local organizations applied for funding under this program and worked in close association with the Combat Poverty Agency, which supervised the scheme. The partnership aspect came mainly to the fore in relation to the employment and training schemes offered by FÁS, the statutory training agency. But the latter operated according to its own rules, for instance, in terms of the conditions of participation in its training schemes, and it did not always accommodate the special conditions of the antipoverty schemes. The Community Development Programme was established in 1990 to enhance the capacity of local communities to tackle poverty and exclusion. Fifty projects were funded in 1995. The Department of Social Welfare assumes overall responsibility for its management and administration, while the Combat Poverty Agency provides support and monitors standards for the program as a whole.

The partnership idea was formalized with the twelve partnership structures set up between May and November 1990 on a pilot basis at a local level. They carried out the state commitment to deal with the high level of long-term unemployment in Ireland, as formulated in the Programme for Economic and Social Progress (PESP). They are referred to as the Area Based Response to Long-term Unemployment. Community representatives, state agency representatives and social partner representatives (including trade unions, employers, and farming organizations) joined in these partnerships. The political center dominated the partnership in several ways. The partners were national organizations that had vested interests to uphold. State agencies also created difficulties. Local representatives of public agencies enjoyed little discretion and remained very defensive about their areas of responsibility. The PESP Partnership operated within a national context of centralized and compartmentalized decision making.

The third poverty program also relied heavily on this partnership idea. One scheme within this program, the PAUL Partnership (People Action against Unemployment Limited), has been subjected to a detailed evaluation and report (Walsh 1994). The project defined its goals as increasing access to the labor market and empowering disadvantaged communities to direct their future development. It involved the cooperation of four different institutional sectors. Six community-based organizations were chosen to represent the population target. Some of these community organizations formed umbrella groups, which typically embraced twenty or thirty local organizations providing a diversity of services. Other organizations promoted socioeconomic developments in their catchment areas. The social sector included the two national representative bodies for business/ employers and trade unions. The state sector comprised six agencies, ranging from local authorities (Limerick Corporation and Limerick VEC) to national bodies, including the Department of Social Welfare.

Mixed Feelings about Partnership

The evaluation reports relating to these various partnership programs raise a range of questions and point to difficulties in the way that partnership operates. The relationship between the voluntary and the statutory sector, on which this idea of partnership is based, is always presented in such reports as problematic. The first difficulty relates to the localized nature of the program. Few people involved in these projects would nurse illusions about the capacity of such programs to alter drastically the disadvantaged situation at the local level. By definition, poor communities possess very limited resources, and their capacity to create work is itself severely curtailed. It is accepted that broader forces are at work and that local partnership can only mediate the impact of the inadequacies of the labor market, not remedy them or even neutralize them. Partnership will not overcome the inadequacies of the national labor market, although it may improve the position of some people in competing for whatever jobs are available. Even the more indirect goal of community empowerment will be rarely achieved. Referring to the PAUL Partnership, Jim Walsh concludes: "The project had a limited impact on its goal of empowering the target group to become agent of change in the social, political and economic life of their community" (Walsh 1994: 123).

Some commentators take an even more negative view of the exercise in local partnership. It is suspected by some that community development is used to transfer responsibility for some issues (Lee 1989: 99). This occurs, in McCashin's words, when the statutory authorities have only a vague idea of what should be done. The community, or rather the locality, often becomes "a misplaced site for ill conceived social policies" (McCashin 1990: 87). He gives the psychiatric services and diverse schemes to overcome unemployment as examples of misplaced transfers from statutory bodies to the community, in the absence of clear public policy.

Reliance on local communities brings about many difficulties, the least of which is the lack of clarity about what is meant by community. Organizations that are involved in such schemes do not necessarily "represent" the locality, since their function is usually to provide a service or to campaign on some specific issue. The assumption that community actors stand for a coherent and consensual community has been seriously challenged: community actors are frequently divided by intracommunity rivalry and compete for scarce resources (Varley 1998: 395). Some element of deception may even lurk in the assumption that community partners make the whole exercise more democratic. Both words, "partnership" and "community", are heavily loaded terms: they create "an illusion of participation of the community in decision making" (Rafferty 1990: 217). Some would even suggest that the word "community" is used as a kind of symbolic invocation and that its main purpose is to generate support for the state (Crickley and Devlin 1990: 74).

But the main difficulty in these partnership schemes seems to rest with the state itself or, rather, with various statutory agencies. Each agency follows its own rules and pursues its own goals, which, even if not contradictory, are not necessarily harmonized. Furthermore, state agencies operate according to fixed rules and enjoy little discretion in the way that they function at the local level. They are constrained by their own organizational rigidities and display little flexibility. Financial support is often granted to existing programs of public agencies. The latter fix the terms under which people avail themselves of such subsidized services. But the main criticism of the state as partner in these programs is about the unequal power between different groups. Community groups depend totally on public funding, which is granted on a short-term basis. Statutory agencies hardly feel accountable to the other partners, and they sometimes remain quite aloof from the whole exercise. Their views and interests are given priority. Partnership, more often than not, means co-optation of communities by the state (Tucker 1990: 42), and this implies an element of control.

Partnership and the Constitution of Civil Society

The critique of local partnership schemes that has been developed here and that focuses on the state itself often misses a fundamental point: the state has facilitated community development and has encouraged partnership. One would find it difficult to identify a single example of a community program that was set up without state support of some kind and, more importantly, without public financial support. After all, the Youth Employment Agency, incorporated into FÁS, and Combat Poverty Agency constitute the two major statutory backup agencies for community development programs. These schemes cannot be dismissed as purely ritualistic, and they have achieved some results. Critics fail to note that public authorities have their own good reasons for upholding effective community development. The question is: What is in it for the state?

This question relates to the nature of the society that is administered by the state: how it is structured and organized and what kind of activity takes place within it. The term "civil society" is conventionally used to refer to society as organized outside the state. A healthy civil society allows for a communal association of people that is largely self-governing and does not allow the state to exercise too much power. It places many intermediary institutions between individuals and state. "Civil society in its reinvigorated form is presented by its advocates as a democratic movement based on the concept of active citizenship as opposed to the dependent status imposed by the entitled citizenship of the Welfare State. The emphasis of active citizenship is on participation in the decision-making process leading to empowerment of the citizen" (Powell and Guerin 1997: 22).

To a large extent, the discourse that has emerged around community development and partnership draws from such a model of the civil society. But this kind of civil society represents one particular model, which public authorities may not favor. It could be contended, despite the rhetoric of participation and self-empowerment according to which they are presented, that all these partnership projects operate according to a different logic, that is, according to a different model of civil society. It is endlessly repeated that these disadvantaged communities and people have to change if they are to overcome their problems: to change in ways that are spelled out by public agencies, experts, and even community workers. They are asked to train and be educated in all kinds of ways and to alter their attitudes and recast their motivations. In that sense, they are seen as the object of external action, but the success of this transformation depends, in part, on these people's assuming their own transformation.

Modern societies cannot afford to leave a significant part of the population outside the mainstream. People are constantly mobilized economically, politically, culturally, and socially. Such societies always require of their members an additional effort: adjusting to a new situation and acquiring new skills or knowledge; participating in the political game that legitimates the state; complying with its values and norms; and associating with other people in all kinds of ways. Irish public authorities find themselves quite at a loss in connecting with these localities which have become marginalized, which have left the mainstream and risk moving out of the reach of public administration. "The rationale for a community development approach is that local development is dependent on strong local communities taking part in planning and management. In disadvantaged areas the community infrastructure is often weak and a process of community capacity building is required" (Craig and McKeown 1994: 75). It would seem that the partnership exercise, as its main purpose, aims at remedying the serious weaknesses in the social fabric of these marginalized communities, to uphold the infrastructure that will transform them into manageable entities.

The state is keen on the idea of partnership because it offers a mechanism through which the civil society is shaped, at least to some extent. The state does so in several ways. The first one relates to the constitution of voluntary organizations. Partnership requires the emergence of voluntary organizations with definite characteristics: those features favored by statutory funding agencies. For instance, some of the voluntary organizations involved in the Poverty 2 program were specifically set up for the purpose of applying to the program. Furthermore, most of these organizations formed an amalgamation of voluntary associations and acted as umbrella federations for funding purposes. Not only that, but these groups had to organize themselves in a way that conformed to the statutory rules for availing themselves of funds. It even appears that a few of them were actually induced by state agencies. The kind of organizations that operate on the public scene and the way that people organize themselves represent crucial aspects of the way that civil society is constituted. To that extent, consciously or not, the state is engaged in the business of organizing civil society through the partnership projects.

Most of the partnership programs are community-centered, and, for this reason, they carry with them a range of assumptions about the nature and structure of society. This perception of society, once translated into statutory programs, impacts deeply on the way that needs are defined. In fact, many such programs explicitly seek to help disadvantaged people identify their needs, and, of course, the focus remains on local needs or individual needs within a local context. Through local partnership, the state imposes a particular framework for the definition of social needs, and this represents another way of shaping civil society.

But the local emphasis carries with it other implications that have been noted in many evaluation reports. "Communities" have to apply to these programs in order to obtain funding, and this public funding constitutes a very highly valued resource. For this reason, they compete with each other and define from the start their needs as antagonistic. This localization of disadvantages has been recognized as a problem, as some categories of people cannot be reached in that way. Community development focused exclusively on the locality would fail, even in its own terms. For this reason, the term "community" has been extended to cover various categories of disadvantaged people (single parents, homeless, etc.), and relevant organizations have been included in partnership schemes. This, of course, opens up another form of competition between disadvantaged groups. The very mode of intervention of these programs produces or reinforces effects that relate quite directly to the way that these categories of people define their needs.

If a local definition of needs represents the second mechanism through which the state fashions civil society, networking forms a third. An example of the state's using partnership as a mechanism for constituting civil society is given by the analysis of the PAUL Partnership. Jim Walsh (1994: 76) describes the procedure for the elaboration of the partnership. He points to the elaboration of ad hoc alliances of local organizations as part of the preparation for structural funds submissions. New agencies that are seen as having something to offer to the partnership are invited to participate. He finally emphasizes the standardization of partnership, in which some agencies are added or removed to conform to a standard national model of partnership. This represents a revealing example of the way that partnership is used to create a particular social structure.

Also revealing is the involvement of the Combat Poverty Agency in the development of women's networks. This networking program originates in a philosophy of empowerment, in which particular agents are created and a particular type of civil society is shaped. The latter is envisaged in terms of a loose federation of voluntary organizations and, more crucially, as one in which local groups identify needs, provide information, organize self-help, and articulate the views and interests of women participating in such networks. The constitution of the civil society by the state goes even one step further. Groups formed through such schemes, such as women in disadvantaged areas, are also encouraged to develop alliances. This calls, in no uncertain way, for the construction of a sector of civil society, based on all groups generated or upheld by community development schemes, into broader configurations and alliances. This policy is aimed at creating a new social force composed of disadvantaged people but conceived more as an interest group than as a social movement. In all such cases, the state participates in the creation at a macrolevel, through networks and alliances, of a civil society that suits its purpose.

One should note the convergence that arises in this respect between community workers and statutory authorities. Like the state and despite the tension that exists between community workers and public authorities, the former are engaged in a rather similar exercise: constituting civil society. Perhaps they have in mind the kind of democratic civil society that was referred to before, by contrast with the administered civil society promoted by the state. It remains that community workers often militate in favor of their preferred kind of civil society as part of statutory agencies. For instance, the considerable growth in the number of local women's groups is closely related to the fact that many community workers were feminist and participated in the creation of a strengthened women's movement in working-class communities (Tobin 1990: 235). The apparent radicalism of many community workers and the interest of the state have been quite easily reconciled in their joint effort to produce a particular type of civil society through partnership.

A NEW DEAL

"The key argument of this paper is that an official redefinition of the relationship between the voluntary sector and the state is currently taking place. Many organisations are moving from a relationship based on 'separate dependency' to one of 'integrated dependency' (e.g. higher levels of statutory funding linked to agreed results and greater consultation)" (Powell and Guerin 1998: 1). The voluntary sector has, on numerous occasions, expressed its dissatisfaction with the kind of arrangements previously described, and it would seem that the political center is now responding to the demand for change. Is this transformation best analyzed in terms of a shift from "separate dependency" to "integrated dependency"? In the introduction to this chapter, it was emphasized that very different welfare mixes coexist within the welfare system in Ireland. Four such welfare mixes have been identified:

- The first one points to the historical compromise that was effectuated very early in the life of the new independent Ireland, one in which the Catholic Church enjoyed a special position in education and in the provision of health services. In this welfare mix, the state paid, while voluntary organizations, most of the time religious orders or diocesan clergy, delivered the service more or less as they saw fit. We analyzed, in Chapter 4, the decline of this type of welfare mix.
- The second welfare mix relates to the elaboration of social policy at the national level: we have referred to this as welfare corporatism. The state and the major social partners have, for more than a decade, negotiated and agreed upon a national program of development. The agreement covers social policy: the types of services and the level of benefits are matched against economic goals. It is difficult to predict how long such an arrangement will prevail, for it depends on the will of all the major socioeconomic forces to enter such agreements. But the balancing of economic and social benefits, the trade-off between wage moderation and tax and social benefits, has proved too effective to be pushed aside totally.
- The third type of welfare mix is found in the personal social sector: it is characterized by a very informal relation between statutory agencies and voluntary organizations. The state provides, on an ad hoc and discretionary basis, funding to a large number of voluntary organizations. The latter perform a range of social services on their own terms and are not really accountable to the funding agencies. This aspect of the welfare mix is now being challenged.
- Finally and more recently, a mode of organization has emerged that involves statutory and voluntary agencies working together in a tighter relationship. We have seen that the partnership programs are limited in scope, as they deal only with unemployment and poverty. In that respect, they remain quite narrowly focused. The nature of the link between the two sectors has also been submitted to criticism. The statutory sector bears the brunt of the criticism, in that it does not operate as an equal partner but assumes very much a dominant position.

Powell and Guerin use the term "welfare pluralism" when the voluntary sector remains separate from, but subservient to, the state. Do the different welfare mixes in Ireland belong to such a type? Two aspects must be taken into consideration:

1. Does the voluntary sector exist separately from the state, as opposed to their symbiosis? Only in the case of partnership can some element of symbiosis be observed: statutory agencies partly shape the kind of civil society with which they want to deal through the formation of a particular type of voluntary sector. Overall, the externality of the voluntary sector is well protected and not challenged in a fundamental way by the state. But one should not think in absolute terms, for a range of intermediary positions is possible, through diverse forms of integration.

2.   The second dimension points to the nature of the external relationship that prevails between the two sectors. One could hardly speak of the subservience of the Catholic Church toward the state in the context of education and health. But this type of relationship, one of dependence, comes to the fore in relation to the informal financing of voluntary organizations and also in relation to partnership schemes: they both imply a separate and subservient existence for the voluntary sector—although the nature and level of subservience differ considerably. In the first case, the dependency remains mainly financial, while in the second case the subservience involves an increased accountability to statutory agencies. A third type of relationship assumes a contractual form: one in which the state seeks the best providers of a service and pays for the service.

The question then becomes: Is Ireland moving toward a more integrated and contractual welfare mix, in contrast to the external and informal mix of the past? The policy of the state on the question of the relations between state and voluntary sector manifested itself in the formation of the National Social Service Council in 1971; it was meant to stimulate the establishment of regional voluntary social service councils and to coordinate the work of bodies engaged in community social services. It was replaced in 1984 by the National Social Service Board, with the much-diminished function of providing relevant information and offering advice to voluntary organizations. Nevertheless, along with many other organizations, the National Social Service Board has argued for increased consultation and coordination between statutory and voluntary bodies. The role of the voluntary sector was explicitly recognized in the 1992 Programme for Economic and Social Progress (PESP); the government commited itself to prepare a charter on voluntary social services. A partnership program was put forward that delivered social services through the coordinated effort of statutory and voluntary sectors. The Department of Social Welfare produced its Green Paper on this question in 1997.[1] Is the state proposing, and working toward, a new welfare mix in which state and voluntary sector would cease to relate to each other externally and in which dependency would be overcome?

The aims of the Green Paper are presented in ambitious terms: "The objective of this Green Paper is to discuss a framework for the future development of the relationship between the state and the community and voluntary sector and to facilitate a debate on the issues relevant to that relationship" (Department of Social Welfare 1997: 6). Such an undertaking is timely, as an exclusive reliance on the state to provide a range of welfare benefits no longer commands wide support. The state does not seek to redefine the welfare mix in Ireland, for the issue of the relationship between the voluntary sector is considered only in the context of exclusion and marginalized groups. The fact that Ireland forms one of the most centralized welfare systems in Europe is not even mentioned; the whole social security edifice will firmly remain under the control of the Department of Social Welfare. The rhetoric of empowerment, bottom-up strategy, and citizen participation does not apply to nonmarginalized groups. The Green Paper is founded on the idea that social exclusion constitutes a problem that must be addressed with urgency and commitment. Furthermore, it is considered that only the coordinated action of state agencies and the voluntary sector can effectively deal with such a problem. It promotes a strategy of empowering marginalized communities and advocates their direct participation in this process. Fine. But how does the Green Paper intend to achieve such goals?

A closer reading of the text helps clarify some of the reasons that the Department of Social Welfare is engaging in this exercise. The Green Paper explicitly acknowledges that the state has ceased to be effective in addressing some social problems. Public agencies have failed to meet the needs of a wide range of marginalized people. More flexible agencies, closer to excluded social categories, offer a better prospect of reaching them. The call for voluntary agencies to work with the state in order to overcome these problems should be interpreted in this light. But the question remains: What kind of relationship is going to be established between the public and the voluntary sector? What kind of partnership is being sought?

In the first instance, one needs to be clear about which organizations will participate in this framework and why. Many voluntary organizations do not "represent" the social categories that constitute their clients. They follow their own agenda, charitable, religious, or ideological; the way that they define the needs of their clients does not necessarily correspond to the preferences or requirements of such clients. Only those organizations that organize a category of people in need have a legitimate place in this framework. The Green Paper tends to refer to representative associations as "community associations." The assumption that the needs of diverse categories of clients are best dealt with in the context of a communal framework raises some difficulties, and it does not actually fully correspond to practice. Communities, at least in those areas that experience deprivation, are said to be characterized by a culture of mutual help: how much mutual help have those suffering from drug addiction received from their local communities? One should ask Travellers[2] what they think of the inclusive power of neighborhoods. The reliance on communities to achieve social inclusion is bound to have limits.

Community includes various categories of people with very different needs, and the organizations that represent them do not speak and stand for all these people. They have their own agendas, which do not necessarily uphold the needs of some categories of people within them. This, of course, is not to deny that different needs are most effectively met at a local level. Even so, the question of deciding which organizations and networks are recognized by the state as legitimate partners remains open.

The voluntary sector is considered to have great potential for bringing about the inclusion of marginalized social categories. It identifies the needs of these categories more adequately; it delivers services to them more effectively. The involvement of the voluntary sector with the state also brings marginalized social categories into the center: it gives them a voice and an existence within society. The voluntary sector will be consulted, supported, facilitated in providing a range of social benefits, and accepted as a full social partner. Some umbrella associations already participate in the corporatist process of decision making as the fourth partner, along with state, employers, and employees. There are pitfalls with such a strategy, as corporatism can exclude as well as include: it relies on organizations that speak for a whole sector and excludes those that do not quite attain this status. Admittedly, corporatist participation remains limited to decision making at the national level, within the context of recent national agreements, and the Green Paper does not promote a corporatist type of partnership in the welfare field.

The statutory mode of welfare delivery is frequently presented as bureaucratic and inflexible, while a voluntary mode of welfare delivery would manifest greater flexibility and a capacity for innovation. But many shortcomings have also been associated with the voluntary sector, and most of them are implied in the Green Paper. For instance, voluntary organizations show a weak commitment to participation by consumers/users. In order to receive public funding, such organizations will have to become accountable, to respect individual dignity, privacy, and confidentiality, and to facilitate the participation in planning, delivery, and management of the people who avail themselves of services. The monitoring and evaluation of their activity will be carried out regularly in order to ensure the effectiveness of the services provided and to account for public money. The conditions under which the voluntary sector will become a partner of the state are in this way fairly well established. But what about the public agencies themselves? They are urged to be open, to link positively with the community, to recognize and support local initiatives and groups. But who will ensure that they play the game according to this logic of participation, empowerment, and partnership?

Powell and Guerin conclude from their reading: "The suggestions in the Green Paper point towards a more integrated working relationship with the State" (Powell and Guerin 1998: 13), at least in personal social services. The depth of this integration may, of course, considerably vary. It covers at its lowest level a contractual relationship that is advocated in this policy document. But it may also imply a closer coordination of state and voluntary organizations in order to define welfare needs and identify the most appropriate ways of delivering services.

CONCLUSION

Several welfare mixes coexist in the Irish context, although they have emerged at different times in history. How can these be understood in terms of Bourdieu's framework? The first welfare mix that has been identified relates to the historical compromise struck between the state and the Catholic Church. For a long time, the whole welfare field was organized around them. To summarize the conclusions reached in Chapter 4, the position of the Catholic Church in the welfare field has changed quite drastically. Its intervention relied mainly on its control over crucial welfare institutions; now, its symbolic capital originates from its caring orientation, from its expressed commitment to the poor and vulnerable. Approval by the church has become less and less crucial to the state, although useful in some cases. The church's economic capital, in the form of schools and hospitals, is still needed, but religious orders progressively cease to provide such social services. The state continues to draw on the symbolic power of the church, but a symbolic power that is generated on the basis of the critical discourse of the church and paradoxically often critical of the state itself. The mutual bolstering of state and church has given way to a very different and more distant interaction between them that depends on the ability of the church to speak for marginalized social categories and to bring to the state its critique of existing social conditions.

The second welfare mix has developed around corporatist decision making, first at the national level and then in the welfare field. This growing welfare corporatism derives, to a great extent, from the global operation of the state, in that a package is agreed by the social partners, and social policy advances are traded off for economic goals. In this context, each major actor pursues its own strategy. The state, through this procedure of negotiation and compromise, elaborates a policy that commands a broad consensus. National programs have produced a great deal of stability in industrial relations. All this increases the legitimacy of the state, that is, the symbolic capital that it generates. But it loses in the process some control over the social policy that it wishes to pursue, as the other partners contribute in a significant way to the formulation of social policy objectives. These social partners acquire some control over the determination of social policy. They use this control in order to maximize material returns: to maintain or even increase the value of welfare benefits for the trade unions and to contain the cost of welfare for the employers. The objectives of these two groups appear contradictory, and some kind of compromise has to be reached.

The third welfare mix observed relates mainly to one particular sector, personal social services. The ad hoc arrangements between the state and voluntary organizations that characterized this sector for so long are giving way to a new mix. Some kind of partnership has been established, mainly in an attempt to foster community development and to address the problems of long-term unemployment. In this context, the partnership involves the state and the representatives of employees and employers but also voluntary organizations at a local level. It seems, at least from the policy statements that have been formulated, that public authorities also envisage a move toward a contractual type of relationship between state and the voluntary sector.

The failure of public policy to deal effectively with the problems of poverty and long-term unemployment is clearly displayed in the comparative figures that are regularly published about European or even countries of the Organization for Economic Cooperation and Development (OECD). Ireland has fared badly over the years, and the shift toward a new welfare mix could be seen as an attempt, at least in part, to deal more effectively with the issue of poverty and long-term unemployment and to counter any loss of legitimacy. Such a strategy appears all the more desirable for the state as partnership is promoted by the European

Union, and a substantial amount of money is made available from this source. The policy shift in the personal social services sector, from an informal to a partnership arrangement and even to a contractual one, is best interpreted as an attempt to contain a potential erosion of state legitimacy, to stop the decrease of its symbolic capital. The voluntary sector, on the other hand, expects to secure more adequate funding. Entering such arrangements would, in a sense, undermine the autonomy of voluntary organizations, as they would be subject to definite controls and evaluations. But they would enjoy more control over their working environment and operate within a clear, formal framework.

NOTES

1. Based on Peillon 1997.
2. The name Travellers refers to a group of Irish people who traditionally pursue a seminomadic lifestyle.

8

The Irish Welfare Regime

For a long time, welfare systems were classified according to the degree of their development. They were placed along a continuum that ranged from minimum to extensive welfare state, according to the range of social programs that they provided, the proportion of the population that they covered, or, more simply, the amount of money that they spent on welfare. However, the classification of welfare regimes put forward by G. Esping-Andersen (1990) goes beyond a conceptualization in terms of levels of welfare growth. It takes into account the way that social programmes are organized and operate. It considers the delivery of social benefits, the mode of access to services, and the effect of such programs on society. Welfare systems are said to cluster around three types, each displaying a particular profile.

The present chapter aims at placing the Irish welfare system within Esping-Andersen's classification. This does not constitute a major issue for him, and he never looks at Ireland in any detail. However, the location of Ireland within this classification has been raised by several authors. Ireland is presented as a typical example of the conservative (corporatist) type of welfare regime in a book that explicitly sets out to illustrate and apply this typology (McLaughlin 1993). It has also been contended that Ireland, along with other countries, cannot be accommodated within this typology, thus challenging the validity and usefulness of the whole framework (Ragin 1994). The straightforward question of placing Ireland within Esping-Andersen's typology of welfare regime turns out to be far more complex than anticipated. In the following pages, we look at the main social policy programs in Ireland and consider how they fare in the light of the three criteria involved in Esping-Andersen's classification of welfare regimes.

ESPING-ANDERSEN'S ANALYSIS

It may be useful to present the broad outline of the analysis conducted by Esping-Andersen in his book *The Three Worlds of Welfare Capitalism* (1990). His main claim concerns the fact that welfare systems in advanced capitalist societies are best classified according to three main types. He mobilizes a wide range of empirical information, related to many countries, in order to validate his claim. Each type of what he calls welfare regimes involves three dimensions: their decommodifying impact, their stratifying effect and their public–private mix. A welfare regime represents, in that sense, a particular combination of these three dimensions. Table 8.1 gives the general profile of these three welfare regimes.

Table 8.1
The Profile of Welfare Regimes according to Esping-Andersen

	Decommodification	Stratification	State Involvement
liberal	low	low/dualism	low
conservative	high	low/occupationals chemes	high
social democratic (socialist)	high	high	high

The first dimension of welfare regimes taken into consideration by Esping-Andersen concerns what he calls "decommodification." This refers to the extent to which the welfare state, through its diverse programs, removes individuals from the necessity of selling their capacity to work in order to make a living. Esping-Andersen seems to imply that social policy programs are really decommodifying, although to different degrees. But some ways of providing social benefits actually contribute to this process of commodification. Esping-Andersen relies on a range of empirical indicators in order to calculate a score of decommodification. These indicators, which relate to pensions and unemployment benefits, measure the replacement rates of benefits and account for such features as the conditions to qualify for benefits, the duration of such benefits, and so on.

The second dimension in Esping-Andersen's classification relates to the impact of social programs on social stratification. This impact is considered under two different headings: first, but only briefly, in terms of the redistributive impact of such programs and, second, in terms of the extent to which they uphold established class boundaries or create social divisions. Three principles of stratification are identified, and then each assigned to a welfare regime. Each model of stratification is defined according to the prominence of a particular feature. For instance, the liberal model of stratification is characterized mainly by the salience of means-tested services that produce a class of stigmatized welfare recipients. In the conservative model, social programs and benefits vary according to occupational groups. It differentiates social benefits according to occupational categories, and the public sector is sometimes sharply set apart in such regimes. The social democratic regime dissolves social distinctions by ensuring universal access to social benefits and services, and it decreases stratification.

The "nexus of state and market," more particularly the level of state involvement, has been at the core of the debate on the provision of welfare. Peter Flora (1986) has put forward the concept of "stateness" in order to indicate the degree to which the state participates directly in social policy programs. Welfare stateness is given as a basic dimension of the institutional framework of social services. A low level of welfare stateness simply means that welfare services and benefits are not predominantly delivered by public authorities. In a sense, the state is always involved in the setting up of social policy programs. It provides the legislative framework for such services; the issue concerns not so much the opposition that may exist between a state-centered and a private mode of welfare provision but, rather, the balance that is established between them. One is looking at the articulation that exists between public and private modes of welfare provision, at the modality of what has been called the welfare mix. Esping-Andersen argues that countries cluster, in this dimension of the welfare mix, in a way that corresponds to that of other dimensions of the welfare regime. The state weighs heavily in the conservative and social democratic types, while the market prevails in the liberal, residual regime. He reaches this conclusion on the basis of a study of pension programs, which, he notes, represent the largest social program in advanced societies.

OUTLINE OF IRISH SOCIAL POLICY PROGRAMS

The main social policy programs in Ireland are examined in terms of how they fare in the light of the three dimensions considered: the extent to which they decommodify people, structure society, and involve the state.

Health

Health services in Ireland mainly cover hospital care and a medical card scheme. From 1972, a scheme allowed more than a third of the population (around 40 percent) free access to the doctor of their choice and free prescribed drugs. This service is granted on the basis of a means test and is paid out of general taxation. The rest of the population remit their medical visits and their drug bills, although they were able to offset some of their medical expenses against direct income tax. More recently, a monthly ceiling on family expenditure for drugs has been introduced. Such a program is not commodifying, for it does not require any previous contribution based on employment. Medical cards, which entitle recipients to free medical care by a chosen general practitioner, favor low-income households and are, for this reason, redistributive. Finally, such a program relies entirely on public money and is administered by the relevant ministerial department. But private general practitioners provide this medical service and are paid a general fee from the state.

Hospital care constitutes the other main element of the health service: every Irish resident is now entitled to free medical care in public wards. Public hospital care constitutes a universal service and is consequently decommodifying. Although a universal benefit, public hospital care is more availed of by low-income categories, while higher-income categories still rely on private insurance to pay for care in hospitals. The state subsidizes the private medical care of the better-off third of the population through tax allowances for private health insurance premiums. One suspects that, on balance, public expenditure on health still redistributes income. But health care remains highly segmented in social terms. A high percentage of the population does not avail itself of the universal public hospital care and continues to rely on private medical care, based on private insurance. Despite a move toward a more universalist service, health care is highly fragmented and reinforces the significance of social divisions. With its reliance on means-tested benefits, it falls into the category of the liberal principle of stratification.

Several types of hospitals provide medical care, each differently managed. Public hospitals are directly administered by statutory health boards; voluntary public hospitals are usually run by religious orders, although funded by the Department of Health. Other hospitals have remained entirely private and do not receive state subsidies. They cater to patients who enjoy private health insurance. Health boards are responsible for the administration of public health services. They operate largely independently from the Department of Health, but within the strict budgetary limits set by central government and subject to its external supervision.

Education

Access to free education, at both primary and secondary levels, is guaranteed to all children, without fee. Education constitutes a universal service, and only a small number of pupils attend private schools. Payment of fairly high fees was required up to 1996 for university attendance, although such fees were remitted for students from a low-income background. However, the number of places in third-level education is limited, and access to such places relies on competitive academic performance.

If one assigns a financial value to primary and secondary schooling, it is more beneficial to the low-income categories than to the high-income categories. This has mainly to do with average family size, which offsets the slightly higher participation of the middle-class categories in higher levels of secondary schooling. However, a similar conclusion cannot be formulated for third-level education, which clearly advantages the better-off categories. Public expenditure on third-level education benefits those categories that are already socially advantaged. This latter item constitutes roughly one-fifth of educational public expenditure. On balance, educational expenditure is marginally redistributive. However, all statistics have pointed to the exclusion of the lowest social categories from third-level education. Access on merit hides a very severe social selection, with the middle and higher classes seriously overrepresented at that level. This sector of education functions in a way that quite rigidly stratifies access to occupational qualifications. Its quasi-universalist character does not eliminate some significant stratifying effects of education.

One observes a high level of complexity in the way that education is administered. The Department of Education retains a supervisory role in educational matters, but the running of schools is left to the parish for most primary schools and to religious orders for the great majority of secondary schools. However, some purely public secondary schools have been established and are managed by public agencies within the budget fixed by central powers. Central government meets the running costs of practically all schools and pays staff salaries. Third-level education also encompasses a range of diverse institutions. Universities administer themselves, although they are nearly entirely financed by the state. Institutes of technology are run by special public bodies and funded nearly entirely from the public purse.

Income Maintenance

Income maintenance includes two quite different schemes. The first one distributes benefits, mainly old age pensions and sickness and unemployment benefits, to those who have been insured through regular contributions. This constitutes a system of social insurance, in which the insured contributes a fixed percentage of earnings. Benefits are distributed to those who have paid the required amount of contributions. But the benefits are not proportional to the contributions or, ultimately, to the income earned. Social assistance is granted to those who do not meet the insurance requirements. These welfare payments, for instance, unemployment assistance and noncontributory old age pensions, are means-tested and financed from general taxation. Both social insurance and social assistance schemes are administered by the central authorities. Social assistance is entirely funded by the state, while social insurance is financed by contributions from employers and employees with state subsidies. One notes the existence of a different income maintenance scheme for public employees. The latter pay a significantly lower rate of social insurance but are entitled to very few benefits. Public employees participate in various pension schemes, which are considered to bring better benefits than those available to private sector employees. But it does not seem that the state contributes more to the pension of a public employee than to the pension of a private sector employee (Hughes 1988).

Old age pensions are paid to two different categories of pensioners. A pension is received by those who have contributed during their working life, but the pension level is not determined by past wages and contributions. Noncontributory old age pensions are offered to those who do not have sufficient means, independently of past working life. One type of pension (contributory) is commodifying, and the other (noncontributory) is not commodifying. But the amounts of money involved in the contributory and in the noncontributory pensions do not differ very widely. The monetary advantage of receiving a contributory pension is not high: for this reason, pensions as a whole are not very commodifying. However, pensions could contribute to commodification by not providing an acceptable level of living. For a long time, old age pensioners formed a significant proportion of the poor in Ireland. But it has been argued that the pension level has been significantly increased of late: old age pensioners, even those on noncontributory pensions, have been lifted above the poverty level as conventionally defined (Nolan and Callan 1994).

Unemployment payments are also granted on the basis of two different schemes. Unemployment insurance guarantees a benefit to those who have contributed to the fund. It is also commodifying according to the low level of benefits that are offered. The same benefit is bestowed on all those workers who become unemployed, but the benefit does not sustain a level of subsistence sufficient to raise a family in acceptable circumstances. Unemployment is closely associated with poverty in Ireland, although the extent to which it is so depends on other circumstances, mainly familial (Nolan and Callan 1994). Unemployment assistance is given, on the basis of a means test, to those with insufficient contributions or to those who have remained unemployed for a period longer than the one covered by unemployment insurance. This benefit is commodifying mainly because the level of benefit does not sustain a sufficiently high standard of living. It constitutes a strong incentive for those people to seek gainful employment. Unemployment programs are strongly commodifying.

Income maintenance schemes, such as old age pensions and unemployment payments, redistribute income toward the less well-off categories. This conclusion is, in a sense, obvious. Pensions and unemployment benefits are provided to individuals and households that would enjoy no or little income without such benefits. Or else, through regular contributions during their working and earning life, individuals pay for the benefits that they receive when they are not earning. This redistribution takes place within the life span of the same individual. Social insurance itself includes an element of public expenditure, but social assistance depends entirely on it. Noncontributory old age pensions, as well as unemployment assistance, are granted from general taxation to those who have insufficient income. Overall then, income maintenance programs are highly redistributive.

However, the experience of unemployment is strongly patterned according to class position, in that the chances of experiencing unemployment are considerably increased if one belongs to the unskilled working class. Unemployment payments themselves do not uphold social divisions, other than the one between the employed and the unemployed. Unemployment benefits (which derive from social insurance contributions) are marginally higher than unemployment assistance payments (which are means-tested). Insurance coverage is provided for only a relatively short period of unemployment, after which unemployed people receive assistance. The rates of long-term unemployment assistance are, nowadays, actually higher than the rates of unemployment benefits. It remains that unemployment, because of the low welfare benefits that it commands, represents a major determinant of poverty. The distinction between contributory and noncontributory pensions creates two categories of pensioners, but even contributory pensions offer a flat benefit that is only marginally higher than noncontributory pensions. Here one deals with a double system of income maintenance, one based on means tests, and the other, on some form of insurance; one participates in the liberal principle of stratification, and the other in a conservative one.

Child Benefits

Child benefits are paid for all children residing in Ireland, independently of the parent's income. This represents a universal benefit and as such is noncommodifying. This program is administered and funded by the state out of general taxation. Such a benefit is not redistributive.

Housing

Housing policy in Ireland is composed of two elements, each of which is targeted at a very different category of people. Public housing is provided for a substantial minority of the population. The second element of housing policy is directed at those who borrow money to buy their own house. The state encourages the purchase of houses as private accommodations; it allows tax concessions on mortgage interest.

Access to council housing does not depend on past or present participation in the labor force, and it offers an acceptable level of accommodations. On both grounds, this social program is not commodifying. However, access to mortages and to tax remissions requires participation in the labor force. Mortgages are available only to those who prove that they are gainfully employed; the amount that they are allowed to borrow is also limited by the wage that they earn. This aspect of housing policy is highly commodifying.

The provision of public housing is targeted at low-income households and proves very redistributive. However, the second aspect of housing policy involves state subsidizing of homeownership. These subsidies take the form of tax allowances that benefit most those who purchase more expensive houses (although a ceiling has now been introduced) and those who earn high incomes. So housing balances between a highly redistributive council housing service and a highly regressive support of homeownership. But the provision of public housing, in special estates, has also led to the creation of deep social segregation between a large sector of manual workers, often with low skills, and a skilled manual and middle-class category. The latter enjoy access to mortgage finance and purchase houses in private estates. Housing policy can be considered to constitute one of the most significant mechanisms of class structuration in Ireland. It does so by segregating the lower working class into special districts. Housing policy produces a sharp dualism between two categories of people.

The local authorities, county and urban councils, assume direct responsibility for constructing and allocating public housing. But they operate within definite legal and financial constraints set by the central authorities. Furthermore, the latter transfer the necessary finances directly from central funds.

PLACING IRELAND IN ESPING-ANDERSEN'S TYPOLOGY

Esping-Andersen's places Ireland into the category of low decommodification, which corresponds to the liberal welfare regime (the conservative regime is associated with a medium decommodification, and the social democratic regime, with a high level of decommodification). Here are the decommodifying categories that are assigned by him to the relevant social policy programs in Ireland:

old age pensions: low
sickness insurance: low
unemployment benefits: medium/ high

The general score points to the fact that, comparatively speaking, Ireland displays quite a low level of decommodification (Esping-Andersen 1990: 52 table 2.2).

Table 8.2 summarizes the conclusions that we have previously reached about the commodifying character of social programs. Most social programs in Ireland are not commodifying: they do not exercise any pressure on the incumbents to participate in the labor force. Only unemployment benefits display a very strong commodifying character. If we leave mortgage aside, one can then conclude that the welfare system in Ireland is not commodifying. Some of the benefits are universal, while others are targeted to, but do not depend on contributions from or on participation by, the labor force.

Table 8.2
Matrix of the Commodifying Effect of Social Policy Programs

	1	2
Hospital Care	—	
Medical Card	—	
Education	—	
Family Allowance	—	—
Social Housing	—	—
Contributory Pension	+	—
Noncontributory Pension	—	—
Unemployment Insurance	+	+
Unemployment Assistance	—	+

commodifying: + ; noncommodifying: —

Notes: Number 1 in the Table refers to the commodifying effect of the mode of access to benefits (see 1 in next page); number 2 refers to the commodifying effect of the level of benefits offered by social policy programs (see 2 in next page).

The capacity of a social policy program to remove dependence on the labor market may occur in different ways. Two such aspects are taken into account here, and they differ only slightly from those used by Esping-Andersen (1990: 47):

1. Universal access to a social service or unconditional benefit, as of right, is decommodifying. Means-tested benefits are also noncommodifying if they do not depend on participation in the labor force. On the other hand, a program is commodifying if the relevant benefits depend on contributions, which are mainly based on paid employment.
2. If social benefits sustain a sufficiently high standard of living, according to the expectations existing within a particular society, then such a program does not put pressure on the recipients to seek wage employment.

On the basis of the analysis presented in the previous section, we have concluded that, despite the presence of some regressive elements, the general impact of welfare services and benefits in Ireland remains redistributive. This redistributive impact of welfare has been investigated in several studies (Callan and Nolan 1992; National Economic and Social Council (NESC) 1988; O'Connell 1982), and we summarize these findings. A measure of this redistributive effect is given by the Musgrave-Thin coefficient (which represents the percentage reduction in the Gini coeeficient). On the basis of the figures published in Breen et al. (1990), this coefficient reaches 17.59 for the transition from direct income to gross income in 1980 (and this measures mainly the effect of direct financial transfers such as pensions, unemployment benefits, family allowances, etc.). This means that the Gini coefficient, a conventional measure of income distribution, is reduced by 17.59 percent when one passes from direct income to gross income. The Musgrave-Thin coefficient is computed at 3.19 for the passage from disposable to final income, which mainly registers the impact of social services on income.

But social programs have an impact on the stratification of Ireland, above and beyond their redistributive impact. The Irish welfare system contributes to the stratification of Irish society and does so mainly by transforming the lower working class into an assisted class. It targets this category for a special medical care programme and segregates it into separate residential areas. The stratifying principle of the welfare system in Ireland would then correspond to that of the liberal/dualist regime. One has also noted a configuration of welfare elements that points to a relatively weak "conservative" orientation. This does not correspond to Esping-Andersen's characterization of Ireland (Esping-Andersen 1990: 74 table 3.3), which places it quite definitely in the conservative category.

Esping-Andersen provides a range of statistical information concerning the level of stateness for pension schemes. This information covers Ireland, and I extract in the following table the most relevant information (Table 8.3).

Table 8.3
The Relative Weight of Types of Pension Schemes in Ireland

	% of GDP	% of pensions	relative position of Ireland
social security	3.4	54.8	one of the lowest
government employees	2.2	35.5	by far the highest
private occupational	0.1	1.6	very low
individual insurance	0.5	8.1	among the highest

Source: Esping-Andersen 1990: 84 table 4.2, 85 table 4.3.

It is, in fact, difficult to reach any kind of conclusion on the basis of this information. Ireland displays a high level of individual insurance but a low level of private occupational schemes. If we combine both measures, they point to the middle ground of the liberal features. The high level of pensions for employees in the public sector suggests that Ireland scores high on the conservative-etatist dimension. The figures in Table 8.3 are not easily reconciled with available information on pensions in Ireland, as several schemes of public pensions are operating: social security schemes (either insurance or assistance) and occupational schemes. It has been estimated that 47 percent of employed people participate in an occupational scheme, and public employee pensions belong to this category of occupational program. Furthermore, social security pensions (which are given as an indicator of high stateness) remain very ambiguous from the point of view of stateness; the state fully pays for noncontributory pensions and subsidizes contributory pensions. Altogether, it finances about half of pension costs. In any case, on the basis of his own evidence, Ireland is identified by the following features:

> liberal: medium
> conservative: high
> social democratic: low

Ragin's (1994) reworking of Esping-Andersen's analysis assigns to pensions in Ireland the following profile:

> liberal (private pension): medium
> conservative corporatism (civil servants/ number of programs): medium
> social democratic (universal pensions): low

This does not conform to the profile associated with any welfare regime. Both profiles raise the question of the possibility of a particular case, like Ireland, scoring similarly high to medium or even low on two variables. Or said otherwise, scoring high in one respect does not necessarily mean scoring low in other respects, as a sustained classificatory logic would demand.

The welfare mix amounts to more than the balance of public and private pensions. It is not adequately measured by the level of state involvement in social policy programs, for such an approach leaves out the actual configuration of other relevant elements, besides state and markets. We have seen in Chapter 7, nevertheless, that the various welfare mixes that have been observed in Ireland revolve around the state. For this reason, it does not seem inappropriate to focus on stateness as a summary approximation of the welfare mix. State legislation and supervision are not considered, as most programs are performed under some sort of legislative or supervisory control by the state. We have adopted a loose definition of the state/public sector to include all public agencies of local government or independent bodies. Here are the categories that we use:

administration: full state or public administration/ partial state or public administration/ nonpublic administration
financing: full state or public financing / partial state or public financing/ nonpublic financing

This represents a rough scale of stateness, from full state (+) to nonpublic (—).

The main results of this review are given in Table 8.4. They point to the conclusion that the state is heavily involved in the financing of social services in Ireland, while it participates less in the administration of social programs. At the same time, public authorities always participate in one way or the other in the administration or financing of such services. They do so often in partnership with different agencies. The state even finances services that are administered by purely private organizations; this occurs for secondary education and in hospital care, with schools and hospitals actually run by religious orders. We also observe that each social program possesses a distinctive profile in terms of the involvement of the state and public agencies. We then conclude that the state is highly involved in the provision of welfare services and benefits in Ireland, albeit rarely on its own. Such a statement suggests that Ireland does not belong to the liberal type of welfare regime in this respect. But it does not, as such, differentiate between conservative and social democratic regimes.

Esping-Andersen uses the presence of distinct occupational social programs as the criterion for the corporatist regime. Occupational schemes exist in Ireland only for pensions. These schemes do not cover occupational categories as such, at least in the private sector. They constitute company schemes, often negotiated between management and unions. In 1992, 30,746 such schemes were recorded, most of them very small (National Pension Board 1993). Occupational pensions complement social security pensions and have nothing to do with corporatism as conventionally understood. They point more to the operation of a market than to an institutionalization of the social position of large occupational groups. In the same way, the significance of public employee pensions does not necessarily point to an "etatist" welfare system. Public sector pensions themselves fall into the category of occupational schemes. Practically all countries have set up separate pension schemes for civil servants and public sector employees or else have granted such employees a special complementary pension (Department of Social Welfare 1976). It seems difficult to assign Ireland to a conservative-etatist regime on such a basis.

Table 8.4
Matrix of State Involvement in Main Social Policy Programs

Administration → Financing ↓	Full state/ public	Partial state/ public	Nonpublic
Full state/public	social assistance (pension, unemployment) child allowance	housing education	
Partial state/public	social insurance (pension, unemployment)	health care	
Nonpublic			

Table 8.5 allows us to restate the conclusions that have been reached previously. The Irish welfare state is characterized by a high level of state involvement in the provision of welfare benefits and services. At the same time, this involvement appears more definite for the financing of such programs, as opposed to their administration, which is often left to other public agencies or even to private organizations. A clear tendency is observed in relation to the decommodification effects of social policy programs in Ireland, which can be considered, on balance, quite high. The heavy reliance on means tests generates a deep social dualism. In all these respects, it seems possible to identify systematic features in the Irish welfare state, overall tendencies: toward a high level of state involvement, toward low commodification, and toward a dualist stratifying effect.

The Irish welfare state displays a profile that does not correspond to any type. Esping-Andersen himself portrays Ireland in a way that does not fit any of the types that he identifies. But he does not draw any conclusion from such a discrepancy. Ragin (1994) expresses the same view about pensions in Ireland; pension schemes do not conform to any type of welfare regime. On the basis of a very different kind of information and procedure, we have sketched another profile for Ireland: high stateness, quite low commodification, and a redistributive/ dualist principle of stratification. But the conclusion remains the same: Ireland does not fit in Esping-Andersen's classification. Close to the

Table 8. 5
The Value of Social Policy Programs in Relation to the Dimensions of Esping-Andersen's Classification

	A	B	C	D	E
hospital care	high	low	low	yes	dualist
medical cards	high	low	low	yes	dualist
education	high	low	low	yes	universal
family allowance	high	high	low	no	dualist
social housing	high	low	low	yes	dualist
mortgage	high	high	high	no	dualist
contributory pensions	low	high	medium	yes	insurance
noncontributory pensions	high	high	low	yes	dualist
unemployment insurance	low	high	high	yes	insurance
unemployment assistance	high	high	high	yes	dualist

Notes: A: stateness (finance); B: stateness (administration); C: commodification effect;
D: redistributive effect; E: stratification.

social democratic regime in some ways (stateness, decommodification), it differs from it by its stratification effect. Its dualist principle also marks the difference between the Irish welfare system and the conservative regime. On the other hand, the high stateness and fairly high decommodification of the Irish welfare system set it apart from the liberal regime; nonetheless, they share a reliance on means tests and a dualist principle of stratification (Table 8.6).

Table 8.6
The Profile of the Irish Welfare, as Compared to Esping-Andersen's Types

	Stateness	Redistribution/ Stratification	Decommodification
Liberal regime	low	low/dualism	low
Conservative regime	high	low/status maintenance	high
Social democratic regime	high	high/equalizing	high
Ireland (Esping-Andersen	high/conservative	status maintenance	low
Ireland (Ragin)	medium	medium	low
Ireland (present study)	high	low/dualism	high

The Irish case points to a situation in which the redistributive impact of the welfare state is accompanied by a significant stratification effect. This implies that, although it contributes to some income redistribution, the welfare state also participates in the structuration of Irish society into classes. The dual character of this criterion of income redistribution and stratification effect makes it difficult to assign a particular welfare system to a category of welfare regime. The Irish welfare system equalizes income, at least to some extent, but it also strengthens social dualism.

Ireland is not adequately defined in terms of any of the stratification principles formulated by Esping-Andersen. This occurs, as we have seen, because a low score in one respect does not imply a high score in another respect. This surely does not indicate that the Irish welfare system has no stratifying impact. It possibly points to the existence of other principles of stratification. The Irish case suggests that the stratifying impact of welfare systems is not satisfactorily characterized in terms of a single, unambiguous general principle. As it happens, the modalities of state involvement also differ radically according to financing and administration of such programs. This is clearly illustrated in the Irish welfare system, in which the central state or even the public sector contributes far more to the financing of social programs than it participates in their administration.

CONCLUSION

Although not really part of his analysis, Ireland is placed by Esping-Andersen in the category of conservative-corporatist welfare regime. Such a conclusion is not seriously grounded in the empirical information that he presents. It simply derives from the link that he establishes between the predominance of the Catholic Church and the conservative-corporatist regime. Ireland's welfare regime is also identified as conservative-corporatist in a more focused analysis of the Irish welfare regime (McLaughlin 1993). The evidence presented in this chapter does not support this view. Specific occupational welfare schemes exist for the public sector, with separate occupational pensions and a different social security regime. But they form a weak basis for assigning Ireland to the conservative type of welfare regime or even to locate it within this classification.

As a way of accounting for the difficulty of setting Ireland in Esping-Andersen's typology, Mel Cousins (1997) contends that this classification applies to advanced societies and ignores peripheral countries. He calls for the introduction of a fourth category in the classification, that of a peripheral welfare regime. The case for placing Ireland into a fourth category of peripheral welfare regime is developed and discussed in Chapter 9. He also points to the failure of such an analysis to take into account historical and national factors. For instance, the colonial and postcolonial status of Ireland contributed to the shape of its welfare institutions. The neglect of the historical and national paths of welfare formation underlines the fact that Esping-Andersen's analysis does not allow for a deep understanding of the forces that are at work in the respective countries and that fashion their welfare institutions. Such an analysis does not grasp their internal dynamic, and one learns very little about the internal features and functioning of the Irish welfare system by labeling it liberal or conservative.

It would appear that Esping-Andersen's analysis does not account for the internal logic of welfare systems, but it fares better in analyzing the mode of insertion of the welfare system into society. Esping-Andersen focuses on three different dimensions of the welfare system in order to elaborate his classification. The commodification theme refers to the extent to which social policy programs act as an incentive to participate in the labor force. Welfare acquires a direct economic function. But welfare is connected with the economic system in other ways. The low level of commodification of social policy programs in Ireland implies that the welfare system is not used as a way of ensuring the continuity of capitalist social relations. In the past, it performed the function of a safety net in an economy that was grossly underdeveloped and could not secure full employment. More recently, social policy has become a crucial instrument for promoting economic growth and, particularly, for creating the conditions that have facilitated the emergence of a dynamic postindustrial sector in Ireland. Welfare also impacts on the distribution of material resources and contributes to the structuration of society into classes. It constitutes one element, one mechanism through which the structure of society is produced and reproduced in its main features.

Another dimension is concerned with the role of the state in the provision of welfare benefits and services. It considers the relative contribution of state and market mechanisms, without much attention to the voluntary or even the informal sectors. The centrality of the state gives the measure of how closely the welfare system is linked with the structure of power in society: one in which the relations between the various forces in society are structured, through the state, into relations of power. The previous chapter pointed out the existence of several types of welfare mix in Ireland; it showed that the state remains central to the diverse configurations of the welfare mix. This high stateness indicates that the Irish welfare system is closely connected with the general structure of power. Through the three dimensions of welfare regimes, the welfare system is linked with other aspects of society.

These comments bring us back to Pierre Bourdieu with his concept of field, which points to the differentiated character of a sector of activity and also to the way that it relates to other sectors of activity. Bourdieu's framework has been elaborated to account for the internal dynamic of a sector of activity. But this can be done only by understanding the place of the welfare field in society, its relation to other spheres. The double articulation of the Irish welfare system that we have just outlined to the economic and political systems provides the key to understanding the logic of its internal activity. Within the Irish welfare field, economic resources are redistributed in a way that optimizes symbolic capital for a range of actors, particularly for the state. The conversion of material capital into symbolic capital is, to a great extent, effectuated there. One needs Bourdieu's framework in order to analyze both the internal functioning of the welfare field and the way that it is connected with other sectors of activity. Esping-Andersen's analysis helps connect welfare with the economic and political systems. But the internal features of this field are not adequately comprehended by the concept of the welfare regime.

9

Peripherality and Welfare in Ireland

The comparative study of welfare has recently focused on the different ways of organizing the welfare system and the forces that are associated with each type. Such analyses have been based on mainstream capitalist societies; so-called peripheral societies have hardly figured in the picture. Nevertheless, interest has been growing about Mediterranean or Southern European countries and the shape of the welfare state within them. A range of questions is now asked about the welfare system in non-core countries: are they simply less developed, or do they display features that set them apart? (Ferrera 1996). No systematic comparative study has been made of the impact of the peripheral situation as such on the welfare system. This chapter undertakes such a study in the Irish context.

Peripherality is a geographical term and indicates the spatial remoteness of some regions and countries in relation to a center. Ireland, located on the western edge of Europe, constitutes a peripheral country in geographical terms: an island behind an island. But peripherality refers by extension to all forms of marginality. Ireland, as a colony, was definitely located in a peripheral position within the context of the British Empire, although spatially close to Britain. A political system may even be deemed peripheral if its main features do not conform to those of the parliamentary democracy predominant in Western Europe.

The concept of peripherality has acquired its academic pedigree mainly in the context of economic activity. World system theory, as elaborated by Wallerstein, looks at the global process of capitalist development and identifies different positions in this world economy that are referred as central, peripheral, and semiperipheral (Terlouw 1993). Dependency theory also relies on this notion of peripherality. One should even stretch the meaning of peripherality to include any type of underdevelopment. Peripheral countries are economic laggards or in some way "backward." The lack of crucial modern institutions or even partial modernization would imply peripherality in relation to the dominant model of modernity. This may even apply to culture, to mean a marginalized position in the network of cultural exchange that takes place through the diverse means of communication or, more simply, cultural isolation. The present chapter looks at the impact in Ireland of diverse forms of peripherality on the welfare system.

THE WESTERN EDGE OF EUROPE

One wonders, at first, how the location of Ireland within Europe would have influenced the way it elaborated its welfare system. Of course, this location has contributed to Ireland's becoming a colony of Britain; its remoteness from the main economic markets within Europe has also generated its economic marginalization. Both these features have shaped the welfare system. But here we are studying the direct impact of spatial peripherality on welfare institutions.

Spatial remoteness from the centre does affect the welfare system. The literature on clientelism in Ireland has focused on the way that public benefits are distributed, and these include welfare benefits. The theme of clientelism is closely related to the issue of peripherality in two ways. Clientelist practices have been mainly observed in peripheral countries. They are associated with countries that have not achieved full modernization, retain a strong agrarian character, and struggle to establish a formal democratic system. Second, clientelism is prominent in the most remote parts of such countries.

The clientelist system operates in Ireland not around the patronage of local notables but around the benefits granted by public agencies (Bax 1976; Sacks 1976). It revolves around the local politician, who acts as an intermediary between the local electorate and public agencies. As a broker, she or he intervenes on behalf of constituents for the granting of diverse benefits. In exchange, such brokers receive the political support of their clients, come the next local or national election. The benefits sought after concern grants, planning permission, pensions, medical cards that entitle the recipients to free medical care, and the provision of social housing. Brokerage may also include employment in a small range of positions that remain at the discretion of the local authorities: rate collectors, some typing jobs, and possibly occasional laboring jobs. To obtain such benefits, an application must be made to the relevant agencies, and the latter reach a decision on the basis of clear criteria. It has been found that brokers are approached mainly to accelerate the administrative process and avoid delays (Higgins 1981; Kelly 1987).

Students of the clientelist system in Ireland agree that brokers deal mainly with trivial matters. They introduce a personal touch into a bureaucratic process. The administrative agencies involved communicate their decision to the brokers, who then inform their clients and reap in this way the symbolic benefit of their intervention. But brokers rarely influence a decision, and the allocation of welfare benefits follows, by and large, well-defined rules that leave little room for arbitrariness. Their patronage remains largely imaginary (Komito 1984; Sacks 1976).

This clientelist practice was, for a long time, associated with the most remote part of Ireland (Bax 1972). The best-known political machine was located in Donegal, at the top northwest of Ireland and far, indeed, from the political center in Dublin (Sacks 1976). The central powers are perceived as distant, impersonal, and, in a sense, hostile (and this perception fed on the past situation of a colonial power ruling from the center, at Dublin Castle). The broker knows how to operate in the bureaucratic maze of the modern state and secures for constituents what they are entitled to. This type of political practice has also appeared in cities and even in the capital. It has been re-created in Dublin, mainly in the most disadvantaged areas (Komito 1984). Categories of people who may find themselves close to the political center in geographical terms have, nonetheless, been totally marginalized. They have had more and more recourse to political brokers in order to have access to the state apparatus, which is perceived as totally alien to them. Their remoteness is generated by their economic and political peripherality.

Clientelism develops in contexts of peripherality, and welfare benefits occupy a central place in this practice. Brokerage thrives in those areas of decision making that enjoy some discretion in the way that public benefits are distributed. Social housing and medical cards constituted the two main areas in which sufficient discretion was allowed for clientelist practices to emerge. It seems, however, that the scope for clientelism within the welfare system has been reduced nowadays to very little.

THE COLONIAL LEGACY

The integration of Ireland within the United Kingdom deeply influenced its welfare development after independence. When Southern Ireland became an independent republic in 1922, the welfare framework was largely retained in place. This British legacy has been outlined by Geoffrey Cook (1986), and the broad lines of his analysis are followed here. The welfare framework inherited by the new state largely revolved around public assistance directed at the poor. The Poor Law came into operation in Ireland in 1838 and provided assistance for the destitutes in workhouses. But the introduction of some measure of income maintenance at the turn of the century established the foundation for a welfare system based on insurance. Ireland also inherited some elements of a public health service, mainly in the form of dispensaries, and an extensive educational system. In fact, Ireland had acquired a uniform educational system as early as 1831, well before England, and education up till the age of fourteen was made compulsory at an early stage.

Thereafter, the paths of the British and Irish welfare systems separated. Irish authorities inherited a public assistance mentality, in which the welfare state remained minimal and was directed at those in need. The predominantly rural character of Ireland, with its majority of farmers, did not facilitate the introduction either of a universal system of welfare entitlements or of a widespread insurance system for employees. Irish authorities continued to provide welfare on the basis of means tests and social assistance; they were quite slow to move in the direction of insurance benefits. In that sense, the paths of Irish and British welfare development diverged in the aftermath of Independence.

Although Ireland and Britain became two separate political entities, it was agreed to retain freedom of travel and right to work in either country. This, in practice, produced a single labor market in which Irish workers could seek employment in Britain. Not only that, but many Irish trade unions still operated as a branch of a British union. Similarly, Northern Ireland, still in the United Kingdom, formed a point of reference for workers in the Republic. The proximity of Northern Ireland, the integration of Ireland into a British labor market, and the organizational overlap of the trade unions ensured that Irish workers remained acutely aware of the relative wage and welfare benefits in the two countries. To that extent, the United Kingdom exercised some influence on the type of welfare system that was developing in Ireland and on the level of benefits that were offered.

WELFARE AND ECONOMIC UNDERDEVELOPMENT

The peripherality of Ireland also relates to its low level of capitalist industrialization. The latter manifests itself in a large agricultural sector and, more crucially, in the low level of wealth, comparatively speaking—and this is now changing fast. Figures about the per capita GDP, for instance, clearly identify a group of countries that lag behind other European countries in terms of wealth creation; Ireland belongs to this group. Despite that, Ireland possesses all the major institutional features associated with organized capitalism (Peillon 1994): the growing intervention of the state, the coordination of the relations between employers and employees, the development of neocorporatist arrangements, and the large-scale provision of social benefits by public authorities. Although Ireland was relatively poor by Western standards, social expenditure increased faster than national wealth, as measured by the GDP, between 1960 and 1980. It doubled in size in each of these decades, while the GDP was increasing only by one and half times for each period. This means that, although Ireland up to the 1960s trailed well behind in terms of welfare effort, it had made up a great deal of ground by 1980 and followed not far behind Continental European countries.

It has even been asserted that the welfare state in Ireland was far more developed than its level of economic development would warrant. This anomaly, of course, raises the question of why Ireland spent a relatively high percentage of national wealth on welfare benefits. O'Connell and Rottman (1992) contended that the conventional explanations of welfare development do not apply. Neither the level of economic development nor the strength of the labor movement or social democratic parties could explain this relative overdevelopment of the welfare state. They argue that the state has been very instrumental in promoting the development of welfare services, and in this context they point to the high level of autonomy enjoyed by the state apparatus.

The low level of economic development itself generates extensive welfare needs. The chronic high level of unemployment that has characterized the Irish economy for most of its recent history weighs heavily on public finances; it contributes to the swelling of social expenditure. Unemployment must also be linked to the large black economy, which constitutes a feature of the Irish economy. The black economy consists mainly of claimants of welfare benefits engaging in undeclared employment. Such a practice requires the complicity of mainly small employers, who avoid paying social contributions. It is more particularly observed in industrial sectors that depend on casual or seasonal employment. Countries that, like Ireland, retain a strong agrarian sector or are less economically developed contain a large black economy. It may have something to do with the state capacity to regulate such economic sectors and effectively implement its rules. When the Irish state, after a media campaign against the abuses of the welfare system, declared its intention to tighten its control on the granting of welfare benefits, a significant proportion of welfare claimants suddenly ceased to register for social benefits. The rate of unemployment dropped by a few percentage points.

The link between welfare and the black economy can be interpreted in two ways. In the first one, the black economy puts an unfair burden on an already overloaded welfare system. It creates, or at least sustains, a large welfare clientele. In that sense, the underdevelopment of Ireland adds to its welfare burden. But the black economy could be said to form a palliative to an ungenerous welfare system. People on welfare are experiencing a hard time and would not satisfy the basic requirements of living in a modern society without complementing their welfare benefits with some casual employment. In this case, the limited welfare benefits generate a black economy.

DEPENDENT DEVELOPMENT

The economic peripherality of Ireland has been conceptualized, so far, as mere underdevelopment. But many analysts would view the economy of peripheral countries as undergoing a different kind of development. Such economies are said to be placed in a dependent situation in relation to an economic center. The penetration of foreign capital into the local economy and the emergence of a dual economy figure high in the list of features associated with semiperipheral economies (Mouzelis 1978; Seers, Schaffer, and Kijunen 1979; Williams 1984). The presence and possible dominance of foreign capital in the manufacturing and service sectors of peripheral countries create a dualism between a foreign/modern sector and a domestic/traditional sector. The nature of economic development in Ireland bears quite directly upon some aspects of the welfare state.

The first phase of dependent capitalist development in Ireland took quite a conventional form. Multinational corporations were attracted to Ireland for a range of reasons: relatively low wages, state grants, fiscal advantages, and also direct and unhindered access to the large European market. Such multinational corporations set up plants involved in the assembly of a final product and required a fairly unskilled labor force. The public authorities were at this stage committed to a policy of rural industrialization. They encouraged firms to set up in small towns and even rural locations, not in the main cities. This policy of rural industrialization was justified in terms of regional balance and it also sought to avoid a full-scale modernization of Irish society (Gibbons 1988). In the process, the capital city was largely bypassed, and the Dublin working class experienced a serious decline (Breen et al. 1990). A large section of this class became dependent on welfare.

This stage of dependent capitalist development, focusing mainly on electronic and pharmaceutical industries, has been overtaken by another form of dualist economic development. In recent years, Ireland has been transformed into what may be called a dependent postindustrial economy—although this kind of occurence has not been analyzed in any depth in Ireland or elsewhere. Many international companies, mainly in computer-related industries, are setting up in Ireland. They find there a large pool of young, well-educated, English-speaking workers, able to adapt quickly to the changing demands of the postindustrial service industry. For instance, many firms service their customers all over Europe or North America from Ireland. Dublin has also been promoted as a financial center and many international banks have located some of their services there. In all cases, they require a labor force of university graduates. The moving of the Irish economy, or at least some parts of it, in this direction has meant that job opportunities for university graduates have improved considerably; those without skills or recognized formal education have been largely marginalized in the process. The lower working class has once more borne the brunt of this transformation.

Such developments directly contribute to the creation of a large category of people depending on welfare. Chris Whelan (1996) has investigated this question of the existence of an underclass in Ireland. He points to the high level of long-term economic marginality in the republic: 11 percent of nonfarm households are classified as economically marginalized. At the same time, he expresses doubts about the extent to which this marginality is transmitted from one generation to the next. No clear evidence exists for the transmission of unemployment. Neither is the idea of underclass ghettos empirically sustained. Many such families are located in rural areas; and even in urban areas, they form a minority within the county council estates where they typically reside. The deprived material and social conditions experienced by this marginalized social category do not lead to the emergence of a distinctive culture. He concludes that this category of people does not constitute an underclass differentiated from the working class. Rather, these people represent a marginal and poor element within it. Underclass or not, the marginalization of this lower working class makes heavy demands on the diverse social policy programs.

IRISH CIVIL SOCIETY AND WELFARE

Semiperipheral countries are often presented as being characterized by a weak civil society; this weakness would manifest itself in extensive clientelism, social disorganization, and a weak bourgeoisie (Mouzelis 1978; Seers, Schaffer, and Kijunen 1979; Hudson and Lewis 1985). The civil society is weak, mainly because it remains unstructured. This occurs if no social group or class assumes a clear position of dominance and leads the way. Ireland does not fit unambiguously in this category. Although the process of economic development has not originated in a native entrepreneurial class, unable or unwilling to engage in a policy of economic modernization, this does not mean that Irish society was not clearly structured, mainly around property relations. An alliance of the small property class with the large class of farmers at its center and of the professional class has ensured the establishment of a fairly stable structure for Irish society. The process of industrialization was initiated by a faction within the political elite, which was more firmly rooted in the professional category than in the small property class.

The second possible source of weakness for the civil society relates to the inability of the major socioeconomic categories to organize themselves in an autonomous way. However, the number of recorded organized interests has grown quite considerably in the last thirty years, in parallel with the differentiation of Irish society and the emergence of a range of cultural issues as well as material concerns. Many interest groups compete to influence public decisions. The farmers have, from an early stage, constituted an organized and effective force in independent Ireland, even if rivalries have emerged between organizations representing different agricultural sectors. Business interests have never enjoyed the same level of organization; they, nonetheless, display great coherence, as the interests of the business sector are effectively articulated by a few large firms. The trade union movement is characterized by a large number of occupational unions, over 100, each looking after the interests of particular trades or occupations. But the vast majority of them are organized in a confederation of unions, the Irish Congress of Trade Unions, which authoritatively speaks on behalf of the employed labor force.

The very organized character of Irish society is further emphasized by the emergence of neocorporatist arrangements. In fact, the very presence of "peak associations" has made possible the development of corporatist institutions. A policy of centralized wage bargaining developed very early after the industrial takeoff. This took the form of voluntary agreements between representatives of employers and employees about working conditions and pay levels. The state participated in these negotiations not as a representative of the central authority but more simply as a large employer having a stake in the outcome of the talks.

In 1979, as we have already noted, for the first time in the history of the state, a link was established between wage negotiations and a range of measures concerned with employment, social services, and social security benefits. In this process, the budgetary policy of the state was directly linked with an agreement covering wages and social benefits. This meant that the representatives of the major interests in modern Ireland were able to influence in a direct way the public management of the economy. This was followed by a series of national agreements up to the present day. The very existence of such a tradition of centralized tripartite agreements and then more recently of neocorporatist arrangements underlines the organized character of Irish society. It is difficult to conclude from these considerations that Ireland has a weak civil society. In fact, the strength of Irish civil society directly bears upon the determination of social policy.

STATE CENTRALIZATION AND THE WELFARE STATE

In peripheral countries, a weak civil society faces a weak, but overdeveloped, state. The tendency of the state to solve the problems that it encounters by creating employment in the public sector, often as part of a clientelist orientation, generates an "overdeveloped" state. But the size of the state does not determine its strength, which depends on its capacity to decide on goals and pursue them even against the preferences of dominant groups in society. In any case, the strength of Irish civil society does not necessarily imply the weakness of the Irish state; the strength of the state depends on strategic resources and on how these resources are actually used.

Public authority is exercised in Ireland at the central level, with little devolution of power to regional or local levels. Local authorities exist only for counties and larger urban areas. They perform a very limited range of functions and depend on financial transfers from the central authorities: these finances are earmarked, and little flexibility is granted to local authorities in fulfilling their functions. The central state closely supervises the activities of local councils.

A similar centralization and lack of devolution of responsibility are observed in relation to social security programs. These are administered by the Department of Social Welfare. Contributions to social insurance tend to be treated as an element of taxation; they are raised at source by the revenue commissioners from both employees and employers and then transferred to the relevant agencies. The state pays for the shortfall between contributions and social security payments. Once political decisions have been made about the levels of contribution and benefit entitlements, the whole scheme is administered in a bureaucratic manner. Even social assistance is administered in a similar fashion, although the reliance on means tests for the distribution of such benefits introduces an element of discretion in the way that claims are evaluated.

Strangely enough, the high level of centralization in relation to social security programs is accompanied by a high level of decentralization in relation to the delivery of social services, mainly health and education. In this context, the state provides practically all the finance but leaves to private organizations the task of managing the service, independently of the state. For instance, the state finances the construction of the primary schools and foots the bill for school maintenance and teachers' wages. But school management is left to boards that are, in fact, controlled by the parish priest. A similar pattern exists in relation to secondary schools. They are owned and run mainly by religious orders, but the state meets the cost of maintaining and managing them. A similar comment applies to hospital services.

A third aspect of the Irish welfare mix relates to the state subsidizing of some social services. These services are provided by voluntary organizations, but they are given complementary financing by the state. This occurs mainly in the context of personal services, when bureaucratically administered programs do not reach those people who need support. A major beneficiary of state subsidies is the Society of Saint Vincent de Paul: a charitable organization of religious inspiration that offers a range of charitable services to the poorest sections of Irish society. It intervenes where normal assistance fails to solve the problem. A range of voluntary organizations has emerged to deal with problems that are not adequately addressed by statutory agencies. Homelessness is best dealt with by voluntary organizations able to reach such people in a flexible and informal manner. New organizations have been set up to respond to women's concerns, such as battered wives and rape. In the absence of effective statutory agencies, the state often grants subsidies to such voluntary agencies.

The mode of organization of welfare programs in Ireland does not allow any scope for democratic decision making. The only democratic element relates to the fact that the central authorities are elected and represent the majority of the population. After that, the social security system is managed without outside intervention from contributors or beneficiaries. A cozy arrangement between mainly state and churches has evolved in relation to social services. Only recently have the parents of pupils been included in the running of schools. In relation to the subsidization of voluntary organizations to provide personal social services, the central state remains the final arbiter of which organizations will be subsidized and by how much. In none of these cases have the relevant categories of people involved in such social policy programs democratically participated in decision making.

STATE AUTONOMY

The claim has been made that the Irish state has constituted the main force promoting welfare development (O'Connell and Rottman 1992). It has initiated the shift from economic self-sufficiency to export-oriented industrialization; this breakthrough is conventionally said to have ushered Ireland into the modern world. The idea that the state apparatus has been crucial in the development of the Irish welfare state cannot be accepted as self-evident. Other forces in Irish society, particularly the Catholic Church, have been instrumental in tracing the path along which social services have developed. In fact, the Irish welfare system has been shaped by a very narrow range of forces.

The constellation of forces that are active and influential changes according to each sector of the welfare system. Overall, the state has enjoyed a rather low level of autonomy in the health field, and it did not achieve its goals. The Catholic Church effectively blocked, at an early stage, the development of a universalist welfare system, and the battle has been fought and won mainly in relation to health services. In 1951, the introduction by the minister for health of a scheme for free public health care for children and mothers led to a confrontation between the state and a coalition of church and medical doctors. Health services have remained quite segmented up till the present day, with only a third of the population benefiting from free medical care. Despite free hospital care for all, the wealthier third of the population relies on private health insurance and attends private hospitals. The state has led the way on crucial issues in education; it has introduced free secondary schooling for all despite a lack of enthusiasm from the religious orders. But it failed to carry out its preferences in relation to the development of community schools when confronted with strong opposition. It adopted instead a policy that could be reconciled with the preferences of the Catholic Church.

The state plays a more significant role in relation to income maintenance programs. It has progressively extended the range of social categories covered by social security. Directed originally at the poorest sections of the community, then at manual workers, the diverse programs of social security progressively covered all employees and, more recently, the self-employed. Overall, the state enjoys a different level of autonomy in these three welfare subfields. It was given little room for maneuver in the health services, while the picture remains rather mixed in education; but it has displayed a great deal of autonomy in relation to social security.

The Irish state does not constitute a strong state. It possesses a range of capabilities that enhance its power of intervention within Irish society. It extracts substantial financial resources, although it does not ensure an equitable contribution from all economic sectors to public finances; only a low level of taxes is obtained from farmers and from small business in general. Direct taxation is very narrowly based and largely confined to wage earners. The Irish state is also highly centralized and can mobilize effective administrative capabilities; it is staffed by a reliable civil service, although often accused of lacking in imagination and innovative urge (Lee 1989). But all these capabilities are not translated into state strength. Admittedly, the state initiated some policy moves at crucial stages in the history of independent Ireland, mainly because the structuration of Irish society was not conducive to the emergence of a risk-taking and entrepreneurial class. Even within the social field, the state has, from time to time, initiated new policies and promoted radical departures. But the state does not enjoy a high degree of autonomy from society. It can operate effectively within the limits set by the most powerful forces. It has failed, whenever it has tried, to move beyond such limits or attempted to renegotiate them. Within these limits, it removes itself from the direct pressure of groups within society and operates quite effectively. It is not constrained by limits imposed by some powerful force in the economic field; its orientation of action is broadly accepted by employees and employers alike. However, it has had to operate within narrower limits in the social policy sector.

PERIPHERALITY AND WELFARE LEGITIMACY

In Ireland, the welfare state receives a very high level of support. In comparative terms, Ireland figures in the highest category of support for all types of welfare programs (Peillon 1995). No significant antiwelfare voice is heard there. Business organizations may bemoan the increasing cost of social security contributions; they may even express concern about the level of welfare benefits, which, they contend, acts as a disincentive for seeking employment. But no large political party has so far put forward strong antiwelfare views or a program of welfare retrenchment. Only the Progressive Democrats have formulated, in an explicit way, some reservations about welfare and have attempted to make it a political issue, but they represent a small minority of the electorate. Some newspapers have pointed out the high level of welfare fraud, playing on a latent distrust toward some welfare programs. In Ireland, as elsewhere, unemployment assistance receives relatively less support: it is suspected that many who receive such benefits are not entitled to them or do not deserve them. But even in this context, Ireland records one of the highest levels of support for this program compared to other countries, albeit at a lower level than for other social policy programs.

The explanation for this high support for the welfare state in Ireland has not been investigated in any serious way. However, it has been contended that the level of prosperity in a country determines, to a large extent, the level of support for the welfare system. Less prosperous countries express more positive attitudes toward state intervention than prosperous nations (Haller, Höllinger, and Raubal 1990). The rationale for such an explanation would be that the level of welfare dependency or at least the likelihood of having to rely on welfare benefits increases for individuals in poorer countries. For instance, the high level of unemployment in Ireland increases the number of people who think they will experience unemployment at one time or another: such people display highly supportive attitudes toward unemployment benefits and assistance. Such a statistical association may be tentatively accepted: on the whole, poorer countries are indeed more supportive of welfare institutions.

It has also been found that the level of welfare support is related to the scope of social programs: those programs that involve a large clientele of potential beneficiaries receive far more support than those social programs that are targeted at particular categories (Peillon 1996). If one makes the assumption that, in poorer countries, more people depend on welfare, then an indirect link is established between welfare support and the level of economic development. However, this explanation does not easily square with the very high level of support that is also recorded in some rich countries, as in Scandinavia. The relative economic underdevelopment contributes to the high legitimacy of welfare in Ireland, but it does not account for the full picture.

The traumatic experience of the Irish Famine, from 1844 to 1848, when potato crops failed and plunged millions of people into starvation, death, and emigration, has deeply marked the collective psyche of Ireland. The effects of the Famine were made far worse by the refusal of the colonial British authorities to bring relief. The authorities took the liberal view of market economy and contended that any attempt at interference in market mechanisms in Ireland would aggravate the situation. Such a callous policy, rooted in ideological dogma, caused many deaths, and the lesson of the Famine has not been forgotten. The refusal to help, to provide relief or welfare would go against the grain of Irish culture. The positive attitude of Irish people toward welfare reaches deep into its colonial experience.

The high level of support for the welfare system could also be explained, at least in part, by the relative weakness of the state, which was analyzed earlier. The Irish state has found ways of sustaining its legitimacy, but it does not enjoy much leeway in this respect. Its rather mediocre economic performance, up till very recently, its inability to overcome chronic unemployment and migration, and its rather selective tax extraction undermine the level of support that it receives. The provision of a range of welfare benefits and services, even if not particularly generous and often relying on means tests, offers the state a fairly uncontroversial way of bolstering its legitimacy.

To conclude, the very special position of Ireland in terms of welfare legitimacy is potentially related to three features of peripherality: economic underdevelopment, the colonial experience, and the weakness of the state.

CONCLUSION

The extent to which the Irish welfare system has been shaped by the peripheral nature of Irish society has been examined under different aspects. The notion of peripherality is used in a rather loose way, in order to include all its potential facets.

1. The peripheral position of Ireland, on the western edge of Europe, does not seem to have had a deep impact, at least directly, on the development of its welfare system. Although it originally included some clientelist practices that accompany marginality, the welfare state in Ireland no longer harbors such practices and now operates, by and large, in a straightforward, bureaucratic manner.
2. The colonial legacy of Ireland has more directly influenced the Irish welfare system. Not only has Ireland inherited a welfare system that relied heavily on means tests, but it accentuated this feature after independence. The colonial legacy is also manifested by the high level of support for welfare institutions.
3. It has been remarked that Ireland once possessed a welfare system that was overdeveloped in relation to its level of industrialization and wealth: in that sense, it had overcome and negated the effect of economic underdevelopment on welfare effort. However, the low level of industrialization in Ireland and the predominance of both the self-employed and small business in the nonmanufacturing sector, together with a high level of unemployment, have been conducive to the development of a large black economy thriving in the shadows of the welfare system. This large dependent welfare class accounts for both the lack of generosity of welfare benefits and the reliance on means tests but also for the low level of policing of welfare claims. More generally, the relative poverty of Ireland has contributed to the positive attitudes of the Irish population toward welfare institutions.
4. The emergence of economic dualism in Ireland, with a domestic and a foreign sector, has directly structured Irish society. The policy of locating multinational plants outside major cities has marginalized the traditional urban working class. More recently, the change in the nature of the firms setting up plants in Ireland and their reliance on a highly educated labor force have further reinforced this trend, producing a large urban, unskilled category, depending more and more on welfare.
5. Ireland cannot be characterized as having a weak civil society, and the stability of neocorporatist arrangements emphasizes its organized character; social policy benefits are decided through these neocorporatist negotiations. However, Ireland shares an important feature of peripheral societies: that of a relatively weak state. The weakness of the Irish state would occur despite its extreme centralization and despite the level of both financial and administrative capabilities at its disposal. It

enjoys only a small amount of autonomy, chiefly in the welfare field; it effectively acts only within the limits that have been set by major forces within Irish society. The contrast between the welfare mixes observed for social security programs and social service programs is also quite revealing in this respect. The weakness of the state (in the context of a strong civil society) explains in part why it is so willing to play the welfare card, as a way of bolstering its legitimacy without high political costs. This lack of autonomy has blocked the path toward a universal welfare system, at one stage favored by state agencies.

The major features of the Irish welfare system, such as a high reliance on means testing, a rather slow extension of social security coverage, and a contrast in the management of social security programs and social services, are partly rooted in the peripherality of Ireland. The preceding analysis has led to clear conclusions about the characterization of the Irish welfare system as belonging to the peripheral regime. Doubts have been expressed about the reality of such a type of welfare system and, more definitely, about the inclusion of Ireland in such a category. However, the focus has been set on some features of Irish society that derive from its relatively underdeveloped and peripheral nature. These features condition, to some extent, the nature and orientation of welfare.

Peripherality implies that the Irish economy is open to the high winds of global capitalist markets. In such circumstances, welfare determines the global cost of labor and plays a part in the decision of foreign companies to locate in Ireland. The underdevelopment of the Irish economy has also generated a high level of unemployment, as well as a high rate of emigration, which has imposed a high social assistance load. Underdevelopment creates a tightness in public finances, which militates against generous welfare payments.

The peripheral nature of Irish society fashions political relations and the structure of power in Irish society. A weak civil society is given as the mark of peripheral societies; this means that society finds it difficult to organize itself, independently of the state. Instead, society is structured around the state. The state becomes central to the structuration of society. The central position of the state extends to welfare, in which it occupies in Ireland a crucial position. The Catholic Church has, to some extent, supplied an alternative focus for organizing society and for providing social services mainly; but it has not managed to sustain this role into the present day. The central position of the state does not mean that it is strong. In fact, the state of peripheral societies remains weak and reactive. It possesses only low capabilities and finds it difficult to mobilize the kind of resources that would be required for proactive policies. This weakness manifested itself, for a long time, by the high level of clientelism that characterized the exercise of power in Ireland. Clientelist relations render the holders of power dependent on the delivery of short-term and individualized benefits and, by and large, ineffective in tackling collective issues. The systematic ineffectiveness of the Irish state in relation to welfare has been demonstrated by its failure to address the problems of poverty and social exclusion and by the growth of a large class of marginalized people, despite the relative prosperity of Ireland.

The peripheral character of Ireland should not be exaggerated, but it should not be ignored either. In such circumstances, welfare occupies a central place in collective life, and support for the state greatly depends on the kind of social policy that is pursued by central authorities. The peripheral nature of society renders the legitimacy of the state more sensitive to welfare issues. To express this in Bourdieu's terms, the internal dynamic of the welfare field is deeply affected by the peripheral nature of Irish society. The latter, to a greater extent, shapes the economic and political fields and strengthens the role of welfare in connecting these two fields. The conversion of material capital into symbolic capital takes place primarily in the welfare field.

Conclusion

This study has sought to develop a sociological analysis of welfare in Ireland. In order to do so, it has relied selectively on the conceptual framework elaborated by Pierre Bourdieu. The present work has delved into aspects of welfare that were deemed significant for the analysis. But we now need to lift our sights to the broad picture and put together the main elements of a conclusion. What have we learned about the way that welfare has been constructed in Irish society and how it operates? According to which dynamic is the Irish welfare field functioning?

THE INSERTION OF WELFARE INTO IRISH SOCIETY

For a long time in Ireland, welfare performed the task of relieving the worst aspects of social deprivation. Throughout its history, the Irish economy has rarely been able to provide sufficient employment and wealth to look after the welfare of its population. Emigration and welfare constituted the two main and parallel ways of coping with this situation. Welfare programs simply intervened when the economy failed, offering a safety net when needed. This meant that they did not perform an economic function but acted as a palliative in difficult circumstances. They were not mobilized as instruments of economic policy.

This lack of a direct economic role for welfare is further emphasized by the low level of commodification that characterizes Irish social policy programs. The enjoyment of welfare benefits often depends on social contributions that require participation in the labor force, or else, social benefits are fixed at a level that does not ensure survival and constrains individuals to seek employment in order to avoid destitution. In both cases, the welfare programs are commodifying: they press individuals into gainful employment. Welfare acquires in such circumstances a direct economic function. But the analysis of the Irish welfare regime has pointed to the low level of commodification associated with the provision of welfare benefits. Social policy programs in Ireland are not used to sustain a particular type of economic relation.

Not only was welfare uncoupled from the economy, but, in fact, it constituted a highly differentiated domain of activity. This simply means that a very distinctive rapport of forces developed within this sphere of activity: one that was organized around the interaction between church and state, with a few minor players. The welfare field did not reflect the structure of society at large, where a rather different configuration of forces prevailed.

The place of welfare has drastically changed in recent times. Social policy issues are no longer decided within the confines of a differentiatied welfare domain. The development of a welfare corporatism has meant that the major decisions relating to the types and levels of social benefits are decided as part of an overall package. Social policy advances are traded off for economic goals. This way of elaborating social policy links welfare with the economy in a direct way. Social policy has become a crucial instrument in promoting economic growth, particularly in creating the conditions that have facilitated the emergence of a dynamic, postindustrial sector in Ireland. But the economic system is not itself differentiated, operating according to separate market mechanisms. The structure of power in society is directly implicated in it.

Welfare does not stand outside the socioeconomic structure of society, to be influenced by it. It has always had an impact on the distribution of material resources and contributed to the structuration of society into classes. It constitutes one element, one mechanism through which the structure of society is produced and reproduced in its main features. Welfare is now directly connected with, and even part of, the socioeconomic field in which the main social partners come to arrangements about the distribution of material resources or, rather, the redistribution to be effectuated through the state.

The socioeconomic structure represents a structure of power. The centrality of the state in the provision of social benefits gives a further measure of how closely the welfare system is linked with the structure of power in society: one in which the relations between the various forces in society are structured, through the state, into relations of power. The implication of welfare in economic policy and its closeness to the structure of power through its high stateness place the welfare field in a strategic position. The socioeconomic structure and the power field are connected through it. The welfare field becomes the place where material resources and political resources (mainly in the form of legitimacy) are exchanged or, rather, converted into each other. Within the Irish welfare field, economic resources are redistributed in a way that optimizes symbolic capital for a range of actors, particularly for the state. Although not the only place where it occurs, the conversion of material capital into symbolic capital is particularly significant.

An adequate account of the activity that takes place within the welfare field is achieved only by identifying the place that welfare occupies in society. The mode of insertion of the Irish welfare system within society provides the key to understanding the logic of its internal activity, as the strategic place for the conversion of material resources into legitimacy. The crucial role of welfare in the field of power is further accentuated by the peripheral position of Ireland. This peripherality is associated with underdevelopment and a significant level of poverty, which produce a high dependency on welfare. The observation has sometimes been made that people in poorer countries show more support for social policy programs. In such circumstances, welfare occupies a more central place in collective life, and support for the state depends to a greater extent on the kind of social policy that is pursued by central authorities. The peripheral nature of Irish society renders state legitimacy more dependent on welfare issues.

The central position of the state in peripheral societies does not mean that the state is strong. In fact, the state in peripheral societies remains weak and reactive. It possesses only low capabilities and does not easily engage in proactive policies. The weakness of the state explains, in part, why it relies so heavily on welfare to bolster its legitimacy, with limited political costs. But legitimacy is not guaranteed for the state in the welfare field. The ineffectiveness of the Irish state in relation to welfare is demonstrated by its failure to address the problems of poverty and social exclusion and by its inability to thwart the growth of a large class of marginalized people, despite the relative prosperity of Ireland. This, by itself, undermines support for the state.

PLAYERS, STRATEGIES, AND STAKES

The internal functioning of the welfare field depends, in great part, on the way that it is connected with other fields of activity and with the structure of society. This articulation was examined in the previous section. But the game has still to be played by collective actors engaged in various strategies and pursuing their own goals.

The state represents the main player in the welfare field. It is mainly interested in securing and even boosting support for its activity. Approval of its welfare policy adds to the support that it receives from the mainstream of society. Legitimacy constitutes the resource that the state seeks to maximize through its welfare activity. But it needs resources in order to perform this welfare function and capitalize on the benefits: these resources have to be extracted, with a high potential cost of legitimacy. The state, through the procedure of corporatist negotiation and compromise, elaborates a policy that commands a broad consensus. National programs have produced a great deal of stability in industrial relations. All this further increases the legitimacy of the state, that is, the symbolic capital that it generates. But, in the process, it loses some control over the social policy that it wishes to pursue, as the other partners contribute in a significant way to the formulation of social policy objectives. These social partners acquire some control over the determination of social policy. They use this control in order to maximize material returns: to maintain or even increase the value of welfare benefits for the trade unions; to contain the cost of welfare for employers; and to generate specific women's services.

The Catholic Church has, for a long time, constituted a major force in determining public social policy, and, in that context, it has developed a close relationship with the state. It commanded such a dominant position on the basis of resources that in the Irish context were strategic. It had, over a long period, developed a range of social services in a private capacity and retained control over them. The church also enjoyed a high level of legitimacy in social matters, and the political class needed church approval in those areas that, like social policy, were perceived as relevant from a religious point of view. The Catholic Church possessed resources that the state could not disregard, and this placed it in a strong position. The state did not have the economic resources necessary to establish a secular system of schools and hospitals or a range of personal social services. It could not, in any case, risk the loss of legitimacy in front of a church that, to a large extent, commanded the obedience of its followers on moral and social matters.

The church itself depends on state resources. It requires public money to run the institutions that it controls. More importantly perhaps, the church needs the seal of the state for its schools, hospitals, and various social services. Only the state can grant the legitimacy that derives from being a public institution. The dominant position of the Catholic Church in Ireland was, in the past, entirely accounted for by these flows of resources exchanged between church and state. This situation corresponded to a mutual adjustment between state and church in which the conversions of capital created a "positive game," in which both players in the welfare field were gaining.

The position of the Catholic Church in the welfare field has changed quite drastically. Its intervention relied mainly on the symbolic capital that was rooted in its control over crucial welfare institutions; now, its symbolic capital originates from its caring orientation, from its expressed commitment to the poor and vulnerable. Approval by the church has become less and less crucial to the state, although useful in some cases. The church's economic capital, in the form of schools and hospitals, is still needed: but religious orders are anyway disengaging from the provision of such social services. The mutual bolstering of state and church has given way to a very different and more distant interaction between them that depends on the ability of the church to speak for marginalized social categories. The relevance of the church for social policy has been largely eroded, as the welfare system now develops around a system of social security in which the church possesses no stake and about which it has little to say.

Other agents are also engaged in the welfare field, and their main strategy consists in converting political capital into material capital. The strength of the trade union movement hinges on its mobilizing capacity and its internal coherence. The Irish working class is quite effectively organized, and most categories of workers are included in the unified body of the Irish Congress of Trade Unions. The presence of a relatively strong, although not radical, trade union movement has had an impact on the Irish welfare system. Congress has not constituted the driving force in welfare growth, but it figures in the configuration of forces that have shaped the welfare system in Ireland. The activity of the trade union movement in the welfare field follows a simple logic of transforming its political capital into material capital. This material capital takes the form of better social services and increased social benefits. Such conversion, if successful, adds to the symbolic capital of trade unions: they can realistically present themselves as defending the living standards of the working population and of the most vulnerable among them.

The women's movement has also used its mobilizing power to generate more social benefits for women. But it has mainly contributed to the development of a parallel welfare system, which comprises a range of services relevant to women and administered by them. It has striven to convert its mobilizing capacity into resources for these parallel services, as well as ensuring its continuing control over such services.

Employers operate in the welfare field on the basis of a different kind of political capital. Their economic resources, those of investment and employment creation, are easily transformed into political capital. The latter is actually enhanced by the close association that employers enjoy with the political elite. They bring into play this double capital, material and social, mainly to curtail or at least contain the level of social expenditure that they incur. But they also endeavor to increase their participation and involvement in services that are directly useful to them.

The welfare field is structured around the accumulation of several types of capital. This accumulation rests on exchanges through which actors endeavor to employ the resources that they possess in order to acquire the resources that they seek to maximize. Several such flows dominate the welfare field. The state is concerned with the generation of symbolic capital, and it utilizes economic capital in order to generate this capital of legitimacy. The latter is given, mainly, in the form of generalized support to the central authorities by those actors that aim at securing better social benefits and services. The trade unions, the employers, and the feminist movement are all involved in this conversion of political support into material resources. The Catholic Church was engaged in a more complex strategy of capital conversion. It relied on the control of a range of institutions in the welfare field in order to increase its moral authority and ultimately its symbolic capital. But it also used this legitimacy in order to secure its control over such institutions. More recently, the church has engaged in a new strategy: to generate its own type of legitimacy, not on the basis of institutional control but by voicing the needs of those who are vulnerable and marginalized in society. This represents an attempt at expanding the symbolic capital with which it operates in the field, a strategy that appears sustainable only in special circumstances.

Each agent endeavors to maximize capital returns. For each participant, the main stake in the welfare field remains the rate at which a particular type of capital is converted into another one. This raises a significant question: How fixed is the rate at which capital is converted, and which factors participate in the fixing of rates? It seems futile to look for an overriding factor, for an explanation that would apply to all conversions. The analysis has shed some light on this issue, and several relevant factors have been identified:

- The degree of differentiation of the welfare field plays an important role in this context. It constitutes in itself a stake in the welfare field, for the very reason that it influences the bargaining power of the respective actors and consequently the rate at which they succeed in converting the resources that they possess. For instance, the value of the resources on the basis of which the Catholic Church operates increases when the welfare field is differentiated and uncoupled from the main field of socioeconomic power: in these circumstances, its resources matter more for the functioning of the welfare system.

- The values according to which people live in a particular group have an impact on the amount of legitimacy generated by the material resources that are invested by the state in welfare. They generate little symbolic capital if they are used in a way that does not conform to shared beliefs. A similar comment applies to the Catholic Church.

- Power, in its diverse forms, is used in its own right to acquire other forms of capital. But power also represents a crucial factor in determining the rate at which resources are exchanged. For instance, closure of the professional providers of social services and the alliance with other forces have increased the rate at which they managed to acquire their material capital.

- The ability to separate responsibility for social problems from the policy addressing such problems appears crucial for the state.

This outline of some of the factors that influence the rate at which types of capital are traded does not add up to a sustained account of these exchanges. The analysis presented in this book would find its logical continuation in a systematic investigation of the conditions under which capital is exchanged and accumulated in the welfare field.

References

Accardo, A., and Corduff, P. 1986. *La sociologie de Pierre Bourdieu. Textes choisis et commentés*. Bordeaux: Le Mascaret.

Alber, J. 1988. "Continuities and changes in the idea of the welfare state." *Politics and Society* 16, 4: 451–468.

Barrington, R. 1987. *Health, medicine and politics in Ireland 1900–1970*. Dublin: Institute of Public Administration.

Bax, M. 1972. "Integration forms of communication and development: centre-periphery relations in Ireland, past and present." *Sociologishe Gids* 19, 2: 137–145.

Bax, M. 1976. *Harpstrings and confessions. Machine style politics in the Irish Republic*. Assen, Netherlands: Van Gorcum.

Beedle, P., and Taylor-Gooby, P. 1983. "Public opinion about taxation and welfare." *Policy and Politics* 11, 1: 15–39.

Bourdieu, P. 1990. *In other words. Essays towards a reflexive sociology*. Cambridge: Polity Press.

Bourdieu, P. 1993. *Sociology in question*. London: Sage.

Bourdieu, P. 1994. *Raisons pratiques. Sur la théorie de l'action*. Paris: Editions du Seuil.

Bourdieu, P. 1996. *The rules of art. Genesis and structure of the literary field*. Cambridge: Polity Press.

Breen, R., Hannan, D.F., Rottman, D.B., and Whelan, C.T. 1990. *Understanding contemporary Ireland. State, class and development in the Republic of Ireland*. Basingstoke: Macmillan.

Calhoun, C. 1993. "Habitus, field and capital: the question of historical specificity." In C. Calhoun, E. Lipuma, and M. Postone (eds.), *Bourdieu: Critical perspectives* (61–88). Cambridge: Polity Press.

Callan, T., and Nolan, B. 1992. "Income distribution and redistribution: Ireland in comparative perspective." In J. Goldthorpe and C.T. Whelan (eds.), *The development of industrial society in Ireland* (173–203). Oxford: Oxford University Press.

Callan, T., Nolan, B., and Whelan, C. 1994. "Who are the poor?" In Brian Nolan and Tim Callan (eds.), *Poverty and policy in Ireland* (63–77). Dublin: Gill and Macmillan.

Callender, R. 1988. "Ireland and the implementation of Directive 79/7 EEC. The social, political and legal issues." In Gerry Whyte (ed.), *Sex equality, community rights and Irish welfare law* (1–15). Dublin: Irish Centre for European Law.

Central Statistics Office. Various years. *National income and expenditure.* Dublin: Dublin Stationery Office.

Central Statistics Office. Various years. *Statistical abstract.* Dublin: Dublin Stationery Office.

Coakley, A. 1997. "Gendered citizenship: the social construction of mothers in Ireland." In Anne Byrne and Madeleine Leonard (eds.), *Women and Irish society. A sociological reader* (181–195). Belfast: Beyond the Pale Publications.

Commission for the Status of Women. 1972. *Report.* Dublin: Dublin Stationery Office.

Commission on Social Welfare. 1986. *Report.* Dublin: Dublin Stationery Office.

Confederation of Irish Industry. Various years. *Annual report.* Dublin: CII.

Confederation of Irish Industry. Various years. *Newsletters.* Dublin: CII.

Confederation of Irish Industry. 1982. *The first fifty years, 1932–1982.* Dublin: CII.

Conference of Major Religious Superiors, Education Commission. 1992. *Education and poverty.* Dublin: Conference of Major Religious Superiors.

Connolly, L. 1997. "From revolution to devolution. A social movement analysis of the contemporary women's movement in Ireland." Doctoral thesis, National University of Ireland, Maynooth.

Conroy Jackson, P. 1993. "Managing the mothers: The case of Ireland." In J. Lewis (ed.), *Women and social policies in Europe. Work, family and the state* (72–92). Aldershot: Edward Elgar.

Cook, G. 1986. "Britain's legacy to the Irish social security system." In P.J. Drudy (ed.), *Ireland and Britain since 1922* (65–85). Cambridge: Cambridge University Press.

Coughlan, A. 1984. "Ireland's welfare state in crisis." *Administration* 32, 1: 31–41.

Coughlin, R.M. 1980. *Ideology, public opinion and welfare policy. Attitudes towards taxes and spending in industrialized societies.* Berkeley, Cal: Institute of International Studies.

Council for Social Welfare. 1972. *A statement on social policy.* Dublin: Council for Social Welfare.

Council for Social Welfare. 1976. *Planning for social development. What needs to be done.* Dublin: Council for Social Welfare.

Council for Social Welfare. 1980. *Submission to Commission on Taxation.* Dublin: Council for Social Welfare.

Council for Social Welfare. 1987. *Comments on health: the wider dimensions (A consultative statement on health policy).* Dublin: Council for Social Welfare.

Council for Social Welfare. 1989. *Unemployment, jobs and the 1990s.* Dublin: Council for Social Welfare.

Council for Social Welfare. 1990. *Response to the Report of the Commission on Health Funding.* Dublin: Council for Social Welfare.

Council for Social Welfare 1992. *Emerging trends in the social welfare system.* Dublin: Council for Social Welfare.

Council for Social Welfare. 1993. *Submission on the Green Paper "Education for a changing world."* Dublin: Council for Social Welfare.

Council for Social Welfare. 1996. *The dole truth. Voices of the unemployed.* Dublin: Council for Social Welfare.

Council for the Status of Women. 1981. *Irish women speak out.* Dublin: Co-op Books.

Cousins, M. 1995. *The Irish welfare system. Law and social policy*. Dublin: Round Hall Press.

Cousins, M. 1997. "Ireland's place in the worlds of welfare capitalism." *Journal of European Social Policy* 7, 3: 223–235.

Craig, S., and McKeown, K. 1994. *Progress through partnership*. Dublin: Combat Poverty Agency.

Crickley, A., and Devlin, M. 1990. "Community work in the 80's. An overview." In *Community work in Ireland. Trends in the 80s. Options for the 90s* (53–80). Dublin: Combat Poverty Agency.

Cullen, B. 1989. *Poverty, community and development*. Dublin: Combat Poverty Agency.

Curry, J. 1993. *Social services in Ireland*. Dublin: Institute of Public Administration.

Dáil Report. Various years.

Daly, M. 1989. *Women and poverty*. Dublin: Attic Press/ Combat Poverty Agency.

Daly, M. 1999. "The functioning family: Catholicism and social policy in Germany and Ireland." *Comparative Social Research* 18: 105–133.

Department of Health, 1995. *Health statistics*. Dublin: Stationery Office, 1995.

Department of Social Welfare. Various years. *Report*. Dublin: Dublin Stationery Office.

Department of Social Welfare. Various years. *Statistical information on social welfare services*. Dublin: Dublin Stationery Office.

Department of Social Welfare. 1976. *A national income-related pension scheme. A discussion paper*. Dublin: Dublin Stationery Office.

Department of Social Welfare. 1978. *Social insurance for the self-employed. A discussion paper*. Dublin: Dublin Stationery Office.

Department of Social Welfare. 1997. *A Green Paper on the community and voluntary sector and its relationship with the state*. Dublin: Dublin Stationery Office.

Esping-Andersen, G. 1990. *The three worlds of welfare capitalism*. Cambridge: Polity Press.

Eurostat. Various years. *Basic statistics of the Community*. Luxembourg: Office for Official Publication of the European Community.

Fahey, T. 1998. "The Catholic Church and social policy." In S. Healy and B. Reynolds (eds.), *Social policy in Ireland* (411–429). Dublin: Oak Tree Press.

Fanning, B. 1999. "The mixed economy of welfare." In G. Kiely, A. O'Donnell, P. Kennedy, and S. Quinn (eds.), *Irish social policy in context* (51–69). Dublin: University College Dublin Press.

Faughnan, P., and Kelleher, P. 1990. *The voluntary sector and the state. A study of organisations in one region*. Dublin: Community Action Network/ Conference of Major Religious Superiors.

Ferrera, M. 1996. "The southern model of welfare in social Europe." *Journal of European Social Policy* 6, 1: 17–37

Flora P. 1986. "Introduction." In P. Flora (ed.), *Growth to limits. The Western European welfare states since World War II*, vol. 2 (11–36). Berlin: Walter de Gruyter.

Flora, P., and Heidenheimer, A.J. 1982. "The historical core and changing boundaries of the welfare state." In P. Flora and A.J. Heidenheimer (eds.), *The development of welfare states in Europe and America* (17–34). New Brunswick, NJ: Transaction Publishers.

Gibbons, L. 1988. "Coming out of hibernation? The myth of modernity in Irish culture." In Richard Kearney (ed.), *Across the frontiers: Ireland in the 1990s* (205–218). Dublin: Wolfhound.

Gilligan, R. 1993. *Child care and family support. Choices for the church*. Dublin: Conference of the Major Religious Superiors.

Habermas, J. 1976. *Legitimation crisis*. London: Heinemann.

Habermas, J. 1984, 1987. *The theory of communicative action*. Vols. 1 and 2. Cambridge: Polity Press.

Haller, M., Höllinger, F., and Raubal, O. 1990. "Leviathan or welfare state? Attitudes toward the role of government in six advanced Western nations." In J.W. Becker, J.A. Davis, P. Esta, and P.P. Mahler (eds.), *Attitudes to inequality and the role of government* (33–62). Rijswijk, Netherlands: International Social Survey Programme, Social and Cultural Planning Office.

Higgins, M.D. 1981. "The limits of clientelism: Towards an assessment of Irish politics." In C. Clapham (ed.), *Private patronage and public power* (114–141). London: Frances Pinter.

Hudson, R., and Lewis, J. (eds) 1985. *Uneven development in Southern Europe. Studies of accumulation, class, migration and the state*. London: Methuen.

Hughes, G. 1988. "The Irish civil service superannuation scheme." Paper 139. Dublin: Economic and Social Research Institute.

Inglis, T. 1998. *Moral monopoly*. Dublin: University College Dublin Press.

Irish Business and Employers Confederation (IBEC). Various years. *Annual review*. Dublin: IBEC.

Irish Business and Employers Confederation (IBEC). Various years. *IBEC news*. Dublin: IBEC.

Irish Business and Employers Confederation (IBEC). 1996. *Social policy in a competitive economy*. Dublin: IBEC.

Irish Catholic Bishops' Conference. 1996. *Work is the key*. Dublin: Veritas.

Irish Congress of Trade Unions. (ICTU) 1959–1995. *Annual report and proceedings of annual conference*. Dublin: ICTU.

Irish Episcopal Conference. 1975. *Human life is sacred, pastoral letter of the archbishops and bishops of Ireland to the clergy, religious and faithful*. Dublin: Veritas.

Irish Episcopal Conference. 1983. *Christian faith in a time of economic depression*. Dublin: Veritas.

Irish Farmers Journal. Various years. Dublin.

Irish Times. Various years. Dublin.

Irish Trade Unions Congress (ITUC). 1949–1958. *Annual report and proceedings of annual conference*. Dublin: ITUC.

Kelly, V. 1987. "Focus on clients: A reappraisal of the effectiveness of TD's interventions." *Administration* 4, 2: 130–151.

Kennedy, F. 1997. "The course of the Irish welfare state." In Fíonán Ó Muircheartaigh (ed.), *Ireland in the coming times. Essays to celebrate T.K. Whitaker's 80 years* (129–155). Dublin: Institute of Public Administration.

Komito, L. 1984. "Irish clientelism: A reappraisal." *Economic and Social Review* 15, 3: 173–194.

Lee, J. 1989. *Ireland 1912-1985:Politics and society*. Cambridge: Cambridge University Press.

Lewis, A. 1980. "Attitudes to public expenditure and their relationship to voting preferences." *Political Studies* 28, 2: 284–292.

Maguire, M. 1986. "Ireland." In P. Flora (ed.), *Growth to limits: the West European states since World War II*, vol.2 (241–384). Berlin: Walter de Gruyter.

Maguire, M. 1987. "Ireland." in P. Flora (ed.), *Growth to limits: the West European states since World War II,* volume 4 (407–474). Berlin: Walter de Gruyter.

Mahon, E. 1987. "Women's rights and Catholicism in Ireland." *New Left Review* 166: 53–77.

Marks, G. 1985–1986. "Neo-corporatism and income policy in Western Europe and North America." *Comparative Politics* 18: 253–277.

Marshall, T.H. 1950. *Citizenship and social class and other essays.* Cambridge: Cambridge University Press.

Mayntz, R. 1975. "Legitimacy and the directive capacity of the political system." In L.N. Lindberg, R. Ashford, C. Crouch, and C. Offe (eds.), *Stress and contradiction in modern capitalism* (261–274). Lexington, MA: Lexington Books.

McCashin, T. 1990. "Local communities and social policy." In *Community work in Ireland. Trends in the 80s. Options for the 90s* (81 –94). Dublin: Combat Poverty Agency.

McDevitt, D. 1987. "Marriage maintenance and property." In C. Curtin, P. Jackson and B. O'Connor (eds.), *Gender in Irish society* (224–248). Galway: Galway University Press.

McLaughlin, E. 1993. "Ireland: Catholic corporatism." In A. Cochrane and J. Clarke (eds.), *Comparing welfare states. Britain in international context* (205–237). London: Sage Publications/ Milton Keynes: Open University Press.

McLaughlin, E., and Yeates, N. 1999. "The biopolitics of welfare in Ireland." *Irish Journal of Feminist Studies* 3, 2: 49 -69.

Millar, J., Leeper, S., and Davies, C. 1992. *Lone parents. Poverty and public policy in Ireland.* Dublin: Combat Poverty Agency.

Mishra, R. 1990. *The welfare state in capitalist society.* Sussex: Brighton.

Mouzelis, N. 1978. *Facets of underdevelopment. Modern Greece.* London: Macmillan.

National Economic and Social Council. 1988. *Redistribution through state social expenditure in the Republic of Ireland (1973–1980).* Dublin: National Economic and Social Council.

National Pension Board. 1993. *Final report. Developing the national pension system.* Dublin: Dublin Stationery Office.

Nevin, D. 1994. "Decades of dissension and divisions 1923–1959." In D. Nevin (ed.), *Trade union century* (85–98). Cork: Mercier Press.

Nolan, B. and Callan, T. (eds.). 1994. *Poverty and policy in Ireland.* Dublin: Gill and Macmillan.

Nordlinger, E. 1981. *On the autonomy of the democratic state.* Cambridge: Harvard University Press.

Ó Buachalla, S. 1988. *Education in twentieth century Ireland.* Dublin: Wolfhound Press.

Ó Cinneide, S. 1993. "Ireland and the European welfare state." *Policy and Politics* 21, 2: 97–108.

Ó Cinneide, S., and Walsh, J. 1990. "Multiplication and divisions: Trends in community development in Ireland since the 1960s." *Community Development Journal* 25, 4: 326–336.

O'Connell, P. 1982. "The distribution and redistribution of income in the Republic of Ireland." *Economic and Social Review* 13, 4: 251–278.

O'Connell, P., and Rottman, D. 1992. "The Irish welfare state in comparative perspective." In J. Goldthorpe and C.T. Whelan (eds.), *The development of industrial society in Ireland* (205–239). Oxford: Oxford University Press.

O'Connor, J. 1973. *The fiscal crisis of the state.* New York: St. Martin's Press.

O'Connor, J.S. 1988. "Convergence or divergence? Change in welfare effort in OECD countries 1960–1980." *European Journal of Political Research* 16: 277–299.

Offe, C. 1984. *Contradictions of the welfare state*. London: Hutchinson.

Peillon, M. 1993. "Welfare and state centralisation." *West European Politics* 16, 2: 105–121.

Peillon, M. 1994. "Placing Ireland in a comparative perspective." *Economic and Social Review* 25, 2: 179–195.

Peillon, M. 1995. "Support for welfare in Ireland: Legitimacy and interest." *Administration* 43, 3: 3-21.

Peillon, M. 1996. "A qualitative comparative analysis of welfare legitimacy." *Journal of European Social Policy* 6, 3: 175-190.

Peillon, M. 1997. "The Power of inclusion. An analysis of the Green Paper on Supporting Voluntary Activity." *Poverty Today* 38: 6–7.

Peillon, M. 1998. "Bourdieu's field and the sociology of welfare." *The Journal of Social Policy* 27, 2: 213–229.

Pierson, C. 1991. *Beyond the welfare state?* Cambridge: Polity Press.

Pöntinen, S. 1988. "Stability and change in the public support for the welfare state; Finland 1975–1985." *International Journal of Sociology and Social Policy* 6, 1: 1–22.

Powell, F., and Guerin, D. 1997. *Civil society and social policy*. Dublin: A. and A. Farmer.

Powell, F., and Guerin, D. 1998. "The Irish voluntary sector and the state: The blossoming of civil society or a crisis of identity?" Paper presented at the Sociological Association of Ireland Conference, Wexford.

Raftery, M. 1990. "Community response to unemployment." In *Community work in Ireland. Trends in the 80s. Options for the 90s* (216–234). Dublin: Combat Poverty Agency.

Ragin, C. 1994. "A qualitative comparative analysis of pension systems." In T. Janoski and A. Hicks (eds.), *The comparative political economy of the welfare state. New methodologies and approaches* (320–345). New York: Cambridge University Press.

Retail News. Various years.

Ringen, S. 1987. *The possibility of politics. A study in the political economy of the welfare state*. Oxford: Clarendon Press.

Rosanvallon, P. 1988. "Beyond the welfare state." *Politics and Society* 16, 4: 533–543.

Rottman, D., Hannan, D., Hardiman, N., and Wiley, M. 1982. *The distribution of income in the Republic of   Ireland: A study in social class and family-cycle inequalities*. Paper no. 109. Dublin: Economic and Social Research Institute.

Ruddle, H., and O'Connor, J. 1993. *Reaching out. Charitable giving and volunteering in the Republic of Ireland*. Dublin: National College of Industrial Relations.

Ryan, L. 1979. "Church and politics. The last twenty-five years." *The Furrow* 30, 1: 3–18.

Sacks, P. 1976. *The Donegal Mafia. An Irish political machine*. New Haven, CT: Yale University Press.

Second Commission for the Status of Women, 1993. *Report*. Dublin: Dublin Stationery Office.

Seers, D., Schaffer, B., and Kijunen, M.L (eds.). 1979. *Underdeveloped Europe: Studies in core -periphery relations*. Atlantic Island, NJ: Humanities Press.

Skocpol, T. 1985. "Bringing the state back in: Strategies of analysis in current research." In P.B. Evans, D. Rueschemeyer, and T. Skocpol (eds.), *Bringing the state back in* (3–37). Cambridge: Cambridge University Press.

Smith, B.C. 1985. *Decentralisation: The territorial dimension of the state*. London: Allen and Unwin.

Smyth, A. 1988. "The contemporary women's movement in the Republic of Ireland." *Women's Studies International Forum* 11, 4: 331–341.

Stephens, J. 1979. *The transition from capitalism to socialism*. Basingstoke: Macmillan.

Sweeney, P. 1990. "The churches and business influence on community work." In *Community work in Ireland. Trends in the 80s. Options for the 90s* (182–192). Dublin: Combat Poverty Agency.

Taylor-Gooby, P. 1983. "Legitimation deficit, public opinion and the welfare state." *Sociology* 17, 2: 165–183.

Taylor-Gooby, P. 1985. *Public opinion, ideology and state welfare*. London: Routledge and Kegan Paul.

Taylor-Gooby, P. 1988. "The future of the British welfare state: Public attitudes, citizenship and social policy under the conservative government of the 1980s." *European Sociological Review* 4, 1: 1–19.

Terlouw C.P. 1993. "The elusive semiperiphery: A critical examination of the concept semiperiphery." *International Journal of Comparative Sociology* 34, 1–2: 87–102.

Titmuss, R.M. 1974. *Social policy. An introduction*. London: George Allen and Unwin.

Tobin, P. 1990. "Women in community work." In *Community work in Ireland. Trends in the 80s. Options for the 90s* (235–247). Dublin: Combat Poverty Agency.

Tucker, V. 1990. "Community work and social change." In *Community work in Ireland, Trends in the 80s. Options for the 90s* (34–52) Dublin: Combat Poverty Agency.

Varley, T. 1998. "More power to the people? The politics of community action in late twentieth-century Ireland." In S. Healy and B. Reynolds (eds.), *Social policy in Ireland. Principles, practice and problems* (387–409). Dublin: Oak Tree Press.

Walsh, J. 1994. *Summary report on the implementation of the third EU poverty programme by the PAUL Partnership Limerick*. Limerick: PAUL Partnership Limerick.

Whelan, C. 1996. "Marginalization, deprivation and fatalism in the Republic of Ireland: Class and underclass perspectives." *European Sociological Review* 12, 1: 33–51.

Weber, M. 1978. *Economy and society* (edited by G. Roth and C. Wittich). Berkeley: University of California Press.

Whiteley, P. 1981. "Public opinion and the demand for social welfare in Britain." *Journal of Social Policy* 10, 4: 453–476.

Whyte, J. 1980. *Church and state in modern Ireland, 1923–1979*. Dublin: Gill and Macmillan.

Wilensky, H. 1981. "Leftism, Catholicism, and democratic corporatism: The role of political parties in recent welfare state development." In P. Flora and A. Heidenheimer (eds.), *The development of welfare states in Europe and America* (345–382). New Brunswick, NJ: Transaction Publishers.

Williams, A.M. (ed.). 1984. *Southern Europe transformed. Political and economic change in Greece, Italy, Portugal and Spain*. London: Harper and Row.

Wilson, M. 1993. "The German welfare state: A conservative regime in crisis." In A. Cochrane and J. Clarke (eds.), *Comparative welfare state. Britain in international context* (141–171). London: Sage.

Yeates, N. 1997. "Gender and the development of the Irish social welfare system." In Anne Byrne and Madeleine Leonard (eds.), *Women and Irish society. A sociological reader* (145–166). Belfast: Beyond the Pale Publications.

Index

About the Author

MICHEL PEILLON teaches Sociology at the National University of Ireland, Maynooth. He has written extensively on many aspects of Irish Society and has been published in many Irish and international journals. He has authored or edited four other books.